BRITISH FICTION TODAY

Edited by
Philip Tew and Rod Mengham

continuum

Continuum International Publishing Group
The Tower Building, 11 York Road, London SE1 7NX
80 Maiden Lane, Suite 704, New York, NY 10038

British Library Cataloguing-in-Publication Data
A catalogue record for this book is available from the British Library.

ISBN: 0-8264-8731-9 (hardback)
       0-8264-8732-7 (paperback)

Library of Congress Cataloging-in-Publication Data
A catalog record for this book is available from the Library of Congress.

Typeset by Aarontype Limited, Easton, Bristol
Printed and bound in Great Britain by MPG Books Ltd, Bodmin, Cornwall

In memory of

Nigel 'Buzz' Burrell

and

Frank Whitbourn

Contents

Acknowledgements

Our respective families, friends and colleagues; editorial staff at Continuum; all other individuals and institutions who assisted the efforts of the two editors and the contributing academics; and finally, Dr Fiona Tolan, whose contributions in preparing the manuscript were invaluable.

Contributors

Sonya Andermahr is Senior Lecturer in English at the University of Northampton. Her publications include *A Glossary of Feminist Theory* (1997) with Terry Lovell and Carol Wolkowitz, and *Straight Studies Modified: Lesbian Interventions in the Academy* (1997) with Gabriele Griffin. Currently she is preparing a monograph and an edited collection of critical essays on Jeanette Winterson.

Tamás Bényei is Professor of English at the Institute of English and American Studies, University of Debrecen, Hungary. He has published widely, including an essay, 'The Novels of Graham Swift', which appears in *Contemporary British Fiction* (2003). Bényei's six books include one in English: *Acts of Attention: Figure and Narrative in Postwar British Novels* (1999).

Joseph Brooker teaches Modern and Contemporary Literature at Birkbeck College, University of London. Author of *Joyce's Critics: Transitions in Reading and Culture* (2004) and *Flann O'Brien* (2005), he co-edited a special edition of *New Formations*, on *Remembering the 1990s* (issue 50, Autumn 2003). Subsequently he co-edited a special interdisciplinary issue *Law and Literature* of the *Journal of Law and Society* (31:1, March 2004). He has published several essays on contemporary British fiction.

Robert Eaglestone works on contemporary and twentieth-century literature, literary theory and philosophy at Royal Holloway, University of London. His publications include *Ethical Criticism: Reading after Levinas* (1997), *Doing English* (1999, 2nd edn 2002), *Postmodernism and Holocaust Denial* (2001), *The Holocaust and the Postmodern* (2004) and articles on a range of contemporary philosophers and writers. He is a Literary Advisor to the British Council, and the series editor of *Routledge Critical Thinkers*.

Dominic Head is Professor of Modern English Literature at the University of Nottingham. His books include *Nadine Gordimer* (1994), *J. M. Coetzee* (1997) and the *Cambridge Introduction to Modern British Fiction, 1950–2000* (2002). Most recently he has edited the third edition of *The Cambridge Guide to Literature in English* (2006). A monograph on Ian McEwan is forthcoming.

Nick Hubble is a Research Fellow at the Centre for Suburban Studies, Kingston University. His recently published monograph, *Mass-Observation and Everyday Life: Culture, History, Theory* (2006), is a cultural history and theoretical exposition of the surrealist and anthropological social research organization of the 1930s and 1940s. He has also written essays and chapters on various writers including William Empson, Ford Madox Ford, B. S. Johnson, George Orwell and Christopher Priest.

Rod Mengham is Reader in Modern English Literature at the University of Cambridge. His various publications include books on Emily Brontë, Charles Dickens and Henry Green, and *The Descent of Language* (1993); edited collections of essays, *The Violent Muse: Violence and the Artistic Imagination in Europe, 1910–39* (1994), *An Introduction to Contemporary Fiction: International Writing in English since 1970* (1999), *The Fiction of the 1940s: Stories of Survival* (2001), and *Contemporary British Fiction* (2003). He is co-editor and co-translator of *Altered State: the New Polish Poetry* (2003) and co-editor of *Vanishing Points: New Modernist Poems* (2004). His collected poetry appears as *Unsung: New and Selected Poems* (2001).

Kaye Mitchell is Lecturer in English at the University of Westminster. Her publications include 'Bodies that Matter: Science Fiction, Technoculture and the Gendered Body', in *Science Fiction Studies*, March 2006, and *A. L. Kennedy* for Palgrave Macmillan (2007). A member of the UK Network for Modern Fiction Studies, she also reviews for the *British Journal of Aesthetics* and *Radical Philosophy*.

Christopher Ringrose is a Principal Lecturer in English at the University of Northampton, and editor of both *The Journal of Postcolonial Writing*, and *CCUE News*. He has published variously in *Canadian Literature, Encyclopedia of Life Writing, English Studies,* and *Children's Literature in Education*. His recent research has been concerned with Barbary slavery in eighteenth-century literature, and representation of history in children's fiction.

Philip Tew is Professor of English at Brunel University, and founding Director of the UK Network for Modern Fiction Studies. His publications include *B. S. Johnson: a Critical Reading* (2001), *The Contemporary British Novel* (2004) and *Jim Crace: a Critical Introduction* (2006). Currently he is co-editing two series, *The New British Novel* with Palgrave Macmillan, and *Literary and Cultural Handbooks* with Continuum, and additionally preparing a study of Zadie Smith. He is co-editor of *Symbiosis: a Journal of Anglo-American Literary Relations*.

Pamela Thurschwell is a Senior Lecturer in English at University College London. Author of *Sigmund Freud* (2000) and *Literature, Technology and Magical Thinking, 1880–1920* (2001), she co-edited both *The Victorian*

Supernatural (2004) with Nicola Bown and Carolyn Burdett, and *Literary Secretaries/Secretarial Culture* (2005) with Leah Price. Currently she is working on representations of adolescence in Britain and America in the twentieth century.

Fiona Tolan is a Lecturer and Postdoctoral Research Fellow in English at the University of Northampton. Her publications include 'Feminisms', in *Literary Theory and Criticism* (2005), Patricia Waugh (ed.), 'Anglophone Canadian Literary Studies', in *Twentieth Century North American Criticism* (2006), Julian Wolfreys (ed.), *Margaret Atwood: Feminism and Fiction* (2006). She is to co-edit *Writers Talk: Interviews with Contemporary British Novelists* (forthcoming) for Continuum, and is an advisory editor of the *Journal of Postcolonial Writing*.

Lynn Wells is Associate Professor in English and Associate Dean in the Faculty of Arts at the University of Regina, Saskatchewan, Canada. She is the author of *Allegories of Telling: Self-Referential Narrative in Contemporary British Fiction* (2003), as well as a number of articles on contemporary English writers, Gothic Fiction and literature and technology. She is currently completing a monograph on Ian McEwan for Palgrave Macmillan.

Wendy Wheeler is Reader in English at London Metropolitan University. Her many publications include *A New Modernity? Change in Science, Literature and Politics* (1999) and *The Whole Creature: Complexity, Biosemiotics and the Evolution of Culture* (2006). She is an editorial board member of *New Formations*; she has co-edited two special issues: *Diana and Democracy* (36, 1999) and *Complex Figures: Art and Science* (49, Spring 2003). Forthcoming is a monograph on A. S. Byatt.

Leigh Wilson is a lecturer in the Department of English and Linguistics at the University of Westminster. She is co-editing an issue of *Anglistik und Englischunterricht* on 'Teaching Contemporary British Fiction' (with Philip Tew and Anja Muller-Wood). Both her introduction to modernism and *Writers Talk: Interviews with Contemporary British Novelists*, with Philip Tew and Fiona Tolan, are forthcoming from Continuum in 2007.

Mark Wormald is Director of Studies and Fellow in English at Pembroke College, University of Cambridge. He has published various essays on contemporary fiction in *An Introduction to Contemporary Fiction: International Writing in English since 1970* (1999), Rod Mengham (ed.), and in *Contemporary British Fiction* (2003), Richard Lane, Rod Mengham and Philip Tew (eds).

General Introduction

ROD MENGHAM AND PHILIP TEW

Consider two novels that exemplify certain recent changes in fiction's aesthetic dynamics or dispositions, not only in terms of narrative mood, but also of certain larger perspectival qualities that characterize the historical differences between the pre-millennial and post-millennial phases of British creativity that are the focus of *British Fiction Today*. First, in a London Square in Jeanette Winterson's *Art and Lies* (1994) one of the author's recognizably archetypal trans-historical female narrators, the poet Sappho, identifies an excess in nature itself, a breaching of the average, which is to be found in a cornucopia of fruitfulness, the materialization of an almost violent beauty (88). There is something Woolfian in the range of consciousness disclosed in shifting identities and locations, and something Arnoldian in a later scene by the seaside, where the narrator notes how rain transforms the water's surface (93). This aesthetic is not exactly harmonious, but is organized around a reconciliation of woman and the world, with a lingering note of optimism.

Around ten years later one sees a more fractious, dissonant apprehension of the world in which reconciliations are absent. At the beginning of Ian McEwan's *Saturday* (2005), in a similar London Fitzrovian Regency Square, another excessiveness has entered the human world, but one turning towards a more anarchic and destructive violence. In a location identifiable as where Virginia Woolf once lived with her brother is the home of successful surgeon, Henry Perowne. His house overlooks a façade reconstructed after wartime Luftwaffe bombing, but behind this evocation of violence and trauma is a submerged awareness of the history shattered by the war, and of the Woolfian aesthetic reveries it extinguished. There is also a reassertion of certain masculine principles; at the least, an unembarrassed and confident investment in male middle-class identity. McEwan's protagonist awakes from his sleep nakedly in motion, in the middle of being drawn to his window, at a time just prior to the Iraq War. Thus, McEwan encapsulates and symbolizes the uncertain emergence of the present from the past, in a narrative full of introspec-tive self-absorption. Perowne's nakedness conveys mankind's vulnerability. Disturbing his reveries is a flaming object in descent, difficult to make out at first but subsequently identified as a plane, evoking a time eighteen months before, when 'half the planet watched, and watched again the unseen captives driven through the sky to the slaughter, at which time there gathered round the innocent silhouette of any jet plane a novel association. Everyone agrees, airliners look different in the sky these days, predatory or doomed' (16). Perowne's notion of a penumbra of fear and uncertainty signifies a more general perspective, a post-millennial vulnerability and unease.

The present collection of essays responds largely to the pre-millennial and post-millennial periods, reacting to what are seen increasingly as new eras in literary production, exhibiting new dispositions, exploring new contexts. Our contributors, like most literary critics, respond primarily to texts, teasing out contexts and pretexts, engaging with a range of British authors whose work exemplifies themes central to contemporary aesthetic culture. These novelists engage variously in a critique of an intensely commodified world, a resurgent register of the historical imagination, a need to contend with referentiality in a period obsessed with obstructions to mimesis, and the knowing stylistics of an age so reflexive that identity appears both uncertain and yet totally self-obsessed. As Martin Amis indicates in *Yellow Dog* (2003), there is a superficially democratic cult of celebrity, a banalization of experience where even 'People who weren't famous behaved famous' (8).

Many of the novels featured are very recently published ones, appearing since 1990 and indeed some after the millennium, although naturally in certain cases it is necessary to supplement the critical readings by reference to certain antecedent landmark texts. However one might contest theoretically the legitimacy of any literary periodization, the plain fact is that a new century is upon us, already recognizably distinguishable from the old one in a cultural and aesthetic sense. As Amis says concerning his protagonist, Xan Meo, after he has been beaten up and is recovering in hospital: 'His condition felt like the twenty-first century: it was something you wanted to wake up from − snap out of. Now it was a dream within a dream. And both dreams were bad dreams' (37).

Certainly a series of global traumas, such as the 9/11 disaster to which McEwan alludes, the Bali bombs, the Gulf and Iraq Wars, the late-2004 Tsunami, the 2005 London bombings, Hurricane Katrina and the floods in New Orleans have together brutally asserted the material origins of ideas and conceptions, and the limits of linguistic determination of historicity. As ever, although ephemeral in its nature and scintillating in its possibilities, literature coexists with such hard external realities; it offers a zone of mediation, reflection, and perhaps, as some assert, transcendence. In a text haunted by uncanny manifestations of disaster and conflict, by their strange iterations, McEwan's protagonist perceives in supernatural beliefs 'an excess of the subjective, the ordering of the world in line with your needs, an inability to contemplate your own unimportance' (17). In *Yellow Dog*, Amis has a charmless tabloid journalist, Clint Smoker, survey a symbol of the preceding period's gloomy and insistent orthodoxies: 'the room − the hotel — was postmodern, but darkly, unplayfully so. It seemed that the gunmetal furniture was trying to look like the refrigerator, the television, the safe' (163). Amis designates the end of the postmodern, reducing it to a series of stylistic gestures. Many writers conceive that major world events have reshaped both aesthetic and cultural sensibilities. McEwan's narrative reflects upon the impact of the twin towers on the protagonist's 16-year-old son, who begins to become aware of the international scene, and on Perowne, who has tried to think of it as a historical aberration: 'No going back. The nineties are looking like an innocent decade, and who would have thought it at the time? Now we breathe a different air' (32). The selfsame traumatic event serves as an underlying motif in Amis's *Yellow Dog* (2003), with its evocations of entrapment and disaster.

Moving to the detail of this book, *British Fiction Today*, its chapters are divided into four sections, each of which responds to certain key features of a group of four authors, ordered alphabetically within their sections. The groupings are provisional approximations of shared themes, and are intended to be useful rather than prescriptive. Each section is prefaced by a brief explanatory introduction of critical and thematic contexts. The first section, 'Modern Lives, Contemporary Living', is introduced by Joseph Brooker's chapter 'The Middle Years of Martin Amis'. Amis's breadth is undoubted and he is a problematizer par excellence of certainties. Brooker's chapter offers a cartography of the coordinates of what he argues might be the quintessential contemporary writer, whose work is characterized by its contradictory relation with referentiality, realism and truth. These are key elements with a resonance that goes well beyond Amis; as Brooker demonstrates, Amis's quirky stylistic brilliance has influenced a generation of writers, as have his evocations of male crisis. As Brooker concludes, this is a writer whose art may have become recursive and self-parodying in the course of his mature career.

In concluding Chapter 2, 'Julian Barnes and a Case of English Identity', Dominic Head judges the significance of Barnes's avowal and problematizing of an Englishness still dragging its imperial baggage. While such ambiguities are traced in various of Barnes's works, particularly *England, England* (1998) and *Arthur & George* (2005), Head details Barnes's major themes as the question of history, the construction of its narratives, his relationship to French 'high' theory, and the relationship between art and life. Building upon his critique, Head deftly interprets *Arthur & George*, demonstrating that the complications of imperial identity, racism and self-conscious Englishness in the 1890s might lead the reader to question the need to cultivate a contemporaneous 'nationalism' to counter such prejudices.

In Chapter 3, Pamela Thurschwell's analysis of Jonathan Coe's *What a Carve Up!* centres in part upon the details of the text's architectonics, the formal aspects that engage in a frantic genre-mixing and double-structuring which are, as Thurschwell indicates, reminiscent of Dickens's *Bleak House*. This frames what Thurschwell describes as the 'semi-autistic withdrawal' (32) of protagonist Michael Owen. In a subtle reading of both the historical repetitions and the personal compulsions that characterize this landmark novel, together with the two subsequent novels, Thurschwell concludes that Coe creates both a postmodern commentary on the loss of utopian promise in Britain, and a cartography of the inhospitable nature of history. As a consequence of being unable to process its tragic-farcical iterations, Coe's exasperating but likeable protagonists are thwarted in their youthful desire. As Thurschwell implies, it is in this fashion that one can perceive continuity underlying certain aspects of Coe's work.

Chapter 4, Kaye Mitchell's 'Alan Hollinghurst and Homosexual Identity' relates the public reception of the Booker Prize success of *The Line of Beauty* reflected by headlines in two national newspapers, offering a further account of the relationship of both the author and that of his text to gay identity. Mitchell assesses the elusive relationship of Hollinghurst's protagonist to aestheticism, and his revision of that tradition by 'aestheticising sex and the object of desire'. Mitchell traces these themes in Hollinghurst's depiction of artwork and voyeurism as a libidinal phenomenology of new identities related to past historical practices, an eroticization of an increasingly commodified set of sexual practices, 'a defiant queering of the public realm' (47–8) central to Hollinghurst's oeuvre.

In the second section, in 'Distortions and Dreams', Tamás Bényei explores the limitations of the over-generalizing perception of Peter Ackroyd as a postmodern writer in Chapter 5, 'Reconsidering the novels of Peter Ackroyd'. Bényei situates the novelist's work as a 'centripetal counterforce to the dizzying, centrifugal (inter)textuality and non-identity of postmodern pastiche' (56). Significant for the placement of Ackroyd in this section with its emphasis on extensions of the novelistic genre into explicitly foregrounded archetypal understandings of the world and the pyche, Bényei highlights both the mythological and the mystic elements in these novels, their conscious transcendence of both the codes of realism and postmodern playfulness. Bényei traces Ackroyd's anarchic longings in an intriguing and theoretically informed fashion; in situating Ackroyd's fiction as using metaphor as a synthesis of language, tradition and place he offers an original and incisive reading of major texts in Ackroyd's oeuvre.

In Chapter 6, 'Jenny Diski's Millennial Imagination 1997–2004', Philip Tew examines the apparently changing concerns of Diski's pre-millennial and post-millennial fiction, examining how within a highly personalized quasi-autobiographical narrative form, she addresses at first obliquely her Jewish identity, which is transformed into two novels based upon the biblical accounts of the *Akedah* and Pentateuch. Tew situates these novels adeptly in an exegetical and philosophical tradition culminating in the later writing of Jacques Derrida, and demonstrates Diski's reverence and irreverence towards that tradition and the 'original' scriptural texts. She identifies a gendered perspective that needs to be retrieved and reconfigured without distorting the cultural authenticity of these archetypal sources. Tew's critical strategy allows a nuanced reading of an under-acknowledged writer of profound fiction.

Intriguingly, in Chapter 7, 'Assessing Ben Okri's Fiction 1995–2005' Christopher Ringrose indicates how the novelist, even in a quasi-realist stance, articulates ideas of imaginative and political renewal through what he regards as the visionary and dreamlike potential of the novel, a genre that effectively and increasingly interrogates postmodernism as both a form and ideological consciousness. Subtly Ringrose perceives an oscillation between demands of the material and spiritual worlds, situated in a persistent preoccupation with domestic space in Okri's more recent fiction. Such a reading of the texts, with its allusions to romantic contexts whose underlying radical implications animate Okri's own creativity, broadens the interpretative context of the author's work and demonstrates how his continued commitment to the imaginary as an active and engaged mode finally resists irony.

Robert Eaglestone's Chapter 8, 'Salman Rushdie: Paradox and Truth' assesses the critical reception of Rushdie's notion of migrancy, and moves to consider the relationship of the author's work to the complexities and paradoxes of the experiential, particularly that of the postcolonial subject that renders such texts as implicitly and characteristically uninterested in aesthetic mimesis. This chapter insists that the author's works have been distorted in their general critical reception, and that crucially they remain aware of the fragility of existence, and of the world's fury and destructiveness. In these readings, Eaglestone's innovative loosening of critical expectations allows both a revision of the overall position of, and a greater understanding of, the nature of Rushdie's work and of literary texts considered more broadly, as decisively indecisive, confused and contradictory, allowing Rushdie to identify an ethical positivity in the aesthetic rendering of the incompleteness and complexity of which migrancy is part.

In the third section, 'States of Identity', Leigh Wilson's fascinating account in Chapter 9 of the novels of Toby Litt focuses on the identity of the reader; or rather, on the condition of a reader caught up in a first reading of Litt's *Ghost Story*. Her own attempt to recover a sense of being caught unawares by writing is both complicated and authenticated by the circumstance of her insertion in the narrative (she is Litt's partner), and by her gauging of the distance crossed from a first, affective, experience of the text, to a second, intellectualized, reading. Although writing in an academic context herself, she reveals the scope of what is lost and gained in the movement from one to the other, recognizing the inevitable tendency of academic criticism to attempt to 'write a second reading to contain the pain of the first' (113).

Lynn Wells's survey of the career of Ian McEwan in Chapter 10 places a broadly similar emphasis on McEwan's strategic enlistment of the reader's moral judgement. She approaches with reservations the conventional view of this novelist's development, by resisting the idea of a steady progression from adolescent to adult themes, arguing that every stage of McEwan's work reflects the complicity of both men and women in the reproduction of structures of dominance, as well as insisting on the need for 'compassionate interaction among people in the difficult moral terrain of contemporary life'. If the central dilemma of McEwan's fiction is contained in the tension between selfishness and self-sacrifice, the frequency with which the fictional characters try but fail to rise above their self-interest is offset by the author's provocation of reader response, his staging of scenes 'that enjoin readers to reflect on their own ethical practices' (123).

There is a surprisingly close parallel to this emphasis in Fiona Tolan's analysis of Zadie Smith's latest novel, *On Beauty*, in Chapter 11. Echoing the distinctions between first and second readings, Smith organizes the debates between her characters in terms of over-intellectualized and instinctual responses to beauty. Tolan outlines the preoccupations of critics with the nature of E. M. Forster's influence on Smith, but turns more revealingly to this writer's indebtedness to the thinking of Elaine Scarry in her text 'On Beauty and Being Just'. Scarry's perception that the 'primary response to the experience of beauty is the desire to replicate it' complicates the opposition between adherents to the ideal of transcendent beauty, and those who understand a preoccupation with beauty as a form of distraction from politics. Scarry argues that the desire to replicate beauty actually assists in the work of addressing political injustice, by requiring of us 'constant perceptual acuity'. Tolan demonstrates the full extent of Smith's exploration of this seeming paradox, showing how an engagement with aesthetic concerns can inform an ongoing ethical enquiry.

In Chapter 12, Sonya Andermahr's investigation of intertextuality in Winterson's *Lighthousekeeping* reflects back on the readings of Toby Litt and Zadie Smith supplied by Wilson and Tolan. All three novelists analysed here induct the reader in a means of overcoming the limitations of identity based on systems of binary oppositions. Winterson's retellings of the generically various narrative discourses of her predecessors Charles Darwin, Robert Louis Stevenson and Virginia Woolf, not only valorize the renewal of story as a means of clarifying the most influential and enduring models of Western selfhood, they also activate the differences between the three writers in order to project new, previously unimagined states of being. If Darwin is aligned with the objective and scientific, and Woolf with the subjective and poetic, Stevenson is positioned irresolvably on the axis of these two poles. It is only by establishing a dialogue between all three texts (and others) that Winterson imagines an alternative multiplicity in identity, that hopes to go beyond the binary oppositions of her source texts.

Although the final section of this book concerns the historical imagination, Nick Hubble's account of the psychosocial landscapes of Pat Barker's fiction in Chapter 13 makes clear the extent to which the fictional treatment of epochal moments in British and European history conceives of these moments as history in the making as much as memorialization. The novels of the trilogy and *Another World* focus on the ways in which the meanings of the First World War persist and change for successive generations, identifying the questions they pose about agency and passivity, power and powerlessness, within the process of a long and unfinished transition from

pre-industrial to post-industrial society. Barker's fascination with the supernatural, with the imagining of her characters' engagement with different
planes of existence, provides a means of confronting her characters with
questions they are unable to ask themselves, and only rarely able to answer.

Wendy Wheeler's examination of A. S. Byatt's Frederica Potter quartet in
Chapter 14 traces the career of her main character not only against the
changing cultural and intellectual landscape of postwar Britain but also in
the context of dominant philosophical concepts since the Reformation. Her
discrimination between intellectual and embodied forms of knowledge
gives a decisive importance to phenomena acting like Pat Barker's ghosts
to disturb the fixities of 'ungrounded intellectual abstraction' (175). The role
of art in response to history as it unfolds is divided between embodied
and disembodied alternatives; with the tension between these diverging
traditions of response (reference is made in the novels to T. S. Eliot's
'dissociation of sensibility') becoming unbearable without periodic breaks
in the circuit, whether in the shape of supernatural interventions, fits of
passion, or 'knowing or unknowing possessions'; impulses towards a
materialization of knowledge earthing the characters' understanding of their
experiences in the physical world.

Rod Mengham's discussion of three novels by Adam Thorpe in Chapter
15 illustrates the workings of a historical imagination that supplies an array
of interpretative perspectives on the same sets of relations. These
may confirm or contradict one another, but make equal amounts of sense
whatever their terms of reference; whether of psychology, mythology,
social anthropology, or the uncanny. Thorpe's novels investigate the process by means of which the materials of everyday life become fictionalized
by memory, but equally they recognize the power of fiction to determine
the patterns that govern individual lives. They are as curious about the
effects of narrative whose reach extends beyond literature (familial narratives, national narratives, colonial narratives) as they are insistent upon
the necessity for literature to reflect the totality of such narrative activity,
in the context of any given historical moment.

In the final chapter, Mark Wormald identifies the crucial perspective
disclosed in Sarah Waters' novels as that of a 'compound ghost' (196),
combining elements of nineteenth-century literary material (Wilkie Collins,
Robert Browning, Henry James) with the interpretative techniques of more
recent critical and theoretical accounts of nineteenth-century culture, such
as those that Waters herself has elaborated elsewhere. The movement
backwards and forwards between modern and 'period' sensibilities induces a
sense of interpretative responsibility in the reader of these historical
romances, the awareness of a contract with the writer who partly uncovers
and partly infers the nature of hidden sexual subcultures. Wormald's
reading of *Affinity* monitors skilfully the likely complicity of the reader who
emulates in aesthetic form the culture of surveillance of which the novel so
carefully counts the cost.

For the editors of this collection, echoing the once-fashionable post-structuralist jargon of the 1980s, this book is an 'intertext', in that it supplements and acknowledges their previous work in the field, specifically: Rod Mengham (ed.), *An Introduction to Contemporary Fiction: International Writing in English since 1970* (1999); Richard J. Lane, Rod Mengham and Philip Tew (eds), *Contemporary British Fiction* (2003); and Philip Tew, *The Contemporary British Novel* (2004). All three broke new ground and were well received. To supplement such earlier work, we offer this group of innovative, informative and freshly conceived readings of the literary texts that some of today's key critics feel worth reading, and believe them to offer some intriguing perspectives upon the age in which we live.

Bibliography

Amis, Martin. *Yellow Dog*. London: Jonathan Cape, 2003.

McEwan, Ian. *Saturday*. London: Jonathan Cape, 2005.

Winterson, Jeanette. *Art and Lies: a Piece for Three Voices and a Bawd*. London: Jonathan Cape, 1994.

Section One:
Modern Lives, Contemporary Living

Introduction

ROD MENGHAM AND PHILIP TEW

The following chapters share two focal points: first, they consider authors who have been regarded as exemplifying the crises of contemporary identity and ways of living, and second they interpret the ideological imprints of such lifestyles, affected as they are by cultural and historical changes that are reshaping Britain. Moreover, it seems increasingly that postmodern dogmatism about the impossibility of grounding culture and aesthetics is itself being challenged in fiction, making postmodern irony look like a smug, self-deluding set of intellectual convictions.

Martin Amis exemplifies such transitions both in his shifting literary practice and in his critical reception. Drawing upon various cultural comparisons, Joseph Brooker accounts for Amis's idiosyncratic extravagance and pugnacity, and considers his work in the context of an often mutable and uncertain relationship between fiction and reality, suggesting that Amis cannot finally be regarded as a quintessential postmodernist. Ironically, as Brooker observes, Amis appears increasingly threatened by the self-referential nature of the kind of stylized irony that he himself identified as characteristic of that quintessentially mannered English writer, P. G. Wodehouse. In maturity, Amis appears drawn into a self-parody that attacks the knowing comedic distance upon which he once depended, becoming so stylized as to lose conviction.

Dominic Head evokes a famous comment by Karl Marx that history occurs twice: the first time as tragedy, the second as farce; specifically in terms of Julian Barnes's *A History of the World in 10½ Chapters*, signifying an incident when the narrator draws a conclusion from the fact that *Titanic* survivor Lawrence Beesley is ejected from the Hollywood set just before the re-enactment of the liner's sinking, after trying to mingle with extras on the set of the boat. In Hollywood, even disaster is transfigured into something less than parody, an utterly unconvincing history based upon sentimental banality. Such ambivalence informs Head's analysis of Barnes's literary expositions of identity and historical national consciousness. Pamela Thurschwell prefaces her consideration of Jonathan Coe's *What a Carve Up!*

with Marx's selfsame allusion to history as farce. For Thurschwell, Coe reflects the dynamics of the political class of a nation animated by reductive low comedy, in a sub-parody of the notion of history. Coe's novel reconsiders both the convictions and the traumas of the Thatcherite decade upon which the contemporary world is predicated, and suggests that its underpinnings were not only ethically dubious, but ultimately grotesque. As Thurschwell observes, in Coe's condition-of-England novel the author sifts and winnows the almost farcical possibilities inherent in lives during the collapse of communality and consensus that have led to contemporary British culture; but as Thurschwell indicates, there are nevertheless within such a history many individuals who still acquire almost perversely the status of victims of a Hardyesque tragedy.

Rather than focus upon a collective sense of national identity, in *The Line of Beauty*, Alan Hollinghurst dissects social meaning in the actions and thoughts of one particular individual excited by both power and a quasi-narcissistic sense of his gay identity. The protagonist's self-absorption allows a disassociation from many of the ideological consequences of Thatcherite government. His conciliation of such power is symbolized by his very proximity, since he lodges as a house guest with the family of a Thatcherite cabinet minister. Nevertheless, given its cultural significance as representative of a change broader than the narrowly political, Kaye Mitchell ponders on how the category of 'homosexual' acquires significance through reciprocation in terms of gay identity. Mitchell argues that Hollinghurst conceives the nature or mode of such narratives as constitutive, creating in Judith Butler's terms a species of 'intelligibility'. She shows how the very ambivalence or self-interrogating quality of such 'queer' narratives are situated in the cultural history and complex construction of gay subculture, particularly in the milieu of late-nineteenth-century aestheticism. According to Mitchell, Hollinghurst's consciously articulated indebtedness to Henry James provides a vocabulary through which one can comprehend the juxtaposition of the 1890s and the 1990s that informs so much of his writing, exhibiting his 'nostalgia for the idealized and aestheticized homosexuality of Wilde and, later, Forster ...' (43). This contrasts with the present situation in which the conventional political and public spheres appear bankrupt and jaded, as if irrevocably corrupted by the 1980s with its contradictory cult of the individual, and with its theoretical emphases upon the subversion of any commonly apprehended sense of subjectivity. Contemporary living might exude ambivalence, yet certain literary intelligibilities do emerge.

CHAPTER ONE

The Middle Years of Martin Amis

JOSEPH BROOKER

A fancied newcomer in the 1970s, a defining voice in the 1980s, Martin Amis entered the 1990s as a leading player in British fiction; the young talent had grown into a dominant force. Following his debut *The Rachel Papers* (1973), he subsidized his fictional output through the 1970s with journalistic work, notably as literary editor at the *New Statesman*. His work has remained wryly knowledgeable not only about literature but also about the modern literary world, of magazines and manuscripts, impecunious poets and alcoholic editors. Amis's fifth novel, *Money* (1984), won him special attention and respect. It conjured the distinctively new voice – offensive and amusing, by turns or at once – of John Self, a pornographic film director who seemed emblematic of Thatcher's decade. Much of *Money* takes place in New York, but its primary English setting is Notting Hill in west London. Amis has patrolled similar ground in subsequent novels of equal or greater scale: *London Fields* (1989), *The Information* (1995), and his longest post-millennial fiction to date, *Yellow Dog* (2003). These large novels look like the main landmarks of Amis's career; their tone of black comedy and their milieu of urban vice feel like his default setting. However, he has also published a host of other works, including not only novels (three more before *Money*; the novellas *Time's Arrow* in 1991 and *Night Train* in 1997) and short stories (two collections: in 1987 *Einstein's Monsters*, and in 1998 *Heavy Water*, which gathered both old and new stories), but also a memoir, *Experience* (2000), and a work of historical analysis, his indictment of Stalinism, *Koba the Dread* (2002). His extensive journalism has also been collected, in *The Moronic Inferno*, devoted to America (1986), *Visiting Mrs Nabokov* in 1993, and the extensive collation of reviews *The War Against Cliché* in 2001. Amis has lately become a less prolific journalist, presumably freed from financial necessity. But as the dates above make clear, his rate of publication has not abated.

Typical rhythms: Amis and the contemporary

Amis is a writer of queer contrasts, and like everything else in his work these opposing impulses are taken to extremes. He is at once the most loftily aloof of British writers, and the most committed to busting the *zeitgeist.* A strong case can be made that he is better at this journalistic trade than at fiction, always succinct, mordant and informed. Yet even when making television appearances or offering opinions in newspapers, he has seemed to stake his own guarded ground; his persona has long worn a certain *hauteur*. His collections of reviews and interviews include far more encounters with American authors, of the grade of John Updike, Norman Mailer or Philip Roth, than engagements with his British contemporaries and juniors. Interviewing Nicholson Baker in 1992, Amis noted that he had never before interviewed a writer younger than himself (*Visiting* 190). By the turn of the century, past 50, Amis was becoming an elder statesman of English fiction, admitting that 'You don't really read your youngers' (Keulks 260). Increasingly, Amis has shunned deadline and assignment, and sought a notion of the solitude of art. He speaks of the literal seclusion of the novelist; as opposed to journalism, 'Novels, of course, are *all* about not getting out of the house' (*Visiting* ix). Resulting from the isolation of the dedicated artist, the frequent repetition of phrases, characters and ideas from one text to another has the effect of threading them together into a totality. At times Amis's work seems autotelic, referring as much to itself as to any external reality or literary context.

But Amis also insists on the reference of fiction – to the contemporary world around it, or even to 'the near future': 'It is about the *Zeitgeist* and human evolution, particularly of consciousness, as well as furniture and surroundings. It's how the typical rhythms of the thought of human beings are developing' (Reynolds and Noakes 17). He continues to want a piece of contemporary action. *Yellow Dog* arrived with an ominous blaze of 'Amis Is Back' publicity after his protracted excursion into non-fiction; in its pages a tabloid journalist arrives 'at his workstation, with his latte and his brioche' (111), and receives emails that read 'u ask also 4 my name' (103) and 'y o y, clint, do people use 6 2 infl8 their own gr&iosity?' (75). *Money*, with its subargot of handjobs, sack artists and rug rethinks, had been not merely on the money, but prophetic of a social mood. Two decades on, some were doubtful that Amis could be so sensitive to his moment. Yet he could plausibly respond that the novel was not simply an attempt to mirror contemporary Britain, but an imaginative distortion of it. Where *Money* refers to the wedding of Charles and Diana, *Yellow Dog* contains the invented royal family of Henry IX, confirming our arrival in an alternate universe. This feint from the actual notwithstanding, Amis remains confident of his ability to render the present: 'it's a very transparent kind of culture, it doesn't hide itself away' (Brockes 4).

Amis has always provoked controversy. The queue of complainants against him is so long-suffering that he probably views it as a sign that he is doing his job. In earlier decades, he would kindle disapproval by his explicitness, his cheerful depiction of sexist slang and degrading vice, his books' glee in male bravado; his heedless disobedience of literature's 'do not enter signs' (Bigsby 36). By 2000, he was more likely to offend by his apparent conservatism. The introduction to *The War Against Cliché* is openly elitist, sceptical of the contemporary 'equality of the sentiments' and certain that literature will ultimately 'resist levelling and resort to hierarchy' (xiii–xiv). *Koba the Dread* arraigns Stalinism – a project with which few would argue, though Christopher Hitchens did muster an impassioned public reply – but also complains that trades union power in the late 1970s was 'profound and retroactive', a 'political deformation' which 'made me believe that the people of these islands had always hated each other' (23).

Jason Cowley has mused that Amis, following his father Kingsley (1922–95), might be moving slowly towards the political Right. In truth, Amis is ageing along long-visible lines. Even at its most youthful, his writing craved the disdainful wisdom of the old. In his second novel, at 26, he satirized his own generation; by 1980, at just 31, he could reckon the liberal 1970s a time of 'thronging credulities' (*Visiting* 184). The humiliating decay of the body has been an endlessly insistent theme, not a recent addition. But this dimension has coexisted with, and somewhat been obscured by, his urge to be contemporary. His prose of restless rhythm and riff has made him seem the most streetwise of writers, even as his cultural values have remained icily mandarin. Amis has been a slumming aesthete, a coruscating penman who elects to make art not from country house and dinner party but from gutter and sidewalk, garish off-licence and fraying pub. The airgun wedding of style and subject ('describing low things in a high voice' – Bigsby 23) has made him celebrated as the laureate of *fin-de-millennium* planet panic. It has been a deft double to pull off, but as a younger generation assumes the task of describing modernity, the sternness and canonical rigour grow more visibly central to his persona.

In another coupling of extremes, Amis is the most comic and the most solemn of writers. His native modes are mockery, wit and bathos, rapidly and relentlessly deployed. *The Information*'s protagonist smokes heavily: 'he had long quit thinking about quitting .... Paradoxically, he no longer wanted to give up smoking: what he wanted to do was take up smoking. Not so much to fill the little gaps between cigarettes with cigarettes (there wouldn't be time, anyway) or to smoke two cigarettes at once. It was more that he felt the desire to smoke a cigarette even when he was smoking a cigarette' (111). The passage is pure sport, laughter for its own sake; Amis's ability to keep finding further logical steps in this sequence is ostentatiously marvellous. But such riffs can also ring with truth: Amis is at his most piercingly authentic when anatomizing the humiliating conundrums of addiction, temptation and failure. That is why John Self's massive monologue remains his finest hour: for it is in *Money* that Amis's affinity with stand-up comedy – energized, manic, absurdly excessive yet plausibly observational – is most openly displayed. His comic gift has tended to follow his fascination with masculinity, and this has been among Amis's most influential legacies in the last two decades. Elaine Showalter identifies 'Ladlit' as a key sub-genre of the 1990s, and presents the two Amises' *Lucky Jim* (1954) and *Money* (1984) as its major precursors. She persuasively proposes that a younger generation of male novelists – among them Nick

Hornby, Tony Parsons, Tim Lott and a congeries of former stand-up comics – have followed Amis in their preoccupation with the newly marketable theme of masculinity. His mixture of sexual confession, cheeky humour and anxious introspection has been vital in shaping the sub-genre, though as verbal craftsmen none of the other writers mentioned by Showalter are fit to light Amis's cigarettes.

The swaggering lad and the crumpled bloke are both frequently sighted in Amis's pages, and they are often the same character. *Money* was the keenest instance of this combination: John Self is both a cocksure oaf and an insecure narrator eager for the reader's approval. More recently, male sexual appetites and success are extensively portrayed – in the promiscuous thug Keith Talent in *London Fields*; in the giftless but bestselling author Gwyn Barry in *The Information*; in Xan Meo who begins *Yellow Dog* as Amis's image of a perfect husband. But Amis generally gets more capital from imagining failure and decline, and in his work sexual and financial omnipotence can swiftly topple into their opposites. Reviewing *Money* in 1984, Eric Korn already complained that it must be 'retiring age for the worry about falling teeth and falling hair' (Tredell 58). In fact such worries have had ever more work to do in the subsequent two decades. Richard Tull in *The Information*, five years older than Self, is a physical wreck: three minutes after having a picture taken for his passport, he is 'shredding the strip of photographs with his fingernails – photographs in which he looked, at once, incredibly old, incredibly mad, and incredibly *ill*' (294). Spared no male frailty, Tull is also impotent: 'In the last month alone, he had been impotent with [his wife] on the stairs, on the sofa in the sitting-room and on the kitchen table. Once, after a party outside Oxford, he had been impotent with her right there on the back seat of the Maestro' (90). Tull is a plaything especially abused in the novelist's hands, but his plight is not entirely his own: characteristically, Amis seeks to present it as part of a wider male predicament. *The Information* begins with a panoramic evocation of modern cities in which men cry in their sleep, immune to their partners' comforting words (9). Even when he is not alleging crisis, Amis still offers opinions on supposedly universal male experiences; when Tull and Gwyn Barry enter a pub, we learn that 'All men are eternally confronted by this: other men, in blocs and sets' (103).

Here is one quality that marks Amis out from his imitators: even during a deadpan digression, we are not reliably far from portentous assertion. We can observe this characteristic mix of tones in *The Information*, when the 'spiritual bond' between junk novels and airports stirs Amis toward syllogism:

> Junk novels were about people in airports, in as much as junk novels needed airports to shift their characters round the planet. ... Some junk novels were *all* about airports. Some junk novels were even *called* things like *Airport*. Why, then, you might ask, was there no airport called Junk Novel? Movies based on junk novels were, of course, heavily reliant on the setting of the

airport. So why wasn't one always seeing, at airports, junk novels being made into movies? Perhaps there really was a whole other airport, called, perhaps, Junk Novel Airport, or with a fancier name like Manderley International Junk Novel Airport, where they did them all. (317–18)

The writer drives his terms through numberless hoops; the sheer accumulation of reflections – trivial, yet plausible – builds comic force, the reader wonders how long Amis can maintain this. The notion that 'Junk Novel Airport' would be a fancy name if only 'Manderley International' were added to it is a characteristic throwaway absurdity. Yet the whole passage closes in a different key, with the assertion that 'Airports, junk novels: they were taking your mind off mortal fear' (319). The tone is still cool, but the thought now stares levelly at doom.

Amis wants to be prophet as well as stand-up. While his collapsing men look into toilet bowls, he strains to stare into the abyss. If one feature divides his later from his earlier work, it is its relentless pursuit of gravity. The early funny stuff gives way, from about the late 1980s, to furrowed introspection and wintry warning. Admittedly, Amis has continued producing hefty comic novels, and an entropic and apocalyptic tone has sounded through them at least since *Money*. But alongside this accustomed mode, he has steadily added a body of work devoted to death and catastrophe: *Einstein's Monsters*, *Time's Arrow*, *Experience*, *Koba the Dread*. While solemnity punctuates all the later novels, *Time's Arrow* is boldly distinctive. It pursues a Nazi doctor backwards through time, from death to birth. and value, as well as time, turns out to be inverted. The doctor's legitimate medical work appears to involve maiming defenceless citizens; Auschwitz, by contrast, becomes a massive industry for creating Jews, who are then released into a progressively harmonious German society. To apply such an outlandish narrative strategy to history's most notoriously unspeakable episode is plainly risky. But the book's inverted motion is powerfully utopian, and by the same token a devastating indictment; 'only if you reversed the arrow of time', Amis explains, 'would Auschwitz be what they thought it was, which was something good' (Bigsby 35). The book's inbuilt structural elegance, the simplicity of a lone conceit, allows it to make an unmitigated, if uncontroversial, moral case.

Since *Time's Arrow*, Amis has pursued historical horror through non-fiction. Here again he meets a contemporary trend: the drift into documentary and memoir. Jonathan Coe frets in 'Nothing But The Truth' that the public's appetite for true stories may now exceed its desire for invented ones. Some writers in this period (Iain Sinclair, W. G. Sebald) have not so much favoured fact over fiction as creatively blended the two. Amis's foray into fact is somewhat different. *Experience* is carefully wrought, intricately subdivided; Amis notes that the book demonstrates 'the novelist's addiction to seeing parallels and making connections' (7). Yet it is clearly labelled as a memoir, and not to be confused with his fiction. We note the artist's skill that shapes the book, but this does not mist its factuality, as Sebald's enigmatic reveries do. More substantial genre trouble derives from the frequency with which material from the fiction shows up in the memoir. *The Information*, in particular, shares many motifs with *Experience*. Yet the effect of this is not to make Amis's facts into dubious fictions: rather, it demonstrates the extent to which his fictions are crammed with his own opinions, stuffed with vignettes and intellectual set-pieces he thought too good to leave out. The repetition of material dilutes the impersonality of the novels, yet next to Sinclair, Amis still seems a writer who values fiction as a distinct genre: who retains a certain traditional respect for the Novel. The contemporary trend of which *Experience* really partakes is the confessional, the survivor's tale: the genre at the heart of what Roger Luckhurst terms our 'Traumaculture'.

Amis admits this. 'We live in the age of mass loquacity. We are all writing it or at any rate talking it: the memoir, the apologia, the c.v., the *cri de coeur*. Nothing, for now, can compete with experience – so unanswerably authentic, and so liberally and democratically dispensed' (6). A note of disdain for the loud, inartistic public sounds here, though it is somewhat spoiled within a page when Amis admits that his reasons for writing include 'the same stirrings that everyone else feels' (7). The book relates in detail the death of Amis's father, and also addresses the murder of his cousin by the serial killer Frederick West. Both episodes could raise questions of propriety – of Amis's right to narrate them at such length. His main answer seems to be that these matters were already public: his own contribution merely sets the record straight. Still, his readiness to do this is framed by an era of self-revelation and literary catharsis. In *Experience*, as Luckhurst puts it (36), 'exceptionality is precisely what renders his writing so generic'.

Amis's willingness to dramatize his own life continues in the sequel, *Koba the Dread*, where an account of the deadly tolls of Stalinism is juxtaposed with family reminiscences and open letters to Christopher Hitchens and the shade of Kingsley Amis. In one quite superfluous bout of self-advertising self-criticism, Amis goes out of his way to inform us of his shame at comparing his baby daughter's cries to those of Stalin's prisoners (258–61). *Experience* includes a 'Postscript: Poland, 1995' describing a visit to Auschwitz, and meditating on the Holocaust and the murders of Fred West. In themselves, Amis's reflections on Nazism are eloquent and thoughtful. But it is hard to see that they belong here: the postscript seems to seek an extra dose of gravitas which the memoir does not need. The prose of these books is careful and clear; the sentences of *Experience*, which Amis warns will not shed 'formality' (7), are as stark and unsmiling as any he had published. And both books carry important literary and political freight. But they also veer into a slack self-indulgence, the distended pages of a writer so celebrated that he can get away with publishing his correspondence. It is understandable that Amis is interested in his father, but the many pages of *Experience* devoted to the older man depict a deeply wearisome character. Significantly, though, *Experience* offers extended airings of an Amis subtly different from his black-comic norm. Its publication stirred some to hope for a different fiction — less immersed in irony, more open to bereftness and pathos — in future (Keulks 245–51).

Morality detailed: style and value

Above all things, Amis is a stylist: a performer in language, an artist of the sentence, a tactician of noun and adverb. He is both unfailingly precise — every last comma and colon in his books is deliberate and decided — and endlessly energetic: he routinely completes linguistic leaps that would sprain most writers. Individual touches may seem unremarkable, but they accumulate into paragraphs of rare verbal intensity. In a London park, 'One man and his dog went by the other way, man as thin as a fuse, dog as cocked and spherical as a rocket'. We note the borrowed cliché with which this starts, then the clipped economy of the linked similes. 'The sloping green was mud, churned and studded, beige and dun, half soil, half shit': adjectives are held in a mobile symmetry. A boy looks 'at the loners, the ranters, the post-pub staggerers, all those born to be the haunters of parks' (*Information* 136): Amis never runs short of another category of the destitute, or misses the rhythm and elegiac irony of that last phrase. His lyric gift, as Adam Mars-Jones astutely sees, is distinctive not merely in its quality but in its application: a poet's ear is cocked to the notes of disgust and decay, verbal finesse renders the world's decrepitude rather than its beauty (Tredell 155). But amid the entropic vistas, he can still conjure sudden glory: 'I know I live on a fierce and magical planet', the narrator of *Time's Arrow* muses, 'which sheds or surrenders rain or even flings it off in whipstroke after whipstroke, which fires out bolts of electric gold into the firmament at 186,000 miles per second' (23). The sorcerer's certainty with which that lyrical line is held is worthy of *Lolita*: 'With a swishing sound a sunburst swept the highway ...' (Nabokov 218).

That is no coincidence: Amis seeks his peers in a gilded past. In *Experience* he dares to make his name the third of a trio of 'noted stylists', after James Joyce and Vladimir Nabokov (113). Genuflecting to his masters, he asserts that his relation to Nabokov demands the deference that Nabokov expresses towards Joyce — though he adds that Nabokov's sincerity is 'by no means complete' (117), so Amis's own is left swinging a little. He is right to assert his inferiority to those forebears, but that he sees himself in this company at all is a sign of how he conceives of his own work. For him more than for any British contemporary, 'to write' is the intransitive verb that Roland Barthes called it. His prose is self-delighting, flaunting a joy at its own capacity. Fredric Jameson once declared that the 'deepest subject' of Ernest Hemingway's work was not courage, love or death but 'simply the writing of a certain type of sentence, the practice of a determinate style' (*Marxism* 409). We might likewise say that even when Amis's books seem to be about nuclear war or urban decay, those themes are pretexts for the sentences that explore them. In a 1991 interview he admits that it is 'writing' that interests him, not 'story': from a plot or structure he seeks 'chances to describe the things that I am interested in' (Bigsby 31). Where Kingsley Amis lamented his son's 'terrible, compulsive vividness', the younger man alertly asserts that 'you should not waste anything. There should be no dead areas . . . . Style is not an icing, it is an ingredient, perhaps the main ingredient of your way of perceiving things' (*ibid.*). That claim is extended – interestingly, but riskily – in *Experience*. A footnote recounts Kingsley Amis's reaction to *Lolita* (1955). Father tells son that Nabokov's writing is 'just flimflam, diversionary stuff ... That's just style'. Martin Amis's response to this view bears the solemnity of a major tenet: 'Whereas I would argue that style *is* morality: morality detailed, configured, intensi-fied. It's not in the mere narrative arrangement of good and bad that morality makes itself felt. It can be there in every sentence' (*Experience* 122).

Amis declares style equates with the measure of morality, surely self-serving for such a 'noted stylist'. Linguistic flair as such cannot provide a guide to goodness. 'You can always count on a murderer for a fancy prose style', declares Humbert Humbert at *Lolita*'s outset (9). Happily for Amis, this claim is untrue. But the criminal Humbert's book-long spree of matchlessly fancy prose suggests that linguistic capacity and moral rectitude need not be united. Perhaps Amis's meaning, then, is that ethical care is reflected in a care for language; that moral responsibility – for people, and for their surrogates, literary characters – demands that the detail of writing should be equally responsible. The issue is clarified somewhat by its negation, when Amis finds his own intuition confirmed by the thought that D. H. Lawrence, 'perhaps the most foul-tempered writer of all time (beater of women and animals, racist, anti-semite, etc., etc.), was also, perhaps, the most extravagantly slapdash exponent of language' (117).

That point is well scored, and Amis's extravagance is anything but slapdash. If his own style carries virtue, it may be in a descriptive capacity that strengthens our sense of the world's quiddity: of the particularity of people and things. When the moral-minded critic James Wood admires such touches as 'a loose flock of city birds reared up like a join-the-dots puzzle of a human face or fist' (*Information* 103), it is partly because re-description is a kind of renewal (Wood 195). Amis himself once spoke of Nabokov's style as 'his tireless attempt to pay full justice to the weird essence of things' (Keulks 44). Some of Amis's own writing can seek that ethico-aesthetic justification, but this formulation understates another element: aggression. Adam Mars-Jones finds 'both a fear and a desire' in Amis's writing: an anxious propensity to attack, in which each sentence must pugnaciously 'declare the presence of its author' (15). No writing, perhaps, is entirely disinterested. However, Amis's is peculiarly wired and spiky, primed for strafing, ready for combat. Such writing lacks vulnerability, ready for any-thing, retaliating first. It is not coincidental that Melvyn Bragg on the front of the paperback edition of *The Information* dubbed Amis 'faster on the phrase than any of the other inky cowboys on the streets', or that such a description would feel inappropriate if applied to most other noted writers.

It bespeaks Amis's stylistic status. His ascendancy also encodes a weakness: a dearth of peace, an inability to write with calm attention to the world, which must instead be outblazoned. Phrase-making can teeter from revealing the real to obscuring it, as the task of looking is forsaken for the thrill of the riff. Amis is a devotee of literary tradition, but the traditional virtue he most signally lacks is John Keats's 'negative capability': a readiness to sublimate his bristling literary ego into the world's rich alterity. To return repeatedly to characters plainly different from himself – unlettered bruisers, abused floozies – is not a solution to this but part of the problem, for such monstrous and garish figures are a diversion from the difficulty of imagining life-sized, life-like people.

Amis's creative relation to reality is variable. He will speak of the novelist's responsibility to the present – 'We write about change, planetary change, changes in consciousness' (Reynolds and Noakes 18) – as though his vocation were eagerly mimetic. But he also declares his impatience with life as literary material. 'The trouble with life (the novelist will feel) is its amorphousness, its ridiculous fluidity. Look at it: thinly plotted, largely themeless, sentimental and ineluctably trite. The dialogue is poor, or at least violently uneven. The twists are either predictable or sensationalist' (*Experience* 7). The complaint is tongue-in-cheek, but the nature of Amis's fiction makes it look more telling than it should. There is indeed a running conflict in fiction – discussed by Terry Eagleton in *The English Novel: an Introduction* (2004) – between the reality effect and the yearning for form (10–21). Yet it would be a sleight of hand to assert that 'the trouble with life' makes Amis's fictional method necessary. His alternative to life's 'ridiculous fluidity' has been a ridiculous schematism. A disabling division in Amis has often been observed: between fineness of style and crudity of plot; between perfect phrase and cardboard character; between molecular brilliance and molar crapulence. The part (the peerless sentence) is always more impressive than the whole (the creaking plot, many-paged but still motive-hungry). In this light, Amis's assertion that 'morality' can inhere 'not in the mere narrative arrangement of good and bad' but in style looks like a self-interested defence, as well as an important truth. For once we rise above the level of the sentence and consider his husbandry of fictional worlds – their 'narrative arrangement of good and bad' – then Amis leaves far more to be impatiently desired.

Grotesques, vamps and thieves; working-class women who say 'Eez me yusband' and aristocrats who declare 'It may interest you to know that my inamorata happens to be ... "bleck"' (*Heavy* 127, 105). An endlessly unfortunate writer whose work hospitalizes its every reader, and his talentless but endlessly fortunate nemesis: as James Wood remarks (190), one 'expects to be able to peel them off the page'. A 'dream husband' (*Yellow* 5) who is transformed by a blow to the head – with yawning essentialism – into a stinking, snarling yob. Not all these conceits would be worth a short story. Spread over 300 or 500 pages, they leave the reader not only weary but mystified. Why is his generation's prose master so dedicated to absurd binary oppositions, chimerical extremes, characters and stories with so tenuous a toehold in the real? Amis once wrote of P. G. Wodehouse's fiction as an autonomous world which reflects only its own norms (*War* 204–6), but he seems not to have worried about this fate overtaking his own work — even as he regularly avers the responsibility of fiction to bring us the world's news. A similar dereliction is visible in Amis's dismissal of the idea of human motive. 'Fuck the why', *The Information* advises (169); the theme is picked up in *Night Train*, and is at least as old as *Money* (370). This sounds like a cool-headed determination to face life's real complexity, in which stagey motives have no place. But of course Amis is not really seeking that difficult richness ('thinly plotted, largely themeless'), but evading it altogether: producing, not the over-determined subjects of a Virginia Woolf, but a conveyor belt of conveniently motiveless cartoon thugs and inexplicably lascivious belles. It is all too often in his own work that 'the twists are either predictable or sensationalist'.

To tax so severely this instinctively comic writer may appear a category mistake, but it is disappointing that after 30 years of publication he still sees *Yellow Dog* as his paradigm. The returns have diminished since the cheeky, gross brilliance of *Money*; it is unlikely that Amis can better that performance in his favourite sub-genre. Other writers seem to sense the self-imposed limitation. Alan Hollinghurst in 'Leader of the Pack' observes *Yellow Dog*'s descriptive highlights — 'moments of magical vigilance' — and ponders the different writer Amis could have been. Or could yet be? The best recent evidence for a different kind of Amis novel (as against the non-fiction in which he has been soberly effective) is among his least-mentioned books, *Night Train*. That novel is modest: 150 quick pages, a muted pastiche of the American police procedural. Its initial surprise is its female narrator, the unglamorous, and detective *sans* illusions, Mike Hoolihan. Reviewers understandably scrutinized this strategy in the context of Amis's long strife with feminism. He himself comments that from the first word 'I knew I was much deeper in' (*Experience* 177). But the book's great distinction is not Hoolihan's sex but her air of reality. Amis indeed seems deeper in, simply because he lets his narrator grow into a plausible figure: bruised and resilient, shrewd but not brilliant. The book does possess other aspects. Dedicated to Saul and Janis Bellow, it is a literary performance of American English, in which Amis's relish at the smallest touches can be detected: capital letters after colons, 'too' at the head of a sentence. And it is clouded by the usual metaphysical weather, meditating on human slightness in a forbiddingly vast universe. But it is extraordinary in the Amis canon simply for the author's readiness to make his fictional creature serious and sympathetic.

It is still not too late for Amis to board that train into a different literary terrain. For a writer with such a strong signature, the middle years of Martin Amis have seen a surprising variety of directions essayed. Singular but effective diversions (*Time's Arrow*, *Koba the Dread*) have alternated with works that hint at new tonal possibilities (*Night Train*, *Experience*). But

Amis himself, through it all, seems to cleave to a belief that his metier is in the protracted riffs and compulsive vice of *The Information* and *Yellow Dog*. He has already given the world more than enough of that genre, and the world has begun to tell him so. But as he claims to Emma Brockes not to read his critics, the nature of late Amis must be a decision for Amis alone (3).

Bibliography and further reading

Amis, Martin. *The Rachel Papers*. London: Jonathan Cape, 1973.

———. *Money*. London: Jonathan Cape, 1984.

———. *The Moronic Inferno, and other Visits to America*. London: Jonathan Cape, 1986.

———. *Einstein's Monsters*. London: Jonathan Cape, 1987.

———. *London Fields*. London: Jonathan Cape, 1989.

———. *Time's Arrow, or, the Nature of the Offence*. London: Jonathan Cape, 1991.

———. *Visiting Mrs Nabokov and Other Excursions*. London: Jonathan Cape, 1993.

———. *The Information*. London: Flamingo, 1995.

———. *Night Train*. London: Jonathan Cape, 1997.

———. *'Heavy Water', and Other Stories*. London: Jonathan Cape, 1998.

———. *Experience: a Memoir*. New York: Hyperion, 2000.

———. *The War Against Cliché: Essays and Reviews, 1971–2000*. London: Jonathan Cape, 2001.

———. *Koba the Dread: Laughter and the Twenty Million*. London: Jonathan Cape, 2002.

———. *Yellow Dog*. London: Jonathan Cape, 2003.

Bigsby, Christopher. *Writers in Conversation: Volume One*. Norwich: EAS Publishing, 2000.

Brockes, Emma. 'Amis: I don't read my critics.' The *Guardian*, G2 section, 29 August 2003: 1–4.

Coe, Jonathan. 'Nothing But The Truth.' The *Guardian, Review*, 17 June 2005, http://books.guardian.co.uk/samueljohnson2005/story/0,,1508741,00.html.

Cowley, Jason. 'Catastrophe Theories.' The *Observer*, 8 September 2002, http://books.guardian.co.uk/departments/politicsphilosophyandsociety/story/0,,787961,00.html.

Eagleton, Terry. *The English Novel: an Introduction*. Oxford: Blackwell, 2004.

Hitchens, Christopher. 'Don't. Be. Silly.' The *Guardian*, 4 September 2002, http://www.guardian.co.uk/g2/story/0,3604,785574,00.html.

Hollinghurst, Alan. 'Leader of the Pack.' The *Guardian*, 6 September 2003, http://books.guardian.co.uk/reviews/generalfiction/0,,1036460,00.html.

Jameson, Fredric. *Marxism and Form: Twentieth-Century Dialectical Theories of Literature*. Princeton, NJ: Princeton University Press, 1971.

Keulks, Gavin. *Father and Son: Kingsley Amis, Martin Amis, and the British Novel since 1950*. Madison, WI: Wisconsin University Press, 2003.

Luckhurst, Roger. 'Traumaculture.' *New Formations*, 50, 2003: 28–47.

Mars-Jones, Adam. *Venus Envy: on the WOMB and the BOMB*. London: Chatto & Windus, 1990.

Nabokov, Vladimir. *Lolita*. London: Penguin, 2000 [1955].

Reynolds, Margaret, and Jonathan Noakes. *Martin Amis: the Essential Guide*. London: Vintage, 2003.

Tredell, Nicolas (ed.). *The Fiction of Martin Amis: a Reader's Guide to Essential Criticism*. Cambridge: Icon, 2000.

Wood, James. *The Broken Estate: Essays on Literature and Belief*. London: Jonathan Cape, 1999.

CHAPTER TWO

Julian Barnes and a Case of English Identity[1]

DOMINIC HEAD

Following England's 2003 rugby World Cup victory, Julian Barnes penned an article of muted celebration in the *Observer*, evoking some of the ambivalences of his novels. Accustomed to the propensity of English rugby teams to fall at the final hurdle, Barnes discerns a typical national capacity to snatch defeat from the jaws of victory in the moment when a forward knocked the ball on, when it seemed he needed only to fall over the try-line to score:

> Only an Englishman – at least this is what it always feels like at the time – could have produced Ben Kay's cardiac-arrest fumble two centimetres from the line (but then perhaps only an Englishman would have nicely made a joke of similarly fumbling his winner's medal when he received it). (28)

The first qualification here – 'at least this is what it always feels like at the time' – admits the possibility that the dashing of expectations only *seems* specific to English supporters; but the article enshrines a national identity characterized by disappointment and under-achievement. Yet interestingly self-deprecation is seen as a national virtue (the fumbling of the medal) – humility in the winner is as important as winning – and a broader notion of (undefined) national virtue hovers over the article, invulnerable to its ironies.

The contradiction I locate in this article is the construction of a positive national characteristic rooted in humility, presented as somehow innate. Yet if the *construction* of the virtue is emphasized, then we have an instance of conscious identity building that is intriguing, both in itself, and in its connection with the treatment of English national identity in Barnes's novels.

The important works here are *England, England* (1998) and *Arthur & George* (2005), though critics invoke earlier concerns with national identity. Daniel Bedggood, for example, finds in Barnes's first novel *Metroland* (1980) an 'introduction to the trope of national identity and its history' that figures more prominently in the later novels (most especially in *England, England*) (211). There may also be an important connection with Barnes's favoured topics: the question of history, and the relationship between art and life.

Several critics, like Bedggood, have found in Barnes an emphasis on the constructed nature of narrative. Barnes's two most celebrated novels, *Flaubert's Parrot* (1984) and *A History of the World in 10½ Chapters* (1989), both expose the unreliability of the historical account. In the former, narrator Geoffrey Braithwaite's search for authenticity in his account of Flaubert reveals the difficulty inherent in the reverence of a writer as *persona*. The different perspectives on Flaubert that Barnes assembles indicate that biographical writing may be a distinctly unreliable form of historical record. Yet the book remains a celebration of Flaubert the writer as personality, not just a shadowy figure from whom notable texts are known to have emanated.

A similar paradox – the debunking of the historical record coupled with an insistence on the pursuit of some form of 'truth' – is discernible in *A History of the World in 10½ Chapters*, which demonstrates both the unreliability of history and that familiar trope of modernity: history as a recurring nightmare. This is particularly evident in the story of (the real life) Lawrence Beesley, 'a second-class passenger on the maiden voyage of the *Titanic*.' There is speculation that he must have impersonated a woman in order to board one of the lifeboats, since his name did not appear on 'the initial list of those saved' (173). Later, he is employed as a consultant on a Hollywood film of the disaster, and flouts union rules in an attempt to join the 'extras' on the deck of the replica *Titanic*. Discovered and ordered off the set by the director, 'for the second time in his life, Lawrence Beesley found himself leaving the *Titanic* just before it was due to go down' (175). The precocious narrator draws a conclusion from this story that goes to the heart of Barnes's novel:

> Being a violently-educated eighteen-year-old, I was familiar with Marx's elaboration of Hegel: history repeats itself, the first time as tragedy, the second time as farce. But I had yet to come across an illustration of this process. Years later I have still to discover a better one. (175)

It is possible to read this – as Jackie Buxton does – as the driving principle of the novel, in which 'Barnes figures human history as a flotilla of shipwrecks, failed arks adrift' (65). Much in these novels, then, suggests that history is (at best) a competing clamour of dissonant perspectives, or (at worst) a nightmare in which tragedy is apt to descend into farce. However, critics have tended to retreat from any such conclusion. *A History of the World in 10½ Chapters*, for example, is often seen to find a way out of the bleakness, signalled in the 'Parenthesis', where Barnes's authorial narrator considers the values that might oppose the oppressiveness of history as fabulation: truth and love. For Andrzej Gąsiorek, these qualities extend beyond the personal: 'In *A History* the civic virtue predicated on the "imaginative sympathy" that embraces otherness finds its source in a love that is linked to truth' (164). The pursuit of a qualified truth then has a significant political dimension:

For Barnes, to surrender to fabulation is not only to embrace relativism, thus refusing to differentiate the less accurate from the more accurate, but also to submit to the metanarratives of those who are all too willing to falsify history in the interests of power. (165)

Bedggood suggests that metafictional awareness, combined with the analysis of national identity in *England, England*, enables a focused satire of the promotion and commodification of perceived national traits and icons (213). But can one retrieve a redeemed version of 'Englishness' that transcends the commodified world?

Barnes may, in fact, be attempting a reinvention of Englishness that deliberately courts the kind of nostalgia that many commentators find problematic. Globally, a surge of new nationalistic energy followed the collapse of communism in Eastern Europe, for instance, and the demise of Apartheid in South Africa. Indeed, the status of nations has begun to seem more fluid. Declan Kiberd suggests that the number of recognized nation-states has risen from about fifty in 1945 to 'something more like two hundred' at the end of the century (47). The view of nationalism as a consistent and reactionary force has, therefore, been the focus of a revisionist view, especially in the field of postcolonial studies. Neil Lazarus, for one, has questioned the notion that national feeling is intrinsically undemocratic. He suggests instead that the nationalism of emergent states can tend towards new forms of social organization, especially where the emerging state can be seen as 'a relatively open site of political and ideological contestation' (76).

This positive dynamic in the construction of emergent or transforming states, however, has no direct bearing on Englishness. Indeed, it has been unfashionable in the postwar era to contemplate positively the elements that might comprise an English national character. After Empire, the assertion of Englishness has become tainted with imperialism. The period of postcolonial migration begins a new process of cultural (and biological) renewal and hybridity, apparently making stable national identities problematic. Yet all is not flux, and the development of a genuinely multicultural society is a long-term project. Consequently, the intellectual reticence over what constitutes 'Englishness', as the transition unfolds, is regrettable.

England, England clearly registers this historical moment, with its critique of national identity, and tentative investigation of a more positive construction of Englishness, rooted in humility. Barnes imagines the essential features of England, including all the major tourist attractions, reproduced on a theme park on the Isle of Wight. Sir Jack Pitman, a caricature of the business tycoon, buys the island for this entrepreneurial scheme, and supplements his simulacra of architectural landmarks — Big Ben, the Tower of London, Buckingham Palace — with aspects of reality, for example in the part-time employment of actual Royals. Soon, 'England, England' comes to supplant 'old' England, with unintended effects. The culture of the simulacrum is roundly condemned: the replica has a potentially disastrous effect on national identity; where it supplants the original, however, Barnes's serious purpose, in a book of conflicting moods, is to generate a less conclusive view of the fake and the authentic.

Despite its satirical strand, the novel becomes more engaged in the central character, Martha Cochrane. We are told that she has fabricated her first memory of doing the Counties of England jigsaw puzzle (3–4). The memory has great personal significance as the piece for Nottinghamshire went missing when her father walked out on his family.[2] After his departure, Martha imagines he is keeping the missing piece safe, or that he must have gone to look for Nottinghamshire; but when the truth dawns, she disposes of the remaining counties, one at a time (14–17). This loss of faith in the jigsaw has an obvious symbolic connotation, introducing the motif of uncertainty about England, and about personal roots.

Originally Martha is one of Sir Jack's lackeys, but she eventually takes control of the 'England, England' venture, after acquiring incriminating evidence of Sir Jack at a brothel specializing in regressive fantasies. He has been filmed dressed as a baby, defecating in an outsize nappy, while being stimulated by a 'nurse' (153–8). Again, the satirical point is underlined: the pursuit of definitive origins is wholly untrustworthy. The 'England, England' project's own historian observes that 'there is no prime moment' (132), some pages before we witness Sir Jack's own fantasy 'primal moment'.

Barnes's problem is how to present an alternative to the strident marketing of English heritage; and in the final section he seeks a way of contesting and displacing the false or artificial elements of history and identity. An elderly Martha lives in old England (now known as 'Anglia'), which has developed in the economic shadow of The Island, and has become a parody of its pre-industrial self. Again, there is a concern with how the fake or the imitation supplants the authentic; but the 'England, England' project might be said to have disposed of the idea of authentic Englishness. Consequently, the evocation of village quaintness has its attractions. The closing scene presents a village fête, with a traditional May Queen, a four-piece band, seed cake and preserves, and so on. Barnes tries here to conjure a pastoral idyll. It is all fabrication of course, but Barnes extends the cliché until we wonder if it might deliver something worthwhile.

Martha has come here to find a traditional churchyard where she might be buried (241), a pursuit of geographical belonging that lends the final episode an elegiac serenity which sits oddly with the preceding brash comedy. Yet these dissonances, in tone, and in the denial of originary myth and the pursuit of tradition, typify the novel. As Barnes suggested in an *Observer* interview, it is an 'idea of England' rather than a 'state of England' novel (15).

Ultimately there is no stabilizing force for Martha, nothing in which identity might be rooted. On the contrary, the artificiality of this village life is insisted upon. Even so, a kind of authenticity does emerge, through the response of children to the local publican, Ray Stout, dressed as Queen Victoria for a fancy-dress competition at the fête. The children are able to believe in both Queen Victoria and Ray Stout at the same time, thus displaying a 'willing yet complex trust in reality' (264). The children's reaction reveals a form of duality in *inhabiting* the present: the capacity to make conscious use of the past in embracing the present. This indicates the spirit – fluid and even contradictory – in which national identity might properly be explained. Barnes's novel, with its counterpointed moods, is written in just this spirit.

The content of Englishness becomes secondary to a consideration of how it is put together. This is strikingly clear from the 'Fifty Quintessences of Englishness' where Barnes picks up on the empirical habit of cultural commentators who resort to lists of things that might define the national character by drawing together its disparate elements. John Betjeman's list, originating in a patriotic wartime broadcast in 1943, quoted in Jeremy Paxman's *The English: a Portrait of a People* (151), is probably the best-known of these exercises: it included 'oil-lit churches, Women's Institutes, modest village inns' as well as 'the poetry of Tennyson' and 'branch-line trains'. Betjeman evokes a sense of national stability on the basis of *things*, rather than an explicit statement of attitudes or beliefs. Paxman also resorts to list-making, and includes 'country churches', 'Women's Institutes', 'village cricket and Elgar', as well as 'punk, street fashion', and 'drinking to excess'. The items on this list, admits Paxman, 'may not all be uniquely English'; yet, he claims, any three or four of them taken together will 'point at once to a culture as evocatively as the smell of a bonfire in the October dusk'. Paxman's updating of Betjeman's exercise is strikingly divergent: 'punk' as well as 'Vaughan Williams', 'curry' as well as 'Cumberland sausages'. It points to a heterogeneous culture, which does not lend itself to a single definition (22–3).

Barnes parodies this focus on the *components* of Englishness with his 'Fifty Quintessences of Englishness', ranging from 'ROYAL FAMILY', to 'WHINGEING' and 'FLAGELLATION' (83–5). But Barnes's satirical meta-England also confirms the problem of national identity: the symbols of England, without meaning in themselves, are falsely taken as potent signifiers. Barnes is most interested, however, in exposing the falsity of the pursuit of origins, suggesting that the problem of English identity is not that it has been insufficiently articulated, but that the fluidity and uncertainty that surround any conception of national identity have not been fully embraced.

Critical opinion of *England, England*, it should be acknowledged, is not particularly high. In Matthew Pateman's account, it is a tired rehash of ideas and character traits from Barnes's previous novels. If this implies a principle of compositional self-consciousness, it does not make for good fiction. Pateman suggests that although it is possible to claim that Barnes deploys 'the strategies of simulacra, inauthenticity, and fake in order to tell a story of simulacra, inauthenticity, and fake', ultimately the experiment does not work (75).

Whether the 'mining of one's own previous works' is seen as 'blatant', or a form of 'postmodern self-referential pastiche', there is still the problem of the narrative structure: for Pateman, the story of Sir Jack Pitman's simulacrum of England, and the story of Martha Cochrane, 'do not meld together' (75). Theo Tait in 'Twinkly,' a review of *Arthur & George*, is more condemnatory:

> The novel is written in at least three different modes. It contains a clever satirical parable about national identity; a fairly realistic story about divorced parents and difficult relationships; and a sexual burlesque, occupying the literary wing of the *Carry On* tradition. The realism muddles up the argument of the satire; the burlesque trivializes both. And a novel which very nearly said something about English identity ends up a broken-backed mess. (25–6)

My view is that the novel is a sufficiently amorphous form to accommodate apparently conflicting elements. More important is the issue about writing that the novel reveals. A consistent criticism of Barnes is that he is more of an essayist than a novelist, that the predominance of ideas stifles his creative invention. Perhaps the most explicitly frame-breaking aspect of Barnes-the-essayist is his consciousness of literary criticism and theory. Even here, however, one can find artful implementations of peculiarly literary ideas. As Daniel Bedggood observes, 'Barnes' own academic focus on French writing and culture' places him 'inside the contemporary debates about literary and historical theory' (204). Indeed, it is towards Barnes's 'postmodernist stylistics' that Bedggood looks to explain the success of *England, England*: 'as a postmodern reassessment of national identity, ... this novel works as an effective satire of both the selection of what constitutes 'essential' national characteristics, and the processes of commodification that go hand-in-hand with marketing these for tourist consumption' (213).

Attitudes to literary theory are sometimes taken to signify national traits and predilections. In *Englishness and National Culture*, for example, Antony Easthope seeks to scrutinize the received idea that the English character, and the English intellectual tradition, are both governed by a common-sense empiricism, dismissive of continental theory. For Easthope, discourse has a primary role in the formation of national identity and he effectively debunks the notions of the English empiricist, whose identity is adopted as a 'given'. Therefore, this is not an identity that is sufficiently self-conscious to understand the manner of its own construction. Hence, it cannot know itself (10, 208). On the basis of *England, England*, one might wonder if Barnes is situated somewhere between the two poles: the 'Fifty Quintessences of Englishness' is a potent sending-up of the empiricist approach to Englishness; yet a self-conscious empiricism creeps back in at the village fête, with its resurrection of traditional crafts and traditions.

A similar ambivalence characterizes Barnes's treatment of the relationship between fiction and criticism. In John Mullan's account of this relationship in *Flaubert's Parrot*, Barnes is shown to be working in an established tradition in the English novel, in which 'the novelist's disdain for critics is expressed' (7). What Mullan also shows, however, is that the Barnes of

Flaubert's Parrot is producing a new form of criticism: 'Barnes's narrator can parody literary criticism, but cannot get away from it. ... The puzzle is to know whether the narrator sees as well as the author himself that literary criticism is fiction's necessary companion' (7).

Barnes was clearly also engaging with a specifically *academic* criticism. Writing in 1989, D. J. Taylor stated – wrongly in relation to Barnes – 'no novelist who aims at a wide public and a sustained level of reader interest is going to care much about the lucubrations of French theorists. One of the failures of academic criticism is that it frequently expects everybody to move in the same direction' (45). Barnes, however, is more informed about literary theory than Taylor supposes. *Flaubert's Parrot* demonstrates Barnes's awareness of some of French theory's lucubrations, and their ramifications:

> Contemporary critics who pompously reclassify all novels and poems as texts – the author to the guillotine! – shouldn't skip lightly over Flaubert. A century before them he was preparing texts and denying the significance of his own personality. (88)

This is a broad response to Roland Barthes' argument about the Death of the Author. It also simultaneously confirms and repudiates the critical position it takes issue with: there is nothing radically innovative about emphasizing literature as 'text' and effacing the role of the author, since one can find the same tendency in Flaubert. Of course, it takes an old-style biographical critic – Barnes's narrator, Geoffrey Braithwaite – to demonstrate the parallel, thus undermining the validity of the idea. Barnes remains elusive, conscious of the claims of textual construction, yet not relinquishing the empirical idea of historical evidence.

Barnes's fiction is redolent with such paradoxes; and there is a further paradox in an English Francophile expressing a stereotypically English distrust in French theory. Barnes, in short, is having much fun in the development of a recognizable intellectual English type, but without asserting anything substantial or enduring about the Englishness he presents.

The relationship between fiction and criticism – between art and life – is the express concern of Barnes's most respected books, *Flaubert's Parrot* and *A History of the World in 10½ Chapters*, and he returns to it in *Arthur & George*, in which he examines the issue of national identity, connecting religion, colonialism, racism and the construction of Englishness. The novel recreates an episode in the lives of Arthur Conan Doyle and George Edalji, whose father is a Parsee Church of England vicar, and whose mother is Scottish. At the end of the nineteenth century, George's father begins to receive anonymous hate-mail, and the family becomes the target of a series of hoaxes. The letters and the hoaxes suddenly stop. After a period of seven years they recommence, however, now linked to a series of attacks on animals in the parish. When the victimization was first reported, the incompetent and prejudiced local police suspected George Edalji; and when the hate campaign recommences, Edalji, now a solicitor, becomes, incredibly, the prime suspect.

A miscarriage of justice ensues, resulting in a sentence of seven years' penal servitude for Edalji; but, following public outrage, he is released early, after three years. But with no public pardon, his reputation is besmirched. Conan Doyle, accustomed to requests to play detective in the manner of his famous creation, Sherlock Holmes, always declines. When Edalji contacts him, however, the great writer, in need of diversion, accepts the challenge.

The two men, Arthur and George, are shown to have more in common than one initially supposes. Edalji is 'taken aback' when Conan Doyle proclaims they are both 'unofficial Englishmen', since he considers Conan Doyle to be 'a very official Englishman indeed'; moreover, he considers himself to be English 'by birth, by citizenship, by education, by religion, by profession' (217). However, he has imbibed an understanding of English fair-mindedness, rooted in his faith in the English legal system; and this self-assembled identity has a parallel in Conan Doyle's adopted Englishness:

> Irish by ancestry, Scottish by birth, instructed in the faith of Rome by Dutch Jesuits, Arthur became English. English history inspired him; English freedoms made him proud; English cricket made him patriotic. And the greatest epoch in English history – with many to choose from – was the fourteenth century. . . . For Arthur the root of Englishness lay in the long-gone, long-remembered, long-invented world of chivalry. (23)

An essential aspect of this ideology, for Conan Doyle, is the benign wielding of power, the intervention of the strong on behalf of the weak. This conception of chivalric intervention is a form of humility in which serving others is privileged; but humility can mutate into something disabling where it is taken up as a life code by those without power or influence – and this is what has happened to Edalji. His supporters assure him that 'his case was as significant as that of Dreyfus, that it revealed as much about England as the Frenchman's did about France'; indeed, the miscarriage of justice led to the setting up of the Court of Appeal (332–3).

Yet fame eludes him. Looking back, Edalji is sometimes 'nudged by the thought that he deserved more' than the transition he has experienced 'from villain to martyr to nobody very much' (332). His desire not to appear immodest is partly to blame for this, he realizes; yet he puts his obscurity down, chiefly, to England, which, in comparison with France,

> was a quieter place, just as principled, but less keen on making a fuss about its principles; . . . This has happened, now let us forget about it and carry on as before: such was the English way. . . . The Edalji case would not have arisen if there had been a Court of Appeal? Very well, then: pardon Edalji, establish a Court of Appeal before the year is out – and what more remains to be said about the matter? This was England, and George could understand England's point of view, because George was English himself. (333)

The ideology of undemonstrative Englishness produces a form of quietism, and, in a situation such as this, an internalization of defeat disguised as the adoption of a national trait. By this point readers have been prepared well to reject this ideology, since it is clear that Edalji is consistently blind to racism as a major factor in his victimization.

This is underscored when Conan Doyle attempts unsuccessfully to persuade Captain Anson, Chief Constable of Staffordshire, that Edalji is innocent. In this memorable scene a deep antagonism continually ruptures the veneer of a civilized exchange. Conan Doyle appeals for candour from Anson: 'we are two English gentlemen sitting over fine brandy and, if I may say so, even finer cigars, in a handsome house in the middle of this splendid county. Whatever you say will remain within these four walls' (273). This appeal to a national code of honour elicits from Anson an explanation of the case, underpinned by racism. It is the 'sudden and deplorable miscegenation' resulting in Edalji's birth that Anson sees as the root cause of his criminal behaviour: 'when the blood is mixed, that is where the trouble starts. An irreconcilable division is set up. Why does human society everywhere abhor the half-caste? Because his soul is torn between the impulse to civilization and the pull of barbarism' (275). Conan Doyle observes: 'my own blood is mixed Scottish and Irish ... does this make me cut cattle?' Anson's retort reveals an overt, contradictory, and *conscious* race prejudice: 'You make my argument for me. What Englishman – what Scotsman – what half Scotsman – would take a blade to a horse, a cow, a sheep?' (275). Yet this is the crime of which the half-Scotsman Edalji stands accused, chiefly, it seems, on account of his father's ethnicity.

Early in the novel, we learn how George's father has instructed his son, through a form of catechism, in the repressive English nationalism that justifies the colonial project:

'What is England, George?'
'England is the beating heart of the Empire, Father.'
'Good. And what is the blood that flows through the arteries and veins of the Empire to reach even its farthest shore?'
'The Church of England.'
'Good, George.' (17)

As he goes to sleep, the young George thinks 'of arteries and veins making red lines on the map of the world, linking Britain to all the places coloured pink ... he thinks of blood ... emerging in Sydney, Bombay, Cape Town' (17). The naïveté of George invites us to re-envision his traditional image of England as, instead, a bloated parasite, drawing on the blood of these far-flung places, rather than supplying it.

Such symbolism is embodied in the Counties of England jigsaw in *England, England*. The vacuum consequent upon the end of Empire mutates into a graphic representation of the imperial adventure itself, the interpellation of the colonized, in the interests of the distant greedy heart of the colonial centre. Economically, by sketching the sinister ideological project of map-making, Barnes presents an analysis that is standard in postcolonial criticism; and the really interesting aspect of this is what it suggests about Barnes's literary model.

Postcolonial critics have often sought to expose the unconscious or unexamined racism of Edwardian English fiction, sometimes highlighting its role in the discursive practices of imperialism. Where does Barnes stand on this issue, on the basis of *Arthur & George*? Conan Doyle, as we have seen, is Edalji's champion, convinced of the racist aspect of the case (to which the victim is blind). His own ethnicity is compared to Edalji's, and yet he adopts a form of Englishness – rooted in fourteenth-century chivalry – that presumes dominion, since 'chivalry was the prerogative of the powerful' (23).

Barnes's own gesture in writing this novel is also pointedly ambivalent. Peter Kemp observes that its imitative qualities extend from the obvious – the handsome binding – to the manner of writing:

> *Arthur & George* has strong affinities with Edwardian fiction. Its central figures – contrasting types of social decency – are portrayed with a leisurely fullness redolent of the period. Like many Edwardian novels, it is about close-to-home savagery behind the imperial façade, and unruly impulses festering beneath the veneer of decorum. (38)

Unlike many Edwardian novels, however, the connections between religion, colonialism and racism are acute. Even so, the novel is also a pastiche of Edwardian fiction, by virtue of its appearance and its internal structure, a simulacrum of English literary heritage, in the spirit of the 'England, England' project. Such evaluations are hard to disregard entirely. Yet the important literary comparison is not Wells, Bennett or Galsworthy, but Conan Doyle's Sherlock Holmes stories.

The chief literary-historical effect of the novel is to discreetly qualify or undermine the Holmesian unequivocal detective fiction, and one of the salutary lessons for Barnes's Conan Doyle is that real life is messier than he imagines. When he believes he has solved the case, finding a good deal of circumstantial evidence to incriminate another local man, Royden Sharp, Edalji reflects that the 'case against Sharp strangely resembled the Staffordshire Constabulary's case against himself', relying on the vindictive letters as the chief evidence: just as they had been written to incriminate him, Edalji cannot see why they might not also have been written to incriminate Sharp (304). This, together with the fact that Conan Doyle obtains the only piece of solid evidence by criminal means, thus rendering it worthless, leads Edalji to conclude that 'Sir Arthur had been too influenced by his own creation'. The real case, which remains unresolved, is not susceptible to 'brilliant acts of deduction'; neither does it yield villains 'with their unambiguous guilt written all over them' (305). Jon Barnes sees this inconclusiveness as a virtue, commenting that the story 'is never allowed to build up momentum', because of the 'many frames, caveats, diversions, parentheses and asides'. He suggests that Conan Doyle, a master of the page-turner, 'might have had some suggestions'. Yet, in contrast to Conan

Doyle, 'master of the clockwork plot, arch-practitioner of the blood-and-thunder mystery', he concludes that *Arthur & George* is 'a quieter novel full of the unsatisfactory loose ends and petty injustices of real life' (19).

This chapter's recurring themes are the contradiction and ambivalence of aspects of Barnes's writing, most especially his investigations of the components of English identity; and this is cause for muted celebration. Just as the children's dual reaction at the village fête in *England, England* implies a credulity that might permit the artful construction of identity, so do the contradictions of *Arthur & George* suggest a paradoxical route to something of value. The book debunks the fictional model of Conan Doyle, but presents something messier, a case of English identity less easily resolved. This is very much Barnes's historical point: the Edalji case reveals the full implications for English identity of the obligations of Empire. When these obligations are ignored, prejudice runs rife, producing an oppression that is also internalized in those oppressed. Conan Doyle's self-conscious adoption of an English code of chivalric intervention supplies a way of attacking the iniquities of Edwardian English self-identity. The gesture of publishing this book in the early twenty-first century suggests that, 100 years on, we have the need for a similarly constructed national identity, among those who wield power, if we are to realize the fluid multicultural society for which George Edalji suffered. As with *England, England*, however, the undermining of the possible materials of Englishness – in this case, the literary model that makes the pursuit of justice heroic – is a significant complication.

Krishnan Kumar's work on English national identity is interesting in relation to Barnes's indeterminacy on this question. Kumar's challenging idea is that we should distinguish between the political nation and the cultural nation, and that, in the case of England, the cultural nation did not emerge until the nineteenth century. The 1890s, specifically, emerges as the significant era in the making of Englishness: the Edwardian period of Conan Doyle. In Kumar's account, a crisis of confidence in the Empire stimulates reflection on national identity. Another factor, for Kumar, in the birth of a self-conscious Englishness is the emergence of English literature as a subject.

Kumar's argument that the idea of English national identity does not emerge until the nineteenth century is certainly contentious. However, even if a 'cultural nation' exists in earlier periods, Kumar shows how the 1890s – with, for example, folk revivalism and its cultivation of English pastoralism – embodied a significant phase in the development of the cultural nation that influences our thinking today.

The pastoral vision and the folk tradition are both central to Barnes's concluding scene in *England, England*. Indeed, that novel's investigation of Englishness, finally, seems to accord with a statement from Kumar's concluding chapter:

> The English, having for so long resolutely refused to consider themselves as a nation or to define their sense of nationhood, find themselves having to begin from scratch. ... All that the English can really call upon is the highly selective,

partly nostalgic and backward-looking version of 'cultural Englishness' elaborated in the late nineteenth century and continued into the next. (269–70)

Barnes might concur with Kumar that 'this is not as feeble or class-ridden as many people say' (270). Moreover, the impetus of *Arthur & George* moves the debate forward, again, in the spirit of Kumar's critique:

> [The English] cannot any more protect [England] from the need to inquire more closely into its character as a nation, what it stands for and what face it wishes to display to the world. But in doing so the English should not allow themselves to forget what have been the strengths of their tradition of nonchalance towards nationhood and nationalism. ... England ... can by example still show the world that nationalism need not mean only narrowness and intolerance. English nationalism, that enigmatic and elusive thing, so long conspicuous by its absence, might newborn show what a truly civic nationalism can look like. (273)

The plight of George Edalji, suppressed in official history, indicates the long-term need for this genuine civic nationalism; and Barnes's muscular Conan Doyle, celebrated as Edalji's champion, but intellectually chastened in his failure to make life match art, suggests one way in which that newborn civic nationalism might be embodied.

Notes

1. My title alludes to an essentially unimpressive Sherlock Holmes story concerned with petty deception, 'A Case of Identity', published in *Strand Magazine* in September 1891. Holmes displays his typical characteristics: flawless deduction, undiluted personal conviction, and an unshakeable sense of justice (and how it should be meted out), significant attributes for the latter part of this essay.
2. If England is conceived as a human figure, Nottinghamshire is where the heart might be placed in the popular imagination.

Bibliography and further reading

Barnes, Julian. *Metroland*. London: Jonathan Cape, 1980.
——. *Flaubert's Parrot*. London: Picador, 1985 [1984].
——. *A History of the World in 10½ Chapters*. London: Picador, 1990 [1989].
——. *England, England*. London: Jonathan Cape, 1998.
——. 'Here's Jonny.' *The Observer Sport Monthly*, 46, December 2003: 28.
——. *Arthur & George*. London: Jonathan Cape, 2005.
Anon. Interview with Julian Barnes. *The Observer, Review* section, 30 August 1998: 15.
Barnes, Jon. 'The Pig-Chaser's Tale.' *Times Literary Supplement*, 5336, 8 July 2005: 19.
Bedggood, Daniel. '(Re)Constituted Pasts: Postmodern Historicism in the Novels of Graham Swift and Julian Barnes', in *The Contemporary British Novel*. James Acheson and Sarah C. E. Ross (eds). Edinburgh: Edinburgh University Press, 2005: 203–16.

Beesley, Lawrence. *The Loss of the S.S.* Titanic *and its Lessons*. London: William Heinemann, 1912; Boston, MA: Houghton Mifflin, 1912.

Buxton, Jackie. 'Julian Barnes's Theses on History (In 10½ Chapter).' *Contemporary Literature*, 41, 2000: 56–86.

Doyle, Arthur Conan. *The New Annotated Sherlock Holmes*, volume I. Leslie S. Klinger (ed.). New York and London: W. W. Norton, 2005: 74–100.

Easthope, Antony. *Englishness and National Culture*. London: Routledge, 1999.

Gąsiorek, Andrzej. *Post-War British Fiction: Realism and After*. London: Edward Arnold, 1995.

Hutcheon, Linda. *A Poetics of Postmodernism: History, Theory, Fiction*. London: Routledge, 1988.

Kemp, Peter. 'Conan Doyle to the Rescue.' *The Sunday Times*, 'Culture', 26 June 2005: 37–8.

Kiberd, Declan. 'Reinventing England.' *Key Words: a Journal of Cultural Materialism*, 2, 1999: 47–57.

Kumar, Krishan. *The Making of English National Identity*. Cambridge: Cambridge University Press, 2003.

Lazarus, Neil. *Nationalism and Cultural Practice in the Postcolonial World*. Cambridge: Cambridge University Press, 1999.

Mullan, John. 'Guardian Book Club.' The *Guardian*, 'Review', 24 September 2005: 7.

Pateman, Matthew. *Julian Barnes*. Horndon: Northcote House, 2002.

Paxman, Jeremy. *The English: a Portrait of a People*. London: Michael Joseph, 1998.

Sansom, Ian. 'Half-Timbering, Homosexuality and Whingeing.' *London Review of Books*, 20:19, 1 October 1998. 31 2.

Tait, Theo. 'Twinkly.' *London Review of Books*, 2: 17, 1 September 1 2005: 25–6.

Taylor, D. J. *A Vain Conceit: British Fiction in the 1980s*. London: Bloomsbury, 1989.

CHAPTER THREE

Genre, Repetition and History in Jonathan Coe

PAMELA THURSCHWELL

Hegel remarks somewhere that all facts and personages of great importance in world history occur, as it were, twice. He forgot to add: the first time as tragedy, the second as farce.

Karl Marx, *The Eighteenth Brumaire of Louis Napoleon*

Jonathan Coe's late-twentieth-century condition-of-England novels explore weighty political and moral issues that have emerged from the collapse of communal structures which sustained Britain as a society after the Second World War. *What a Carve Up!* (1994) and *The Rotters' Club* (2001) represent, among other symptoms of cultural stress, the breakdown of the postwar British consensus that the state ought to look after people 'from cradle to grave', a breakdown that for Coe is symbolized by the decline of the labour unions in the 1970s and the dismantling of the National Health Service in the 1980s. To explore these very modern, political themes his novels borrow motifs from classical tragedy: the roles of contingency, chance and destiny; the sense of helplessness that large-scale political and economic forces engender in people; and each individual's potentially catastrophic confrontation with a historical situation he or she cannot control and can barely begin to understand. History and individual tragic fate seem inescapably intertwined for Coe, much as they were for Thomas Hardy.

However, a different and equally valid way of describing Coe's novels is as scripts for 'Carry On' films that have been mixed with a healthy dose of eighteenth-century picaresque, a touch of Dickens, the funny bits of *Ulysses* and a helping of Godard. Coe can't resist any opportunity for a good joke, with an elaborate set-up, and is even more susceptible to a literary or film reference, or a creaking pun. Marx's words seem appropriate for Coe's oeuvre; except that in Coe's novels, rather than an originally tragic happening degenerating to farce when it is repeated later by lesser actors, farce itself becomes the modern form of tragedy. In one unforgettable scene from *What a Carve Up!*, Coe's narrator Michael Owen is about to eat a frozen dinner of sausage and mash when he notices a photograph on the back, captioned 'serving suggestion'. It shows the dinner tipped onto a plate, with a knife and fork on either side: 'I stared at this photograph for some time while a nasty suspicion began to creep over me. All at once I had the feeling that someone, somewhere, was enjoying a monstrous joke at my expense. And not just at my expense, but at all our expenses' (258). When manufacturers imagine that consumers are too stupid to know how to put bangers and mash on a plate, or too apathetic to mind that they are being insulted, then the farces of everyday life shade into tragedy. *What a Carve Up!* makes explicit that the people responsible for that 'serving suggestion' are, in the long run, the people who decide who lives or dies. Coe's narrative universe is one where parody Gothic and gritty realism coexist, where Groucho and Karl vie for space on the same page, even in the same sentence.

My intention in this chapter is to explore *What a Carve Up!* and, more briefly, *The Rotters' Club* and its downbeat Blairite follow-up novel, *The Closed Circle* (2004), in relation to Marx's suggestive statement from the *Eighteenth Brumaire* that prefaces this essay above. Marx's three interrelated topics: genre, repetition and history, raise the spectre of postmodernism, and the postmodern novel's engagement, or lack of engagement, with history and politics. In a review of *What a Carve Up!* Terry Eagleton claimed that the book was 'one of the few pieces of genuinely political Post-Modern fiction around ... it is deeply, unwaveringly furious' (12). Eagleton's comment suggests that postmodernism works against a passionate political agenda: distancing us from the individual's inevitable entrapment in the hegemonic forces of late capitalism by using pastiche and irony to highlight the means of textual production. Postmodernism points out that the genres through which we describe the brute 'facts' of history set the terms for how we read our collective past's legacy. If a realm of freedom for the individual or art is unthinkable outside the constraints of a capitalist system, then the artist-author can comment on or critique the existing culture, but never escape from it.

Postmodernism's preference for comic forms can distract from the potential sadness of that dilemma. Farce, as a genre, distances us from the brutality of everyday life. In farce, pratfalls are funny; in real life they might leave you in a wheelchair. In a political novel farce might be seen as quietist, yet Coe's farce is often designed to enrage. *What a Carve Up!*'s fantastical conclusion borrows wholesale from a little-known (except clearly to Coe) 1933 comedy gothic potboiler *The Ghoul* (the source of the 1961 film *What a Carve Up!*), in order to kill off his Thatcherite villains in an appropriately over-the-top bloodbath. However, Coe's fury remains at the forefront of his postmodern pastiching; his abundant borrowings from popular and high-culture genres actually function to feed anger rather than defuse it. The clashing of genres, perhaps, makes the pain more real; the social realist death of one character while waiting for doctors to see her in an overworked NHS hospital is followed immediately by the gleeful massacre of the entire Winshaw family.

Coe gives us a hint as to his strategy when his protagonist sniffily reviews a recent political novel by a left-wing author. Owen writes:

> We stand badly in need of novels, after all, which show an understanding of the ideological hijack which has taken place so recently in this country, which can see its consequences in human terms and show that the appropriate response lies not merely in sorrow and anger but in mad, incredulous laughter. (277)

This might function as a fair description of Coe's project; the question is can Coe's mastery of that 'mad incredulous laughter' combine comfortably with those 'human terms'? And can the echoes of Greek tragedy that resonate through *What a Carve Up!* – its musings on fate and chance via Oedipus and Orpheus – coexist with its, at times, excruciating excavation of the gritty social realities of the 1980s? Can you mix your pop and politics with your high literary leanings and emerge with a coherent message? Can you have your farce and tragedy, and eat it too?

I. Genre: tragedy, farce and beyond

Rod Mengham has suggested that in *What a Carve Up!* 'Coe imagines the extent to which the shared experience of the Thatcher years is one of cultural psychosis' (Introduction 5). It is that shared psychotic laughter which might best categorize the tone of the book's frantic genre-mixing. Psychosis posits a world in which everything is connected, in which the smallest effect can be traced back to malevolent motivating causes; Coe's reliance on the conventions of various literary and filmic genres creates a series of interlocking contained worlds whose inhabitants' lives are governed by generic rules. But finding oneself trapped by genre, unable to escape from a film or bad novel, also functions as a metaphor for the stitching up of narrative possibilities by the ruling classes who control the means of production, textual and otherwise.

The novel first presents the reader with what appear to be two separate plotlines, each in its own genre. On the one hand we are given the larger-than-life saga of the diabolical Winshaw family who, in Margaret Thatcher's 1980s, proceed to carve up Britain's political and cultural resources. Henry Winshaw is a Tory politician whose motto 'quality is quantifiable' forecasts the privatization of everything, including the beleaguered NHS. Dorothy Winshaw's huge livestock conglomerate mass produces brutally treated animals and nutrition-free TV dinners that work to kill off the poor through slow starvation or quick cholesterol-induced heart attacks. Hilary Winshaw's tabloid columns and controlling TV interests set the terms for a sensationalizing and innacurate media. Roddy Winshaw's influential art interests preside over the sexing up and dumbing down of high culture. Mark Winshaw happily deals arms to either side of any political conflict, while Thomas Winshaw's banking interests provide the money and the illegal insider trading tips that finance his family's projects, while his investment in films and, especially in the emerging technology of the video recorder, feed the voyeuristic tendencies he shares with Michael

Owen. The Winshaws en masse are Gothic in their all-encompassing evil; however, the structure of Coe's double-plotted novel, alternating between their very public world and the private, neurotically isolated world of the other narrator, Michael Owen, also owes much to another genre, the Victorian novel.

The structure of *What a Carve Up!* mirrors the double-structure of Dickens's *Bleak House*, in which Esther Summerson's first-person narrative and the omniscient, largely impersonal, third-person narrative are eventually shown to be helplessly entangled. In both books the story of the lone individual's origins are enmeshed in grander historical plotlines. A secret about Michael's parentage connects him to the Winshaws, just as a secret about Esther's connects her to Lady Dedlock, and to Chancery. In *Bleak House* the primary targets of Dickens's rage are society's deadlocked, outmoded structures, such as Chancery and the Aristocracy, but these impersonal structural evils are always in the service of ruthless, greedy individuals. Similarly, the Winshaws are both individuals and representative cultural forces; the six deadly sins of Thatcherism. They are Dickensian villains, to Michael Owen's (apparently) realist, (but certainly) hapless hero.

In the more orderly nineteenth-century world of *Bleak House*, certain characters are given, by the end of the novel, some leeway for escaping the regulatory structures, which initially determine their lives. Esther Summerson finally retreats to the north of England, away from the stifling metaphorical Chancery-bound fog of London. Michael Owen, whose unintentional discoveries about his own illegitimate origins mirror Esther's, is given no parallel way out of the structuring paranoia of his novel. In this sense Coe enforces a violently repetitive ending on his postmodern protagonist, who, at the end of the book, literally seems unable to escape, not so much from the Thatcherite nightmare landscape of the Winshaws, but from the generic knots of the postmodern author, a point to which I will return.

Michael's dilemma is, in a sense, a narrative one. He has withdrawn not just from the world at large, but from any movement forward in his own life, by spending his time constantly reliving one movie-mediated moment from his childhood. Michael repeatedly watches the Kenneth Connor/Sid James B-movie *What a Carve Up!* that has obsessed him ever since his 9th birthday in September 1961. Forced by his parents to leave the theatre at the moment that blonde-bombshell Shirley Eaton undresses, Michael has been held ever since in a state of perpetual sexual expectation. Thirty years later he repeatedly freezes the frame on his VCR at the moment that Shirley Eaton undresses, indulging in that most solipsistic of practices, masturbation, as he rewinds. However, it's not simply that initial voyeuristic sexual thrill that is formative for Michael, but Kenneth Connor's retreat. Although Connor's character is clearly attracted to Shirley, he leaves her bedroom when she suggests that they spend the night together. It is this refusal to act upon what he most desires that affects all Michael's further non-relations with women. Michael's solitary fantasy cuts him off from the unbearable knowledge that the outside world forces on him, whether that knowledge is personal/familial (we eventually discover that his most recent retreat was inspired by his mother's revealing to him that the man he thought was his father wasn't), or political (the creeping certainty of war with Iraq). The TV itself offers vying genres at this point in the novel — do you watch the (certainly uncontrollable, probably unbearable) news which lets the outside world invade your home, or stay safely with the controllable, endlessly repeatable tapeloop of the old movie?

Near the beginning of the book, a knock at his door interrupts Michael's solipsistic viewing of *What a Carve Up!*, forcing him to interact with his neighbour Fiona. He initially can't hear what she's saying but instead focuses on the TV in the background, which has reverted to the news and is now showing the familiar image of Saddam Hussein on the eve of the first Gulf War. However, Michael's isolation is so complete that he can't recognize that image, despite the fact that all he does all day long is watch TV. Fiona's presence gradually jogs him out of the haze, forcing him to shift his voyeuristic gaze from the frozen image of Shirley Eaton, to interaction with a living, breathing woman, against the barely grasped background of the then current catastrophe of world history.

Michael's alienation in the face of world events reflects his incapacity to function in the present; freeze-framing at a moment of unfulfilled adolescent desire will become his preferred method of survival. But, the novel also suggests that Michael's traumatic retreat typifies the shell-shocked reaction of Britain in the 1980s: 'The 1980s weren't a good time for me on the whole. I suppose they weren't for a lot of people' (102). Coe's shuffling of genres and media forms points towards a characteristically postmodern nostalgia for better times — when people seemed capable of really relating to each other; when British culture was based in community structures sustained by government policy.[1] Early on, Michael remembers his parents' 'easy sociability', which he thinks 'had more to do with the times than with any special maturity of temperament' (32), suggesting that his semi-autistic withdrawal is a product of the *zeitgeist*, rather than his specific psychic make-up.

The novel's use of the film *What a Carve Up!* indicates a nostalgia for the 'Carry On' style of British working-class humour, whose community and continuity are shattered by the corporate greed of the Winshaws. (In a cameo appearance in the novel, a chivalric Sid James forcibly removes film investor Thomas Winshaw from the set of the film of *What a Carve Up!* as he is trying to get a peek at Shirley Eaton in the nude.) But there is also another film showing on Michael's fateful 9th birthday. Michael has been interpellated by one B-movie (in his imagination he becomes the Kenneth Connor character), but he originally went to the cinema with his parents to revel in his desire to be his childhood hero, the Russian cosmonaut Yuri Gagarin, the first man to orbit the earth. A short documentary, *With Gagarin to the Stars*, is showing before the feature film, and in the course of watching the two films, Michael shifts from a desire to *be* Yuri to a desire to *have*

Shirley, moving from what might be seen as an outward-looking desire (to float above the earth and see it whole) to the inward-looking masturbatory, time-arresting, compensation of the freeze-frame. Gagarin's early death in a plane crash also haunts Michael; his, and the book's, penchant for conspiracy theories suggest that Gagarin may have been killed off by the Soviet authorities for becoming too Westernized, for bridging the East/West divide and becoming an icon to children like the young Michael. Gagarin represents the possibility of (literally) escaping from a world hemmed-in by Winshaws; he represents the dashed utopian promise of a shared future, something Britain in the 1980s definitively lacks.

Throughout the book, Michael's dreams, desires and destiny are determined by the movies from *What a Carve Up!*, to Cocteau's *Orphée*, to *With Gagarin to the Stars*. Like one of Woody Allen's essays in which his character gets trapped, first in *Madame Bovary* and then in a Spanish textbook, these narrative frames function in *What a Carve Up!* as unyielding Fate (and also like that postmodern, strong-Foucauldian version of hegemony in which juridical structures of power are totally determining and inescapable). Michael's excessive passivity and lack of self-knowledge places him in an eighteenth-century picaresque tradition, but his entrapment by narrative necessity also makes him resemble Oedipus. As he plays a game of Cluedo, assigned the character of Professor Plum, he thinks:

> In my mind, Professor Plum began to take on the characteristics of Kenneth Connor, and once again I had the sense … that it was my destiny to act the part of the shy, awkward, vulnerable little man caught up in a sequence of nightmarish events over which he has absolutely no control. (302)

When Michael discovers that it is his own character, Professor Plum, who is the guilty party in this particular game, he wonders:

> what it would actually feel like, to be present at the unravelling of some terrible mystery and then to be suddenly confronted with the falseness of your own, complacent self-image as disinterested observer: to find, all at once, that you were thoroughly and messily bound up in the web of motives and suspicions which you had presumed to untangle with an outsider's icy detachment. (303)

Michael's destiny, like Oedipus's, will be to uncover truths about himself that tie him to a mystery he thinks he is detached from. He imagines he is approaching the Winshaws simply as disinterested biographer; but in actual fact it is one of the Winshaws (mad Aunt Tabitha) who has chosen him. However, Coe also suggests that Michael is functioning in a 'different *genre* of existence altogether' from the Winshaws (235); by the end he is a part-realist, part-bumbling comic hero trapped in several overlapping narratives; Michael evades the Gissing-esque tragedy of Fiona's death in an overworked, understaffed NHS hospital by imagining he is watching her deathbed scene in a cinema. This is immediately followed by the final pastiche of Frank King's novel, which combines farce, comedy-gothic, Greek myth and prophetic dream.

It is the repetition of various stories, filtered through different genres, which gives the novel's methods of representing recent history their resonance with Marx's farce and tragedy. Both *What a Carve Up!* and *The Rotters' Club* owe a debt to the story of the Fall; positing a prelapsarian time when community and society were active forces, before individuals had become atomized as the novels' protagonists have. What once was the basis for tragedy (for instance, the incest taboo: Oedipus's unknown illicit coupling with his mother) turns to farce in the postmodern, post-Thatcher era (in *The Closed Circle*, Benjamin's brother Paul has an affair with Benjamin's daughter, none of them initially realizing the relationship). In *What a Carve Up!*, narrative events, such as plane crashes, or leaving women in their bedrooms, or even the Western world's focus on Saddam Hussein, never happen only once. Repeated and filtered through the rapidly shifting genres and registers Coe employs, they become a sign of the historically traumatized state of the postmodern subject, a state in which the freeze-frame becomes the only way left to experience history.

II. Repetition, arrest and oblivion

What a Carve Up! ends where it began, with tragedy and repetition: 'Tragedy had struck the Winshaws twice before, but never on such a terrible scale' (3; 498). But why and how does history repeat? And what is Coe doing by trapping the protagonists of his two strongest novels, in a repetition compulsion, unable to progress past one enslaving defining moment of their youths?[2]

History repeats in a variety of ways that bind the personal to the political in Coe's novels. Hilary Winshaw's two tabloid newspaper columns about Saddam Hussein, separated by four years, are an example of how repetition is used in *What a Carve Up!* to reveal the workings of power, and the presumed oblivion of the postmodern newspaper consumer. Her first column, written when Saddam was seen as a congenial Westernized leader, sympathetic to the Winshaws' business interests, makes claims exactly counter to the column written shortly before the beginning of the Gulf War, when Saddam has become a monster for the West. Repetition here is used straightforwardly to reveal the manipulations of the media; the disposable nature of the information we are fed and through which we form our opinions. The Winshaw-controlled media constructs the newspaper reader as a passive recipient of any information, blithely able to forget and accept the exact opposite of what he or she was told only a few years (or a few minutes) earlier.[3] When Michael places the two columns together and questions what he sees, he breaks out of his own repetition compulsion, and recovers cultural memory. Importantly, he manages this shortly after meeting Fiona and making his first contact with another human being in years. Symptomatically, Michael at first tries to turn Fiona off with his remote control, drastically mistaking her genre – she is a human being and not a TV programme (58), but he gradually realizes that she has, in fact, been able to 'unfreeze the frame' (235), pulling him out of his deadly structuring narrative.

Other kinds of repetition in the book are less easily reduced to political points. There are three important plane crashes; Godfrey Winshaw's (shot down in the Second World War thanks to the double-dealing of his brother Lawrence who betrays him to the Nazis) is shadowed by Yuri Gagarin's crash which, like Godfrey's death, represents the violent end of an era of heroic (and communal) aspirations. Michael's dreams of Yuri become prophetic when he dies in the third plane crash, just as the first Gulf War officially begins. Michael's death has its positive side; through Gagarin's dream of flight he symbolically escapes from the Winshaw-run world below, and he also follows the lead of Cocteau's Orphée: '. . . *Si vous dormez, si vous rêvez, acceptez vos rêves. C'est le rôle du dormeur . . .'* (167). But it is also a jarring way to finish a book in which, it is suggested, every action and reaction is motivated. What is the status of dreaming (and the sorts of mystical, prophetic or coincidental connections that dreaming invites) in relation to the postmodern politically paranoid version of history that the book supports?

A mystical sense of fate, above and beyond the machinations of the Winshaw family, seems initially unimaginable in the world of the novel. In the psychotic state of Thatcher's 1980s, everything happens more than once, because everything has a (malevolent) cause. Everyone turns out to be connected to everyone else, because power is invested in the hands of a very few, who pull the strings and control the puppet show. Coe says in a 1999 interview that the paranoid sense of hidden connections between characters had a political motivation: 'It's a book about how, if you have a small group of people essentially running every aspect of the country, which we do, everything is going to connect up. You're going to find that there are the same people with fingers in every pie. That's really the message of the book – not that we're controlled by fate, but by a small group of people who make up the establishment' (78).

But some version of fate – apart from the Winshaws – still holds sway. In the final section of the novel, in which the Winshaws are killed off in various appropriate and gruesome ways, Michael, now literally placed in the role of Kenneth Connor, does manage to alter the course of events. Instead of timidly backing out of her bedroom when Phoebe suggests he stay, he stays, and sleeps with her, finally breaking through his defining psychosexual repetition compulsion. He has changed the course of the film he is caught in. But when Michael finally does leave behind the constricting frame of the film *What a Carve Up!* and the Winshaws are all safely massacred (in fantasy, at least, putting to rest the Thatcher era), instead of a new-found freedom, or happy ending, he finds himself trapped by his other childhood obsession, repeating Yuri Gagarin's fiery aeroplane death.

It may be instructive to compare Coe's postmodern riff on the repetition compulsion in history with a similar structure at the end of Toni Morrison's *Beloved*. The central dilemma of that book involves Sethe, an ex-slave, who, in terror that her children would be reclaimed by slave catchers, killed her baby daughter. At the end of the novel, in a state of permanent temporal arrest, brought on by the haunting presence of her daughter's ghost, Sethe re-enacts the coming of the white slave catchers. But instead of turning on her own children, this time she turns and attacks an (innocent) white man instead. This is progress, in psychic terms, the book suggests. Although fundamentally mistaken in her assumptions (the white man meant her no harm), Sethe's attack still sees a shifting of the rules of engagement away from a self-destructive, traumatic repetition. Sethe's action indicates one way out of an impasse between the individual and a violent history (she is trapped by the legacy of slavery, just as Michael Owen is by the Thatcherite legacy of the Winshaws). *Beloved*'s ending suggests that repeating an action differently, in Sethe's case fighting back instead of turning on her own children, allows for an end to traumatic repetition, and the beginning of working through.

Michael Owen's relation to history, and to genre, leaves no room for working through, or human agency. Despite getting past his frozen frame, Michael only emerges from one repetition compulsion into another, killed off in a sense by the requirements of plot and symmetry. The question of the individual's vexed encounter with traumatic history is left behind at this point. Michael simply must fulfil the dreams from his childhood. In *What a Carve Up!* as in his two linked novels *The Rotters' Club* and *The Closed Circle*, Coe punishes his intensely exasperating but likeable protagonists by making them unable to escape defining events of their childhood (events they use to escape the socio-political world they are exhorted by others to more fully inhabit). Benjamin Trotter in *The Rotters' Club* experiences his own family's brush with tragic history when his sister Lois's boyfriend Malcolm is killed in the Birmingham IRA pub bombings in 1974, and Lois herself is traumatized for years. He also lives tangentially through the labour struggles accompanying the crumbling of union power in the 1970s. But it is solipsistic desire, his yearning first love for the wildly irritating Cicely, that stops him in his tracks. He never gets beyond the moment at the end of *The Rotters' Club* when they sleep together their one and only time, and which is narrated by Benjamin in a single 36-page sentence, set up to recall Molly Bloom's monologue in *Ulysses*. In the sequel, *The Closed Circle*, Benjamin's youthful promise has dwindled. After Cicely leaves him he can't move on, can't write a novel or even his (surely god-awful) progressive-rock operatic masterpiece. He can't even claim the unexpected outcome of that first climactic sexual experience; he first gets the hots for his (as yet unknown) daughter, and then permanently cuts himself off from her when she falls in love with his brother (her uncle) continuing Coe's fondness for incestuous, closed worlds (to the point where even choosing an apparently random sexual partner will never be truly random).

For Coe, being unable to process history may be the defining condition of what it means to live through it. Yet not every character experiences history that way. Coe loves adolescence (one of the joys of *The Rotters' Club* is the way it evokes the details of the 1970s through the baffled gaze of a teenager), but adolescence is also where people get stuck. It's significant that Benjamin, the anti-political dreamy artist, loses his virginity in his brother Paul's bedroom under a poster of Margaret Thatcher, on election day 1979:

> everything seemed hilarious, like the fact that we had done it for the first time in my little brother's bedroom, and that we had done it on election day, because yes!, there is a general election today, the fate of my country hangs in the balance, and that is hilarious too, and yes I refuse, from this moment onwards, to worry about anything more, to take anything seriously any more, there has been too much of that, and we have all been sad for too long. (398)

This is the wrong kind of laughter. A wilful disregard for the political sphere will never lead to happiness in Coe's universe; you may ignore history but it will always find you, cutting NHS funding so that your loved ones die, packing your father full of heart-attack-producing lard via TV dinners, or in Benjamin's case, killing off his sister's fiancé and his friend Claire's sister, indirectly, via the Irish situation, the National Front and the lurking threat of organized racism.

Somewhat like George Eliot, who sinks her strongest heroines in obscure graves (never allowing them, for instance, to become writers, like she did), Coe refuses to let his male fictional alter egos succeed via art; they can't write their way out of their historical predicaments, or break free of their arrested adolescences. They seem trapped by history and chained to early erotic fantasies. Benjamin Trotter and Michael Owen may be representative postmodern subjects (whose destinies are determined by their historical circumstances), but they are also clueless, immature men making the wrong choices (whose tragedies are also farces, both entertaining and painful to read). By contrast Coe's women sometimes react differently, and I will finish by looking very briefly at two such reactions.

Benjamin's sister Lois's story resonates throughout *The Rotters' Club* and *The Closed Circle*. Her initial desire is straightforward; she wants a boyfriend, and finds one by responding to the most generic of 1970s music magazine personal ads ('Hairy guy seeks chick'). Her tragedy is that, via this response, she becomes unwittingly caught up in England's history of colonial injustice in Ireland (the hairy guy dies in the Birmingham pub bombing). Characters in the book, like Coe himself, are interested in tracing lines of historical responsibility, but then are left in a quandary; what can you do about the helplessness history engenders, even if you feel like you know who to blame? Lois never quite emerges from the defining moment of the bombing (although she eventually recovers, marries and has a child) yet perhaps because of her trauma, she becomes a kind of living archive of those days.

She remembers everything from her childhood, especially everything that Benjamin tells her in the years she is mutely recovering in an institution, and she tells it all to her daughter, who similarly repeats it until it becomes the novel, *The Rotters' Club*. Lois's perspective, although itself a traumatized one, is privileged by the very structure of the book.

In *What a Carve Up!* Fiona offers a different perspective to the paranoid determinist history that Michael and the book seem to sanction. Shortly before she dies, she argues against Michael's conspiracy-theory interpretation of Gagarin's death, arguing for the possibility of mere chance in a non-psychotic universe: 'You think you can reduce everything to politics, don't you, Michael? It makes life so simple for you' (354). Fiona suggests that conspiracies are less common than mistakes. Her perspective is a reasonable one, and she is kind: she participates in charity events, attempting contact with people, interacting with the world. However, the book appears to endorse Michael's paranoia, at the expense of Fiona's rational humanism. As Michael watches her on her deathbed he thinks: 'I don't believe in accidents any more. There's an explanation for everything, and there's always someone to blame. You're here because of Henry Winshaw' (412). *What a Carve Up!* uses its final genre, comedy gothic, B-film send-up horror, to punish its guilty parties, sanctioning Owen's paranoid perspective. In Thatcher's 1980s, the book suggests, farcical evil was England's realism. (When I told one of my work colleagues that I was teaching *What a Carve Up!* in a class called Modern Paranoia she said, 'that's not paranoid; that's the way it really was.') But Coe's paranoid world view is also inhabited by characters such as Fiona and Lois, whose desires, to tell stories in different genres to the ones chosen by Michael and Benjamin, are also significant. These women, in some sense, want chains of cause and effect which are both simpler and more difficult; historical explanations which allow some room for human agency, farces or tragedies which aren't all determining.

Finally Coe's novels about 1970s and 1980s Britain make us ask questions such as 'Who is responsible for the current state of Britain and the world?', 'Do individual desires stand a chance against the weight of historical forces?', 'What is the relationship between individual happiness and social misery?' They try and respond to these questions in local, painful (and sometimes painfully hilarious) ways. Frantically mixing genres and conventions, his books lead us towards the recognition of modern history as tragedy, but also towards the incredulous, shared laughter of those of us still in the audience (and on stage) for postmodernism's endless historical reruns: our second time farces.

Notes

1. In his section on Henry Winshaw, the Tory politician, Coe footnotes the *Beveridge Report*, the blueprint for Britain's postwar welfare legislation which the Winshaws and ilk proceed to rip to shreds (120).

2. Freud suggests that repetition is a key element, both in psychic illness such as trauma, and in the possibility of regaining psychic health. In trauma, an event in a person's life which is too upsetting may be unable to be psychically assimilated. The person repeats the event endlessly in fantasy or in dreams, never able to leave that moment behind. However, Freud also suggests that repetition can become an element of a cure which involves returning to the scene of that event, and living through it again, but with a difference, the ability to analyse it and recognize the source of the difficulty. See Freud, *Beyond the Pleasure Principle* and 'Remembering, Repeating and Working Through'.

3. *The Closed Circle* finds us back once more in the realm of repetition with a president named Bush, and another Gulf War.

Bibliography and further reading

Coe, Jonathan. *What a Carve Up!* London: Penguin Books, 1994.

——. *The House of Sleep*. London: Viking, 1997.

——. Interview with Jonathan Coe, 'A Slice of Satire.' *You*, 4 July 1999: 77–9.

——. *The Rotters' Club*. London: Viking, 2001.

——. *The Closed Circle*. London: Viking, 2004.

Dickens, Charles. *Bleak House*. London: Penguin, 1996.

Eagleton, Terry. 'Theydunnit.' *London Review of Books*, 28 April 1994: 12.

Freud, Sigmund. *Beyond the Pleasure Principle*. *Standard Edition* 18, 1920: 7–64.

——. 'Remembering, Repeating and Working Through.' *Standard Edition* 12, 1920: 147–56.

Kureishi, Hanif. *The Buddha of Suburbia*. London: Faber and Faber, 1990.

Mengham, Rod. 'Introduction', in *An Introduction to Contemporary Fiction: International Writing in English since 1970*. Rod Mengham (ed.). Cambridge: Polity Press, 1999: 1–11.

——. 'Fiction's History.' *Leviathan*, No. 1 (September 2001): 110–13.

Morrison, Toni, *Beloved*. Harmondsworth: Penguin Books, 1987.

The Ghoul. Film, dir. T. Hayes Hunter. Gaumont British Picture Corporation, 1933.

What a Carve Up! Film, dir. Pat Jackson. Produced Monty Berman, 1961.

CHAPTER FOUR

Alan Hollinghurst and Homosexual Identity

KAYE MITCHELL

On 20 October 2004, the *Sun* newspaper unexpectedly turned its attention to the literary world as it announced in a bold headline: 'Gay Book Wins Booker' (1); the *Express* was more obviously scandalized in its headline declaration, 'Booker Won by Gay Sex' (1). Setting aside exactly what might constitute a 'gay book' (as opposed to a gay author, or reader, or character), I want to examine the relationship between Hollinghurst's works and the identity and perception of the homosexual male in the late twentieth century. To what extent can Hollinghurst's novels be read as explorations of or reflections on this identity? How far can they be seen to actively *produce* this identity? In what ways do they engage with questions of (and anxieties about) male homosexual self-definition at the end of the twentieth century? In a *Guardian* interview, Hollinghurst comments that:

> From the start I've tried to write books which began from a presumption of the gayness of the narrative position. ... To write about gay life from a gay perspective unapologetically and as naturally as most novels are written from a heterosexual position. When I started writing, that seemed a rather urgent and interesting thing to do. It hadn't really been done. ... I only chafe at the 'gay writer' tag if it's thought to be what is most or only interesting about what I'm writing. ... I want it to be part of the foundation of the books, which are actually about all sorts of other things as well – history, class, culture. (http://books.guardian.co.uk)

Given that his works *are* so often read as being *about* homosexuality first and foremost (rather than being 'merely' about love, architecture, nightclubs, art, drugs, colonialism, public schools and Thatcherism), it makes sense to ask how and what the term 'homosexual' signifies in these novels, what meanings and effects are produced by his depictions of gay characters, relationships and lifestyles. The importance of this signification of sex lies in the fact that, as Jeffrey Weeks so pithily puts it, 'the way we think about sex fashions the way we live it' (Weeks 3). The relationship between the representation of homosexual identity and that identity as it is lived is one of complex reciprocity:

> As gay persons create a gay culture cluttered with stories of gay life, gay history and gay politics, so that very culture helps to define a reality that makes gay personhood tighter and ever more plausible. And this in turn strengthens the culture and the politics. (Plummer 87)

Literary texts (and other cultural artefacts) which identify themselves, or are identified by the culture at large, as 'gay' works help create that gay culture and are, in addition, 'places where our subculture and its myths are constituted and where they may be questioned and developed' (Sinfield 149). This discussion will have ramifications also for our understanding of the way in which, in the course of the last 100 years or so, the classification of gender and of sexual practices has increasingly permeated the realms of art and literature, thereby producing a further level of classification (the gay novel, the lesbian novel, the woman's novel, chick lit, lad lit). Must Hollinghurst's novels always be read as 'gay' novels?

In addition to looking at the way in which homosexuality is narrated in Hollinghurst's novels, I want to examine what kind of narrative 'homosexuality' represents. My tacit suggestion would be that it is both confining (in the way it attempts to subsume and contain a range of practices, personalities and desires) and, paradoxically, excessive: always testing and occasionally overstepping its own boundaries. More speculatively, returning to that troublesome *Sun* headline, it is possible to consider the sexuality of narrative itself: the extent to which a text can be read as embodying a particular heterosexual or homosexual, productive or reproductive or unproductive, 'normal' or 'perverse' logic. Part of my purpose, therefore, is to suggest an implicit, inevitable and reciprocal connection between sexuality and narrative, with sexuality itself figured as a kind of narrative: one of the stories of self that we all resort to in a bid to explain ourselves to ourselves and to each other. This, however, implies an element of choice which is perhaps misleading; for in many ways such narratives choose us and we alter our behaviour and self-perception accordingly.

Narrative can be seen to have a role, not only in the *representation* of sexual practices, but also in the very *construction* of sexuality: that is to say, in its construction as intelligible — it is narrative which, arguably, produces what Judith Butler calls our 'socially instituted and maintained norms of intelligibility' (Butler 23). It is interesting, consequently, to observe how Hollinghurst's novels might serve to render homosexuality 'intelligible' in certain ways — but also possibly and problematically unintelligible — and to speculate on the intelligibility (or not) of any so-called 'queer' narrative. Does 'queerness', in the broadest interpretation of this term, in fact mean 'unintelligibility'? This is certainly what Eve Sedgwick implies when she argues that:

> Queer can refer to: the open mesh of possibilities, gaps, overlaps, dissonances and resonances, lapses and excesses of meaning when the constituent elements of anyone's gender, of anyone's sexuality aren't made (or *can't* be made) to signify monolithically. (8)

So a queer narrative may simply be one which fails to signify in any stable or 'monolithic' way. In fact the very notion of queerness, in the way that Sedgwick figures it here as transgression (boundary-crossing, category-violation, semantic indeterminacy), seems at odds with our traditional understanding of narrative (as something bounded and unified), so 'queer narrative' may be oxymoronic. Intelligibility and signification (the production and delimitation of meaning) can thus be viewed as properly political matters in a world where the 'heteronarrative' still holds sway (Roof xxxiv).

First, though, it makes sense to detail the emergence, at the end of the nineteenth century, of the category of homosexuality and the figure of the male homosexual; this marks the inception of a narrative of which Hollinghurst-as-gay-chronicler is a prime beneficiary. Ronald Pearsall notes that the term 'homosexual' was first used by Karoly Benkert, a Hungarian physician, in 1869 (546) and subsequently a large and varied discourse on homosexuality emerges which attempts to delineate its causes, symptoms, manifestations and practices. As Michel Foucault famously attests:

> The nineteenth-century homosexual became a personage, a past, a case history, and a childhood, in addition to being a type of life, a life form, and a morphology, with an indiscreet anatomy and possibly a mysterious physiology. Nothing that went into his total composition was unaffected by his sexuality. ... It was consubstantial with him, less as a habitual sin than as a singular nature. ... The sodomite had been a temporary aberration; the homosexual was now a species. (Foucault 43)

The transition is from an act (sodomy), unfettered by any association with particular persons and personalities, to a way of being, a nature, which is seen to be entailed by any preference for or practising of this act. Foucault's argument is that towards the end of the nineteenth century, rather than the 'alien' strain of sexuality (whether homosexuality or zoophilia or some other perceived 'perversion') being suppressed, 'it was implanted in bodies, slipped in beneath modes of conduct, made into a principle of classification and intelligibility' (44).

The early sexological works (by figures such as Havelock Ellis, Krafft-Ebing and Karl Ulrichs), like Freud's investigations into sexuality, are notably reliant upon case studies, which are themselves narratives and thus notably concerned to produce a coherent and intelligible account of what homosexuality is and isn't. The purpose of this narrativization and analysis of homosexuality is to render it intelligible, as concept, practice and identity, and thus (for better or worse) to render it controllable and containable. A coherent, bounded homosexuality is one which can be legislated for (or against) and which doesn't threaten to spill into and contaminate the 'straight' world. While Hollinghurst's works can be read as constituting, together, a kind of Foucauldian 'reverse discourse', a positive and defiant appropriation of the homosexual narrative and identity, the gay subculture that he depicts in all his novels sits in an uneasy relation with the (heterosexual) culture at large: *sub*culture can signify both *sub*version and *sub*ordination. I'll return to this point.

At the end of the nineteenth century, the emergent figure of the male homosexual is closely identified with Aestheticism and with a certain philosophy and practice of decadence; indeed 'decadence' was, as Elaine Showalter notes, 'a fin-de-siècle euphemism for homosexuality, the public or cultural façade that marked out one complex and indeed contradictory position along the axis of English homosexual identity formation in the late nineteenth century' (171). Alan Sinfield's take on this is of the 'model of the queer man – dandified, effeminate, leisured, aesthetic, flamboyant that was personified by Oscar Wilde', and he adds that 'Aestheticism fits the model because high culture is regarded, implicitly and perhaps residually, as a leisured preserve, and as feminine in comparison with the (supposedly) real world of business and public affairs' (150). Commentators on Hollinghurst have, of course, frequently noted his indebtedness to, and reverence towards, Henry James, and late-nineteenth-century Aestheticism. Hence Nick in *The Line of Beauty* is pursuing a PhD on James and 'style' at UCL (although he rarely seems to be overburdened with work on this project). When Lord Kessler remarks to Nick that the latter is 'a James man', Nick replies enthusiastically: 'Oh, absolutely!' and he grins 'with pleasure and defiance, it was a kind of coming out' (*The Line of Beauty* 54). The indebtedness to James is evident not only in sly little references to the Master but also in the focus of the writing itself which, rather than merely aping a Jamesian style, attempts a similarly nuanced and wry observation of a particular social world. As Joseph Brooker notes of *The Line of Beauty*, 'the entire novel is inflected with the example of James, a barrage of probing discernments and mutable judgments' (110).

The juxtaposition of the 1890s and the 1990s occurs also in *The Folding Star*, where Edward becomes fascinated by a Belgian symbolist painter of the *fin-de-siècle*, Edgard Orst, setting up deliberate comparisons between the painter's life and relationships and his own. In *The Swimming-Pool Library*, the artful interweaving of Charles Nantwich's biography (which spans the twentieth century) with that of 1980s hedonist Will Beckwith, allows Hollinghurst to situate his work both inside and outside a tradition of what Bristow terms 'homophile writing that developed in England after 1885', the year of the Labouchere Amendment which effectively criminalized homosexuality (171). Hollinghurst's backwards glances invite us to contrast the construction of the homosexual at the end of the nineteenth century and at the end of the twentieth. Although Bristow reads *The Swimming-Pool Library* as 'defining itself ... explicitly against this palpably powerful tradition' (Bristow 172), it is arguable both that Hollinghurst evinces a kind of nostalgia for the idealized and aestheticized homosexuality of Wilde and, later, Forster (of whom he is a clear literary descendant), and that he presents his own work as a critical reflection on this tradition. Hollinghurst's relationship with Aestheticism, much like James's, can thus be read as both desiring and rejecting that movement's thinking on beauty and its perceived effeminacy.

Hollinghurst's link to Aestheticism is most obvious in the foregrounding of his characters' tastes. In the educated snobbishness of Edward Manners, Will Beckwith and Nick Guest, Hollinghurst presents us with protagonists defined by and valued for their supposedly impeccable taste in music, art and antiques. It is striking that Edward, under the emotional duress brought about by Luc's disappearance, cracks only when he is compelled to listen to an inferior, 'muzak' version of Mozart in a hotel restaurant:

> I sat with pounding pulse through the next few bars, crooningly underpinned by Hawaiian guitars, prinked with a cocktail-lounge piano, fouled by slurs of blue. (*The Swimming-Pool Library* 377)

The normally reticent teacher 'raves', shouts, swears and eventually cries, seeing this 'vandalised' music as constituting 'the mockery of all [he] holds dear' (378). Similarly, Nick sits in the kitchen of his hosts, the Feddens, fuming silently about Strauss:

> What the problem was was this colossal redundancy, the squandering of brilliant technique on cheap material, the sense that the moral nerves had been cut, leaving the great bloated body to a life of valueless excess. And then there was the sheer bad taste of applying the high metaphysical language of Wagner to the banalities of bourgeois life, an absurdity Strauss seemed only intermittently aware of! But he couldn't say that, he would sound priggish, he would seem to care too much. Gerald would say it was only music. (*The Line of Beauty* 96)

It isn't 'only music' to Nick, of course, but part of his self-definition as aesthete, observer, outsider; he is one who looks, implying a kind of distance, judgement, perspective; this lends him a certain authority and status but also reflects his lack of real belonging in this world of his wealthy friends. Nick's identity is painstakingly constructed around his tastes – perhaps because in other ways that identity remains, as yet, so unformed and tentative.

Above all it is his homosexual identity which is, at the beginning of *The Line of Beauty*, ideal and imagined, rather than concrete and lived, and this is directly attributed to his lack of sexual experience. So his gayness too is initially aestheticized, and we are told that 'Nick's taste was for aesthetically radiant images of gay activity, gathering in a golden future for him, like swimmers on a sunlit bank' (25). He has not yet fully attained his homosexual identity, and at Oxford mostly flirts with straight boys:

> He wasn't quite ready to accept the fact that if he was going to have a lover it wouldn't be Toby, or any other drunk straight boy hopping the fence, it would be a gay lover – that compromised thing that he himself would then become. (26)

In referring to 'proper queens, whom he applauded and feared and hesitantly imitated' and their suspicion of him, he implies both that he is not yet 'proper' in this way and that he wishes to resist an absolute incorporation into this particular narrative (*ibid.*). It is sex, then (the encounter with Leo in Kensington Park Gardens), which marks his entry into such an identity, but this is an entry both triumphant and marked by anxiety.

The conceptualization of gay man as aesthete, critic and collector takes on a special resonance when sex is added to the equation. Hollinghurst's updating of the *fin-de-siècle* homosexual is achieved by a dual movement of sexualizing the aesthete (who becomes now a collector of sexual experience and, in a more crudely capitalist way, of men) and aestheticizing sex and the object of desire. So the 'line of beauty' which gives the novel its title has both an artistic and a sexual reading: referring to the S-shaped double curve, the 'ogee' which William Hogarth in *The Analysis of Beauty* (1753) considered to be the model of beauty and elegance in painting — but also to the body of Nick's lover. The words 'beauty' and 'beautiful' are repeated over and over in *The Line of Beauty* (the novel ending with this phrase, 'so beautiful'), but the 'beautiful things' that Nick loves cannot be divorced from their economic value: the design magazine which he and his wealthy lover Wani produce (titled *Ogee*) delineates and defines a self-consciously expensive and definitively 1980s aesthetic (*The Line of Beauty* 501, 7).

The aestheticization of the love object is most obvious in *The Folding Star*, where the museum (natural home of the aesthete) becomes a prime cruising ground, providing 'the licence to loiter and appraise, the tempo of pursuit from room to room'; it is here that Edward meets one of his casual lovers, Cherif (*The Folding Star* 9). Subsequently, under the spotlight of Edward's appropriative gaze, his young pupil Luc becomes a work of art to be collected. Edward's first and last glimpses of Luc come in the form of photographs, static images onto which he projects his longings and imaginings. In the photo which first arouses Edward's desire for Luc, the boy's face is described as a 'pale mask' — a blank canvas which reveals nothing of the personality beneath, lest that personality disrupt the attempts of the artist to paint the desired picture (8); later Edward muses that Luc's upper lip looks as if it were 'finished off' with a 'palette-knife' (29). In this distinctly scopophilic relationship it is clear who owns the gaze and, therefore, the power: on seeing him in the market place with his friends, Edward avers that 'it was a turning point in my life, this second sighting of Luc. I knew at once how the shape of him lingered in me, like a bright image gleaming and floating on the sleepy retina' (43). Luc (meaning 'light', but also implying its homophone 'look') is here turned into pure appearance, image, and the subjective nature of the attraction is stressed: it is not Luc himself to whom Edward is attracted (they have barely conversed at this point) but his own image of Luc. Luc is his own, aestheticized creation, although this view of the relationship is perhaps confounded, and Edward is forced to acknowledge his lack of artistic (and not only artistic) control, when Luc escapes him finally — as all artworks, and their possible meanings and interpretations, escape their creators.

In the course of the novel, Luc undergoes a kind of transformation in his role as Edward's proto-muse — he is a 'proto-muse' because Edward is only nominally an artist, a kind of writer-in-waiting; indeed the obsession with Luc appears to take the place of any actual artistic activity in his life. There are clear comparisons made with Orst's fixation on Jane Byron, whom he idolizes but who is replaced, after her death, with a cheaper copy, a prostitute whom he then subjects to various pornographic humiliations in front of the camera. Again, the centrality of the camera in the relationships between Orst and his lovers underlines the importance of looking as an act of aestheticization and control of the love object in this book; Edward's relationship with Luc is mediated by cameras, windows, photographs, paintings, even at one point by a set of binoculars, reinforcing Luc's status as artwork and Edward's as voyeur, and emphasizing the emotional (and, for much of the book, physical) gulf between them. Like the transition from Jane Byron to her replacement, Luc is at first untouchable, and later rather brutally available. Whatever the possible tenderness of this consummation, there is a kind of anger in it too, in Edward's need to possess and dominate the object of his obsession:

> I fucked him across the armchair, his feet over his shoulders; I had to see his face and read what I was doing in his winces and gasps, his violent blush as I forced my cock in, the quick confusion of welcome and repulsion. ... I was mad with love; and only half-aware, as the rhythm of the fuck took hold, of a deaf desire to hurt him, to watch a punishment inflicted and pay him back for what he'd done to me, the expense and humiliations of so many weeks. (337)

There is something finally unsatisfying in this encounter, however, as Edward finds himself 'craving the blessing of his gaze, though his eyes were oddly veiled, fluttering and colourless like some Orst temptress's' (*ibid*.). The artwork does not look back. In the photograph which advertises Luc as missing, the contemplation of which ends the book, Edward notices, ruefully, that 'he gazed past me, as if in a truer kinship with the shiftless sea' (422).

As the *Sun* and *Express* headlines indicate, there has been a great deal of attention paid to the graphic sexual content of Hollinghurst's fiction, and certainly promiscuity seems central to his depiction of the contemporary gay lifestyle. In *Culture Clash: the Making of a Gay Sensibility* (1984), Michael Bronski comments that:

> From earliest times, condemnations of homosexuality focused not on culture, psychology, or emotion, but on *sex*. This historical categorization of homo-sexuality as a totally sexual experience continues today. Homosexuality is considered to represent a pure, unencumbered form of sexuality. Not engender-ing new life, divorced from the social and economic structures of hetero-sexual marriage, and apparently employing sexuality as the primary form of

self-definition, homosexuality represents sex incarnate. In short, homosexuals are obsessed with sex. This obsession, along with the impulse to personal freedom that makes sexual activity possible, is at the center of the gay sensibility. (191)

Furthermore, it is evident that, in the first uses of the term, 'homosexuality' is defined specifically in relation to sex and is figured as a kind of overt and even predatory sexualization; so Benkert describes homosexuality as 'a sexual fixation' (heterosexuals are not seen as similarly 'fixated'), 'which renders them both physically and mentally incapable of achieving normal sexual erection and inspires them with horror of the opposite sex, while they are irresistibly under the spell of their own sex' (Pearsall 546). The narrative of homosexuality, then, is one of pleasure, excess, of an apparently voracious sexual drive which serves no other end; homosexuality, unlike heterosexuality, is not 'redeemable' as reproduction.

In the 1980s, the decade that forms both subject and backdrop of *The Swimming-Pool Library* and *The Line of Beauty*, gay male sexuality is increasingly and obviously linked to capitalism and sex is, arguably, commodified through the practice of cruising. While this practice may have emerged during the years of criminalization when anonymous sex was a necessity rather than a pastime, it continues after 1967, as a significant feature of gay male culture. As Tim Edwards comments:

> The sexual pick-up system is deeply set in a series of modern developments, including capitalism, that limit and shape sexual practices. ... The homosexual pick-up machine is, in fact, equally accurately seen as a reflection of the internalisation of industrial, capitalist values of efficiency and productivity in turn defined in terms of primarily male sexual activity. (94)

While the late-nineteenth-century homosexual man may have been viewed as effeminate, the sexualization of the aesthete — such as we see in Hollinghurst's novels, most notably in the character of Will Beckwith — coheres with Edwards' argument that gay male sexuality at the end of the twentieth century in fact represents the apotheosis of masculinity, and indicates the progressive 'masculinization' of homosexual culture since the 1970s. This 'masculinization', and the impulse towards public and promiscuous sex that he sees as symptomatic of it, he reads as a reaction to increased (but covert and subtle) regulation since decriminalization — Weeks is just one commentator who notes that the Wolfenden Report of 1957, and subsequent decriminalization of homosexuality in 1967, actually provided

> a framework for potentially extending rather than reducing the detailed regulation of sexual behaviour either by new forms of legal surveillance of the public sphere, or by refined modes of intervention (medical, social work) into the private. (55)

Public sex, then, is interpreted as liberationary — a refusal to accept the suppression and containment (domestication) of homosexuality, a defiant 'queering' of the public realm, a defiance of public norms of decency, and a challenge to the attempt to institute clear demarcations of public and private.

So, in *The Spell*, Robin's first encounter with Justin is in a public toilet on Clapham Common while his long-term lover lies dying at home, and afterwards he muses that:

> There was no choice, just as there was no excuse. And the thrilling squalor of it, the blond's expressionless hunger, swallowing and swallowing on Robin's slippery, kicking cock, then crouched forward over the filthy bowl, hands clasped around the down-pipe, the unlockable door swinging open behind them. (33)

And Robin feels 'half guilty, half exultant' (*ibid.*). This encounter, of course, leads to an affair and subsequently to a relationship, but in *The Folding Star* it is made clear that it is the anonymity and transience of cruising that lend it its peculiar charm. So Edward describes his wait at a train station for a delayed friend as 'one of those vacant interludes, when pleasant boredom mixes with anticipation, and six or seven minutes of anonymous sex in the mopped and deserted Gents is what you would like best' (148). In Tim Edwards' reading of public sex as constituting 'the "eroticisation" of an oppressed position', we see his own tacit politicization of erotic activity, yet Hollinghurst, it seems to me, is more concerned with pleasure than politics (109). Furthermore, if cruising is as compliant with the dominant ideologies of capitalism as Edwards suggests, then it becomes rather harder to figure it as straightforwardly 'oppositional' (92); like Nick Guest in *The Line of Beauty*, it is part of the very system that it is purported to threaten (although it does perhaps point up one of the 'faultlines' of that system).

The critical and popular attention paid to Hollinghurst's foregrounding of homosexual sex, then, perhaps masks a more fundamental uneasiness at the author's political ambivalence – particularly his relationship to Thatcherism – and his refusal to present the contemporary homosexual male as necessarily politicized. This is most obvious in the case of Will Beckwith in *The Swimming-Pool Library* who, in the course of the novel, is compelled to acknowledge his own position as an individual within something much bigger that we might call 'gay history' and his own complicity in a specific history of homophobic persecution; nevertheless, the novel closes in a description of Will apparently returning to his life of selfish pleasure and promiscuity: 'And going into the showers I saw a suntanned young lad in pale blue trunks that I rather liked the look of' (288). Similarly, although critics rushed to read *The Line of Beauty* as a satire on Thatcherism, Nick Guest's willingness to suppress any overt displays of his own homosexuality in order to keep his place in the affections of the wealthy Tory family, the Feddens, makes for uncomfortable reading. Nick is an 'outsider' within the family (as a non-relation, but also as a gay man), but one who desperately wants to exchange his own 'far less glamorous family' for this one 'rolling in money' (4, 31). Undeniably, Nick is in thrall to the easy hedonism of that period, a hedonism that has echoes of the decadence of his *fin-de-siècle* forebears; Hollinghurst's relationship with the 1980s is not anything as simple as satirical, because it is always underscored by a coruscating awareness of his characters' complicity in the systems which oppress them.

This 'complicity', however, can be read another way: as indicating the instability of the boundaries separating the homosexual and heterosexual worlds, and thus – to return to my original theme – to the failure of the orthodox narrative of homosexuality to contain and regulate its subject. So in *The Swimming-Pool Library* we are presented with a meditation on the relationship of underground to overground, with Will and Nantwich both inside and outside the establishment, and Colin oscillating treacherously between his roles as policeman and gay porn model; the underground is explicitly identified as homosexual on the first page where Will muses on the 'inverted lives' of London Underground employees:

> Such lonely, invisible work must bring on strange thoughts; the men who walked through every tunnel of the labyrinth, tapping the rails, must feel such reassurance seeing the lights of others at last approaching, voices calling out their friendly, technical patter. (1)

In *The Line of Beauty* Wani leads a double life, and Nick does too – revelling in the 'heterosexual queenery' of the Tories, while concealing what might be 'vulgar and unsafe' about his own sexuality (382, 25); but there is also a crossing of boundaries within the gay world, suggesting the possibility of diverse gay identities – something that is particularly obvious in *The Spell*, where the cloistered aesthete Alex explores the gay 'scene' of drugs and clubbing through his relationship with Danny, and where all the characters shuttle between the liberal, 'gay' metropolis and the more conservative, 'straight' countryside. This idea of boundary-crossing, permeability, is particularly pertinent in the anxious 1980s, where AIDS induces new fears of contamination – and this can be viewed as the late-twentieth-century manifestation of those *fin-de-siècle* fears of homosexuality as, firstly, visible in the body, and secondly, as dangerously corrupting/influential. The narrative of homosexuality which develops in the late nineteenth century exists precisely to establish homosexuality's otherness, its separateness, figuring it as opposed to heterosexuality, rather than continuous with it. Although Hollinghurst's worlds may appear to be almost exclusively homosexual, in showing the gay man as *simultaneously* insider and outsider, visible and invisible, he introduces an ambivalence into homosexual identity which threatens its coherence and intelligibility while also asserting its presence, even its ubiquity. This paradox of being both visible and invisible, inside and outside, is one that interests Jonathan Dollimore, who asks why:

> In our own time the negation of homosexuality has been in direct proportion to its symbolic centrality; its cultural marginality in direct proportion to its cultural

significance; why, also, homosexuality is so strangely integral to the selfsame heterosexual cultures which obsessively denounce it, and why history — history rather than human nature — has produced this paradoxical position. (28)

More pertinently, for our examination of the 'narrative' of homosexuality, he comments that, 'contemporary culture is obsessed with representations and images of homosexuality as something at once excessively and obviously *there* yet eluding complete identification', yet:

> the more homosexuality emerges as culturally central, the less sure become the majority as to what, exactly, it is: a sensibility, an abnormality, a sexual act, a clandestine subculture, an overt subculture, the enemy within, the enemy without? (29, 30)

So, through the proliferation of representations, homosexuality becomes less, rather than more, intelligible; we find ourselves presented with a series of competing, possibly contradictory, narratives, rather than a unified concept.

Hollinghurst's work seems in thrall to the idea of a homosexual identity, while simultaneously problematizing that identity; as such, it stimulates debate on the future of such an identity — the future as regards our thinking of sexuality *as* identity. Says Sinfield, 'we have to entertain the idea that "gay" as we have produced it and lived it, and perhaps "lesbian" also, are historical phenomena and may now be hindering us more than they help us', so 'we may now be entering the period of *the post-gay* — a period when it will not seem so necessary to define, and hence to limit, our sexualities' (5, 14). This raises the possibility of homosexual *behaviour* which does not entail a homosexual *identity*; if this is what the future holds, then it suggests, in the last 150 years, a movement from behaviour to identity and back again as far as homosexuality is concerned; the 'narrative' of homosexuality is a historically and culturally contingent one. The critical pigeonholing of Hollinghurst as 'gay novelist' perhaps has the intention of perpetuating his otherness (to pigeonhole is to classify and thus to contain), but his mainstream success undoubtedly has the effect of counteracting this, allowing for more positive and radical cross-contaminations (both literary and sexual) to occur. Hollinghurst too, then, is both insider and outsider in the literary establishment and the 'gay books' that he produces invite reflection on the construction of the homosexual identity in the late twentieth century and on homosexuality *as a construction*, effected through diverse narratives, with all the ambivalences, contingencies and contradictions which that construction involves.

Bibliography and further reading

Hollinghurst, Alan. *The Swimming-Pool Library*. London: Vintage, 1988.
——. *The Folding Star*. London: Vintage, 1994.

——. *The Spell*. London: Vintage, 1998.

——. *The Line of Beauty*. London: Picador, 2004.

——. 'I don't make moral judgments', Stephen Moss interview with Alan Hollinghurst. The *Guardian*. Thursday 21 October 2004. Viewed at http://books.guardian.co.uk/bookerprize2004/story/0,14182,1332083,00.html.

Anon. 'Booker Won by Gay Sex.' The *Express*, 20 October 2004: 1.

Anon. 'Gay Book Wins Booker'. The *Sun*, 20 October 2004: 1.

Bristow, Joseph. *Effeminate England: Homoerotic Writing After 1885*. New York: Columbia University Press, 1995.

Bronski, Michael. *Culture Clash: the Making of a Gay Sensibility*. Boston, MA: South End Press, 1984.

Brooker, Joseph. 'Neo Lines: Alan Hollinghurst and the Apogee of the Eighties', in *Literary Criterion*, Vol. XLI, No 1, 2006: 104–16.

Butler, Judith. *Gender Trouble*. London: Routledge, 1990.

Dollimore, Jonathan. *Sexual Dissidence: Augustine to Wilde, Freud to Foucault*. Oxford: Clarendon, 1991.

Edwards, Tim. *Erotics and Politics: Gay Male Sexuality, Masculinity and Feminism*. London: Routledge, 1994.

Foucault, Michel. *History of Sexuality, Vol. 1: The Will to Knowledge*. Harmondsworth: Penguin, 1976.

Hogarth, William. *Analysis of Beauty*. Ronald Paulson, ed. New Haven: Yale University Press, 1997.

Pearsall, Ronald. *The Worm in the Bud: the World of Victorian Sexuality*. Harmondsworth: Penguin, 1969.

Plummer, Kenneth. *Telling Sexual Stories*. London: Routledge, 1995.

Roof, Judith. *Come As You Are: Sexuality and Narrative*. New York: Columbia University Press, 1996.

Sedgwick, Eve Kosofsky. *Tendencies*. London: Routledge, 1994.

Showalter, Elaine. *Sexual Anarchy: Gender and Culture at the* Fin de Siècle. London: Virago, 1990.

Sinfield, Alan. *Gay and After*. London: Serpent's Tail, 1998.

Weeks, Jeffrey. *Sexuality and its Discontents*. London: Routledge, 1985.

Section Two:
Distortions and Dreams

Introduction

ROD MENGHAM AND PHILIP TEW

The following essays concern authors that incorporate the historiographic, the intertextual and the sense of a world that cannot be conceived in reductively realist terms. Recent pre-millennial and post-millennial fiction deploys something insistently knowledgeable in its almost instinctual return to narrative archetypes and its mythic patterns. As Bényei indicates, Ackroyd's historiography achieves something 'almost pre-modern in its archaic intensity' (56). Thus Bényei reads Ackroyd as penetrating the past in a meta-archaeological fashion, evoking a spectral phenomenology, and thus challenging the solipsistic limitations of language to offer among the past's 'monumentalism' a view of the trans-historical potential of literary subjectivity.

As Tew explains, Diski moves from the traumatized urban prosaic evocation of collective doubt to archetypal tales that shape the very roots of Western self-identity, exploring narrative impulses concerned essentially with how *homo fabulans* blends memory, fantasy and dream. Ringrose traces how in Okri's texts the dynamics of an ideological poeticism displaces both realism and the postmodern. His novels identify a rich aesthetic tradition of transcendence, appropriating European contexts to explore a differently centred narrative, a very particular placement of and encounter with implicitly metaphysical possibilities. Okri's sense of spatiality, consisting of a materiality interwoven with a metaphysical speculation, identify him as avowing an aesthetic transnationality, blending various traditional formal antecedents from different genres to challenge the invisibility of the postcolonial subject.

Postcolonial debates inform Eaglestone's consideration of a chthonic Rushdie who introduces an underlying reality into the dreamlike and archetypal, and in so doing Eaglestone explicitly reviews Rushdie's critique of hybridity, a concept that conveys only part of his aesthetic engagement with non-Western communities affected by empire and its legacies. For Eaglestone, Rushdie's works are characterized by a notion of transcendent meaning, superseding the localized, and thereby prioritizing the multifarious. Unlike a postmodern aesthetic Rushdie's work persists with an underlying notion of the philosophical possibility of truth, not a narrow realism, but as part of the momentarily existential that accedes to 'an incommensurable opposition, an aporia, between, on the one hand, character and choice and, on the other, inexorable fate, [with] no resolution even in death' (100). Rushdie creates an equivocal aesthetic determined by para-logical thinking and 'dream reasoning' rather than displaying any ambition for consensus and logic. Contemporary British fiction, in its interrogations and symbolic representations, challenges dualistic thought and uses the imaginary to achieve aesthetic and cultural meaning and understanding of the world, as it develops in all its consistencies and inconsistencies.

CHAPTER FIVE

Reconsidering the Novels of Peter Ackroyd

TAMÁS BÉNYEI

I

No assessment of Peter Ackroyd's fiction can afford to ignore the fundamental ambiguity that exists on several levels of his work. Ackroyd has been celebrated or reviled as a thoroughly postmodern writer, a key figure in the belated rise of postmodern British fiction in the 1980s. Accordingly, he duly features as a constant point of reference in what has come to be known as historiographic metafiction, a self-reflexive fiction that explores the textuality of history, the constructed nature of historical facts and narratives, thus blurring the borderline between fact and fiction (cf. Hutcheon 105–23). The steadily growing body of critical work devoted to Ackroyd has variously described him as using strategies typically associated with postmodern fiction, such as metafiction, pastiche, and ludic textual ventriloquism.[1] Although useful in identifying important components of Ackroyd's fiction, such designations prove limited when one attempts to engage with his fiction on its own terms.

While his novels indulge in heightened self-consciousness, pastiche, ventriloquism and a playfully irreverent mixture of fact and fiction, it is also clear that – apart from *Milton in America* and, to a certain extent, *Dan Leno and the Limehouse Golem* – Ackroyd diverges significantly from the canonical version of historiographic metafiction. While the latter invariably has a political agenda, its apocryphal rewritings of history functioning as a critique of established narratives, raising questions like who has the right (the power) to tell history, and attempting to give voice to muted and disempowered communities, Ackroyd's apocrypha – again with the exception of Milton's fictitious American journey – lack this political dimension. The apocryphal nature of Oscar Wilde's confessions, the account of the last day in Thomas Chatterton's life or the alternative version of John Dee has very different stakes: primarily literary and metaphysical. What Ackroyd's pastiche interrogates is, on the one hand, the tradition of English culture, and, on the other, the metaphysical aspect of our relationship with the past.

Thus, to categorize Ackroyd as a postmodern writer is problematic, not only because he himself refutes such a categorization, but primarily because in his fiction there is a powerful centripetal counterforce to the dizzy-ing, centrifugal (inter)textuality and non-identity of postmodern pastiche. Essentially Ackroyd's fiction explores the tension between a 'postmodern' awareness of the textuality of world and self, and a transcendentally, mythologically, even mystically oriented poetic imagination, which for all the ludic qualities of his texts, is never questioned seriously as the founda-tion (or, to use a phrase that will recur, the 'secret mint') of his writing. Undoubtedly Ackroyd is a radically anti-referential and anti-mimetic novelist (Finney 243–4; Gibson and Wolfreys 68), however, his undeniable 'gift for historical ventriloquy' (Todd 169) and the polyphony of his novels are always counterbalanced by a no less genuine desire for a firm – meta-physical and spiritual – centre, for transcendence, for the absolute, a desire that is almost pre-modern in its archaic intensity.

This ambiguity is also tangible in the contrast between Ackroyd's professed critical views and some aspects of his practice (although this chapter is concerned only with his fictional output). His early *Notes for a New Culture* (written in 1973 and published three years later) is a forceful and passionate indictment of postwar English cultural and literary pieties, especially of the survival of what he sees as the obsolete faith in humanism and realism, in the unquestioned identity and coherence of the subject, and in the referential view of language as a transparent instrument.

Opposed to the rearguard attempt to maintain these apparent certainties, Ackroyd champions an internationally inclined modernist impulse which, as he laments, has almost vanished from British culture. Ackroyd's book, together with both his dense and difficult poetry, and his early biographies of Ezra Pound and T. S. Eliot, situate Ackroyd firmly 'within the anti-realist, cosmopolitan, and experimental poetic tradition' (Onega 8). Yet, although the frame of reference of his fiction is both literary and almost entirely English, it is in stark opposition to F. R. Leavis's 'Great Tradition'. As I shall argue with regard to *English Music*, Ackroyd's work is suffused with an essentialist sense of the English tradition as an abiding spirit, a kind of *Nationalgeist*.

Ackroyd's world, despite his experimental, metafictional aspects, is defined and shaped by a profoundly conservative, even anachronistic and essentialist longing for a centre, in terms of both metaphysics and desire for a spiritual essence of the national culture. Although in certain texts the effect of this contradiction has been crippling, seemingly not an auspicious starting point for a major creative achievement, in what is arguably the central segment of his output – *Hawksmoor*, *Chatterton*, and the partly flawed but very important *First Light* and *English Music* – its ambiguity becomes both exciting and productive.

This problematic effect is best approached by considering Ackroyd's main fictional obsessions. Although not among his best, his first two novels establish the themes of Ackroyd's (meta)fictional realm. Concerned with the survival of the past in the present, *The Great Fire of London* is full of activities of relating to the past, ranging from the academic and artistic

(Spenser Spender's film adaptation of *Little Dorrit*, or Job Penstone's course on Victorian social history) through the everyday and the bizarre (the simulacrum 'heritage' world of the Edwardian Eatery and the old female tramp who collects trash in her prams, creating perhaps the 'only history' the area would ever have [14]), to the irrational irruption of the past into the present: one character realizes that she is a medium, possessed by the spirit and voice of 'Little Dorrit'. *The Last Testament of Oscar Wilde*, in turn, is dominated by Ackroyd's other major preoccupation, the relationship between subjectivity and language in an artistic context. Wilde is the first among Ackroyd's ventriloquist figures, proudly proclaiming the multiplicity and fictionality of the self (89), and conceiving of his life as a sequence of fictitious, specular roles or masks (91), even if in his case this ventriloquism and self-performance turns out to be claustrophobic rather than empowering. Wilde opines, 'I became a prisoner of those masks' (171), claiming that his endlessly performative self inhibits his artistic talent. 'My personality destroyed my work' (66).

Although still separated in these two novels, in subsequent work the two issues (the past and the self) appear as not only related to one another but as inextricably entangled. Ackroyd's main recurrent theme is the relationship between the past and the self, examined and dramatized in terms of one of three kinds of medium or field that both filters and articulates this relationship: variously language, tradition or place. All three constantly abut, nevertheless frequently merging into and even metaphorizing each other.

II

A striking feature of Ackroyd's fiction is the preponderance of characters whose lives are dominated by some professional, ritual, artistic, mystical, or other activities related to the past. Besides rag-collectors – the tramp of *The Great Fire of London* returns as Ned, the metempsychotic tramp in *Hawksmoor* – and antiques dealers – the pantomimically Dickensian figures of the Lemo couple in *Chatterton* and the sinister Augustine Fraicheur in *First Light* – there are several 'professional researchers', like Matthew Palmer and his mentor/friend Daniel Moore in *The House of Doctor Dee* (12); even John Cree, perpetrator of the hideous Limehouse murders (or the 'John Cree' persona of his psychotic wife Elizabeth Cree) refers to himself, when addressing one of his prospective victims, as a 'local antiquary' (*Dan Leno* 127). Ackroyd's plots are often structured around the contrasting strategies implied in these past-ridden activities.

The novel that most explicitly dramatizes and juxtaposes contrasting epistemologies and ways of relating to the past is *First Light*, where the central plot is concerned with the discovery and excavation of an ancient tumulus in a Dorset valley. Mark Clare, the achaeologist in charge of the site, conceives of the past as a knowable object which can be retrieved and contemplated somewhat like a drop of resin that has become amber, enclosing the past as a fixed object. Aiming at 'total recovery, objective interpretation and comprehensive explanation,' he wants to understand 'the real nature of the past' (37). As the multiple stories that make up the novel unfold, Clare's Enlightenment confidence is gradually undercut by a number of factors. First, his venture is undermined by radical epistemological doubt. The pervasive scientific parallel, the reference to the uncertainty principle, foregrounds not only the arbitrariness of all human patterns, emblematized by the constellations, 'horses and fishes floating across the sky' (159), and the futility of all pattern-making in the face of an ever-changing and unknowable world, but also something which is a key aspect of Ackroyd's conception of our relationship to the past: just as, in quantum physics, the position of the observer affects the object and delimits the range of possible observations, here also 'as the expectations of the archaeologists wavered and changed, so did the evidence itself' (187). In trafficking with the past, the clear-cut borderline between past and present, object and subject is blurred; one is inevitably involved, not simply by creating the object which one then claims to discover and know, but also by inescapably being part of what one wishes to examine. It is impossible not to be implicated, as is seen in Hawksmoor's relationship with the crimes he investigates.

This is dramatized through the parallel story of the London comedian Joey Hanover. Joey is totally ignorant of where he comes from; his performing self is seen as a symptom of his troubled origins. His story, a quest for identity, is paradigmatic in the sense that, for Joey, the gaining of a true identity (which coincides with the shedding of the performing identity of the ventriloquizing impersonator, stand-up comedian) is possible only through the therapeutic recovery of his past.

The authority of Clare's objectivism is further depleted, not only by the suicide of his crippled wife Kathleen, but also by the finds of the excavation. Rather than an object belonging to a safely isolated past, the tumulus is gradually revealed to be a *site*, also in the Heideggerian sense (Heidegger 150–5) as a place of dwelling that is still in use, the burial place of the Mint family. Apparently a couple of rustic clowns (again a father and a son without a mother figure), with their richly layered telling name ('mint' meaning 'supply' or 'store', and etymologically related to the Latin *moneo*, 'to remind') the farmers become the representatives of an authentic, lived relationship to the past that is constantly renewed by ritual: the past is not a sealed-off object, but a continuity that includes us. Thus, archaeological research becomes 'trespassing' (267) and the desecration of a tomb. From objective scientist, Clare becomes a party involved: it is in the central burial site that he experiences the revelation that leads to his spiritual rebirth, enabling him to come to terms with his wife's death.

It is precisely this latter aspect of the narrative that raises questions concerning the novel's real stakes. Treating the metaphysical issues – especially the astronomical theme – with 'portentous seriousness' (Head 203), *First Light* follows an epiphanic logic, endorsing the authenticity and authority both of Joey's vision of the faces of his ancestors and of Clare's vision in which he is reconciled to Kathleen's death by realizing, perhaps a little too conveniently, that 'nothing is really destroyed. Things just change their form, and take up another place in the pattern. No one really dies' (264). For all its wealth of literary allusions, its polyphonic richness and its juxtaposition of often discordant voices, the impression the text gives is ultimately that of a nineteenth-century novel where the multiplicity of voices is ultimately controlled and contained by the narrator's voice and vision.[2] The world of *First Light* is mythologically structured and conditioned through and through. Discussing in detail the mythological substructure of the novel, seeing Pilgrin Valley as an *imago mundi* and exploring the correspondences between the celestial, the terrestrial and the subterranean regions, Onega concludes: 'It is only within this transcendental logic that the many metafictional and intertextual allusions suffusing the novel acquire their true dimension' (85). Although she means this as praise, the implied hierarchy also suggests that, instead of the tension that is sustained till the end in some of Ackroyd's other texts, in *First Light* the metafictional issues are subordinated to the transcendental theme, leaving the novel's solemnity unrelieved by textual play.

For all this, *First Light* remains an effective and highly readable dramatization of Ackroyd's idea that any engagement with the past involves, in true hermeneutic fashion, a radical crisis and a risking of the self, that any attempt to gain an objective knowledge of the past is doomed to failure because we are always implicated, and because all such attempts are coloured by some conscious or unconscious affective component (for instance, mourning, as in the case of Chatterton). In some of Ackroyd's other novels, the spiritually regenerative function of the quest for one's origins is further complicated by two other factors: one is the role of language, to which I shall return, and the other is the enormous risk involved in encountering the past.

Joey Hanover's successful quest would seem to suggest — and the same trajectory is implied in Ackroyd's spiritual conception of tradition — that immersion in the eternal, timeless essence of the tradition serves to solidify and anchor the self, endowing it with an authentic and firm identity. Yet, on the evidence of what actually happens in the novels, the engagement with the past may easily result in the complete disintegration or loss of self, in ghosting, madness, demonic possession. 'I had become a primitive again' — says Damian Fall in *First Light* — 'One of my own ancestors. This was madness' (177).

Preoccupied with this danger, *Chatterton* dramatizes the crisis of the self as the imitation or replaying of the past: the playfully intertextual world of the novel is overshadowed from the beginning by Charles Wychwood's terrible suspicion that 'there are no souls, only faces' (7, 46), that is, that the subject, lacking a central core, is simply a series of masks, like the histrionic novelist Harriet Scrope, whose life seems to be a feverish series of impersonations, and who represents the comic aspect of the loss of self. The idea of the performing self is embodied on each of the three chronological levels of the novel: in the eighteenth-century plot by the Posture Master, who acts out the letters 'Y', 'O' and 'U' (that is, 'YOU') to Chatterton (202–3); in the nineteenth-century plot by the writer George Meredith, who poses as Chatterton in Henry Wallis's famous painting, and who is 'all pasticcio' according to his wife (160); and finally, the contemporary protagonist's story whose plastic self renders him susceptible to being taken over by the past and whose identity disintegrates as a result of being possessed by Chatterton.

Charles Wychwood is a repetition or reincarnation of the poet Chatterton in the sense that, like Chatterton, Wychwood is obsessed with the past. Acclaimed by Charles as 'the greatest poet' (94), Chatterton becomes a spirit or imp presiding over the fictional world, a name that allegorically stands for poetic tradition seen as a verbal universe, where 'the truest plagiarism is the truest poetry' (87), as words are never fully ours to mean what we want to say, always already belonging to others. Thus, to express oneself is simply to borrow and recombine the words of other poets, whereas absolute originality, as the example of the mad painter Fritz Dangerfield demonstrates, amounts to psychosis, a private language that is inaccessible to anyone else (116). On one level, *Chatterton* is reiterating the well-known Borgesian – and postmodern – point about the impossibility of originality. The difference between Thomas Chatterton and Wychwood is that, while Chatterton is able to master this situation by limiting it to his 'poetic', textual self and thus turning it into poetry, in Charles's case the obsession with the past (with Chatterton) is, in contrast, a symptom of his writer's block, initiating the disintegration of his self. Instead of anchoring him into the timeless, Eliotian world of tradition, the past seems to batten on him.

III

English Music is important in this context because it quite explicitly connects the role of the past (tradition) in the process of subject formation with the affective charge involved in this relationship. This is achieved by invoking a filial drama: in the case of the narrator Timothy Harcombe, risking one's self and sanity in an engagement with the past is dramatized in terms of the troubled relationship with his prodigal father. Timothy recalls his childhood and adolescence in the 1920s and 1930s when his father worked as a healer in Hackney, and Timothy's presence seemed to be indispensable whenever he was effecting the cures. Seeing his father as an almost supernatural figure, Timothy is blind to the obvious fact that the spiritual power is in fact his own, and that Clement Harcombe was thus exploiting his son's talent to make a living. The novel's odd chapters realistically relate the vicissitudes of this relationship; while the even chapters, Timothy's visions or dreams, offer extended meditations on the spiritual significance of tradition, also going over various regions of the textual domain of English literature (and music and painting), placing Timothy in the fictional worlds of Bunyan, Lewis Carroll, Dickens, Conan Doyle and Defoe, among others.

Using the metaphor of paternity in a self-consciously obtrusive way, and linking Timothy's search for identity through a troubled immersion in the tradition with his quest for the father, *English Music* identifies Clement Harcombe with the paternal principle, with the Logos, charging all the vicissitudes of the relationship between father and son with allegorical significance.[3] Thus, the novel's persistent undermining of the authority of Timothy's father also raises doubts concerning the rather sentimental spiritual notion of tradition which the novel seems to celebrate over and over again, reiterating metaphors of the Goethean idea of *Dauer im Wechsel*, permanence through change (cf. 171–2, 225, 254, 259, 358): the loss of the father's authority entails the collapse of the entire symbolic world of signification.

This is obvious already in the first dream chapter, in which Timothy finds himself in a fictional world that is a hybrid between the worlds of *The Pilgrim's Progress* and *Alice in Wonderland*. This, however, as it turns out in the competition between figures of speech (35), is a decentred, unruly textual universe, very emphatically that of writing, where no discernible rules apply, where it is possible to 'switch stories' according to one's whim (38), and where Alice confidently adopts Humpty Dumpty's linguistic solipsism: 'I mean what I say. I say what I mean' (39), making up provisional meanings as she goes along. This textual chaos deprives Timothy of any stable identity. When asked his name, he can only mutter 'I ...' (31), and by forgetting his appellation loses his identity, his assigned place in the system of language. Thus, Timothy's quest for his missing father is also a quest for (his own) meaning, for an authority, a 'Book of Law' (40), that would stabilize the textual world in which he is wandering. He realizes that for meaning to obtain there has first to be authority: 'And who decides what meaning you should have?' (36). Similarly evident from the start is that meaning is the prerogative of the father (specifically his own): 'I wish dad were here. He would know exactly what to do' (29). Overheard by an Oedipalized version of the Cheshire Cat, a floating head, Timothy is immediately warned: 'I shouldn't say dead if I were you. I should say farther' (29). The head goes on to add: 'I should go farther, if I were you', initiating a sequence of events that is fully determined by the logic of writing. This episode simultaneously revokes and reasserts the father's symbolic authority over meaning and identity in a typically Ackroydian fashion. On the one hand, the word 'father' loses its privileged status and becomes caught up in the decentring play of signification (the events themselves are induced by paronomasia, a pun based on writing). On the other hand, however, the father's authority is re-vindicated, for the head's injunction in fact reiterates Clement Harcombe's only paternal imperative: he dislikes his son calling him 'Dad' and warns him several times to say 'Father'.[4]

Clement Harcombe, then, is both physical father and the figure of tradition; or, more precisely, what emerges as the figure (trope) of tradition is not the father but the relationship between father and son. Although the healing power belongs to Timothy and works in the father's absence, it seems that Timothy is able to integrate this power into his self and make it the basis of his identity only in relation to the father: 'the power belonged to neither of us separately, but resided in the very fact of inheritance' (378). Thus, the father's authority is not discredited by the fact that the source of the magic is Timothy; indeed, their last common feat of healing, the curing of Edward Campion, where their roles are already more or less reversed, suggests that the father is not without his genuine healing power (but perhaps only in the presence of the son).

The relationship between Timothy and his father indicates how Ackroyd's conception of the tradition goes beyond the essentialism implied in the endlessly rehearsed celebration of the eternal spirit of Albion: the mystery of the past, which generates and governs the quest plot, is not some secret that took place in the past, but the relationship between the past and the present. Thus, although there is a great deal of what Nietzsche calls the 'monumental' and 'antiquarian' conception of the past in Ackroyd's notion of tradition, the novel is redeemed by the fact that, in the narrative itself, tradition is imagined in a profoundly hermeneutic sense: the origin is not a single point but manifold ('a sense of origin as subtle as the light which moved back and forth across this [landscape] picture' [308]), constantly being created by the very act of retrospection and remembering: the subject continually creates the past and is in turn created by it.

IV

There is one further aspect of *English Music* that suggests a more complex and troubled relation to the past than that which is celebrated by the visionary chapters. The fact that the prime value seems to be tradition itself, rather than anything 'contained' in it (the content of tradition is this awareness of itself) also implies that there is no centre, only a decentred and decentring textuality that obliterates the autonomy and identity of the subject, 'a world in which there [are] only echoes and no voices' (171). *English Music* is pervaded by a constant vacillation between tradition as a quasi-mystical essence or centre and tradition as archive, a textual field of dissemination where the subject appears as a product or effect of language. Although there is ample psychological motivation for the intertextual games (they are all Timothy's visions), the novel is haunted by the duplicity of tradition. Ackroyd's conception of subjectivity and language does not allow him to believe in the 'good' tradition unquestionably: the 'good' timelessness of the imagination is also the 'bad' atemporality of inter-textuality, of writing, just as the decentred notion of tradition is potentially also the disseminating logic of the archive. As Doctor Dee puts it: 'books talk to one another when no one is present to hear them speak, but I know better than that: they are forever engaged in an act of silent communion which, if we are fortunate, we can overhear' (129).

Drawing upon the notion of tradition as that which encourages a conception of the subject as (emulative) imitation, *English Music* is pervaded by a similar duplicity regarding the relationship between subjectivity and the past. As the fictional 'Defoe', expounding the eighteenth-century concept of poetic *imitatio*, explains to Timothy: 'You honour your father by imitating him, just as you honour an author by the same means' (167). Imitation as the basis of the self, however, has darker connotations that are also dramatized in most of Ackroyd's novels. If conscious imitation may serve as a basis for the hard core of identity, to imitate someone unconsciously suggests a more sinister process of losing control over the self: 'I seemed to be taking part in a story which had nothing to do with me, but from which I could not escape' — says Timothy Harcombe when he realizes that he is 'imitating' his dead mother (178). To imitate someone unconsciously is to be inhabited by a ghost, or to become the ghost, of the past.

The dividing line is tenuous, and nowhere more so than in *Hawksmoor*, the finest example of Ackroyd's archival fiction, pervaded by a fundamental ambiguity that is encapsulated in Derrida's insight, according to which it is impossible to divide 'spirit' from 'ghost': the spirit (of tradition, for instance) is always in danger of becoming a ghost and haunting the present. In terms of the topographical metaphor that dominates the novel, the spirit of the place, the *genius loci*, might easily turn out to be a ghost, and the palimpsest of the city, with the sedimentation and traces of past lives, is also a haunted place, a potential source of evil emanation. Hence the ubiquity of houses in Ackroyd's fiction; to inherit a house from one's father — as Matthew Palmer does in the opening sentence of *The House of Doctor Dee* — is literally to come into one's inheritance with all that this entails. 'No house is empty' — says Chatterton (208), while Clement Harcombe makes the opposite claim: 'There are no haunted houses. Only haunted people' (60). On the other hand, as Michel de Certeau put it, 'Haunted places are the only ones people can live in' (108), and Ackroyd's fiction is full of traces of this awareness.

Running along two temporal lines, *Hawksmoor* is structured around a series of murders, all committed between 1711 and 1715 in the vicinity of churches built by the seventeenth- to eighteenth-century architect Nicholas Dyer, based on the historical figure, Nicholas Hawksmoor. In the late twentieth century, Detective Nicholas Hawksmoor, instead of unravelling the murders, is gradually pulled further and further into the mystery, irresistibly drawn into the last church to fuse with the other half of his personality, the demonic Dyer.

In *Hawksmoor*, it is the haunting, sinister aspect of the relationship to the past that prevails, in two senses. First, the self is depicted as the repetition of past selves, and in this text this appears as demonic possession, as the haunting and hollowing out of the subject. Hawksmoor is metaphorically and literally a 'reflection' (109, 119, 161, 217). Second — an aspect which sets this novel apart in Ackroyd's oeuvre – the possession by the past, partly through the spatial and architectural metaphor of the murderous churches, is filtered and articulated through the medium of language.

Ackroyd's most meticulously planned and most architectural novel, *Hawksmoor* is at the same time his most excessive and dense text. It is architectural in the sense that there is a pervasive analogy between Dyer's churches and the text itself, established in Dyer's opening exposition on 'Fabrick' and 'Structure' (5), and sustained throughout, for instance by the verbal elements that link the adjacent chapters like arches. The churches are seen as text and the text as architecture or, to borrow Henri Lefebvre's pun, 'archi-texture' (118).

The novel can indeed be seen as a fabric of text, made up not of characters and events, but of the recurrence of innumerable scraps of language, although not in a way that the reader could systematize; instead of clear parallels and correspondences, textual fragments arise, to be repeated and recombined according to the logic of writing. Full of uncanny echoes of other chapters (and this logic of writing overrides even chronology, as the many temporal loops, instances of the present haunting the past, attest), and refusing to be arranged into a neat structure, chapters are spilling and bleeding into each other, full of floating scraps of language, with the further uncanny twist that, often, there is no speaking subject behind these scraps (e.g. 167): this is the function of children's rhymes, which here become instances of agentless or subjectless language, instances where language clearly exceeds its concrete use by knowing more than its users, 'remembering' its past. As Dyer says: 'We live off the Past: it is in our Words and our Syllables' (178).

Many of the dispersed motifs are also self-referential: for instance, the world of the text is pervaded by 'dust' both as a textual fragment and as a metaphor of language, as the tangible index of time. Dust is also a symbolic substance, connecting the human figures with the other dominant metaphor of 'stone' which, as in Beckett, stands for the absolutely non-human – through the figure of 'ash', and also suggesting the pulverization of the solid characters and objects of the novel into textual fallout; its appearances are often paralleled with those of 'ink', which functions self-referentially as the fluid, textual counterpart of dust, slowly and entropically covering everything, erasing differences and therefore the possibility of meaning. The characters' existence is purely textual: Dyer's discourse is a patchwork of diverse seventeenth-century texts, the tramp Ned is like a momentary solidification of a cluster of textual elements from the rest of the book, and Detective Hawksmoor is made up of intertextual allusions and bits of the preceding chapters.

The crime plot works effectively, partly because it is a more dramatic version of what language does in the novel. As Alison Lee suggests, the really sinister thing about the killings is not that the perpetrator is not caught, but that there seems to be no subject behind the murders (66, 84): to append a name to a murder is to be able to separate the culprit and to remove him/her from the texture of society, thus restoring its integrity. In a way, the figure of Dyer is a necessary supplement produced by the supposed morphology of the murders, of our desire for a pattern and for a subject behind the series of crimes.

Hawksmoor has at least three levels of signification, and the relationship between these is never one of tidy correspondences and parallels. *Hawksmoor* is clearly a metaphysical detective story, with a serious stake in matters transcendental and mystical (as is obvious from Onega's analysis, which, pursuing all the arcane references, comes up with a surprisingly coherent reading). It is also a novel about a mad architect and a disturbed detective who resemble each other in several respects; and third, it is a postmodern novel that flaunts the textuality of its world. To take as an example the climactic fusion of Dyer and Hawksmoor, what is the union of two halves of a single self on a mystical plane is simply the annihilation of the subject on the ordinary plane, and the dissolution of the subject into the endless sea of textuality on a metafictional level (it is not accidental, as Onega also notes, that the church in which this union takes place is Ackroyd's addition to the actual London churches — that is, a fully textual place). Like several of Ackroyd's other novels, *Hawksmoor* maintains a precarious balance and reveals an uncanny parallel between two distant things: the mystical extinction or sacrifice of the self for the sake of entering and dissolving in something larger, and the postmodern/poststructuralist notion of the subject. In this, Ackroyd is like Borges, with his constant wavering between the metaphysical and the textual (*Hawksmoor*, among other things, is an excellent rewriting of 'Death and the Compass').

Ackroyd's fictional world is a strange, unsettling mixture of the postmodern and the archaic, where, in narratives that plot the engagement between the past and the present, the mystical conception of the subject finds its unlikely echoes in poststructuralist theory, and the quasi-mystical notion of a spiritual tradition merges with the postmodern notion of disseminating intertextuality. This disturbing, uncanny, but unique world is well worth visiting, even if encountering this haunted area is beset with the selfsame dangers that confront Ackroyd's characters.

Notes

1. For a critique of the English reception of Ackroyd's fiction, see the opening section of Gibson and Wolfreys' monograph, especially 15–22.
2. Although several critics — most forcefully Gibson and Wolfreys — have commented on the carnivalistic nature of Ackroyd's fiction, such subversiveness of these phenomena is seriously limited by the solemnity of the issues and often of the dominant narrative voice. Ackroyd's only truly carnivalistic text is the first part of *Milton in America*.
3. In Ackroyd's unrelentingly male plots, the relationship between past and present is metaphorized through filiation: there is no matrilinear tradition in Ackroyd's world, just as female writers are absent from his English tradition.
4. The figure of the Old Barren One, the forefather of the Mint clan, represents the same double logic of asserting and revoking paternal authority: although the figure possesses enormous metaphysical authority over the fictional world, this authority is simultaneously questioned

by his 'barrenness'. The climactic episode of the burning of the father ('original Mint') is in this sense the advent of the Symbolic: the spiritual power of the physical body is from this moment entirely and irrevocably replaced by the supremacy of the symbolic.

Bibliography and further reading

Ackroyd, Peter. *Notes for a New Culture*. London: Vision Press, 1976. Revised edition: London: Alkin Books, 1993.
——. *The Great Fire of London*. London: Sphere Books, 1987 [1982].
——. *The Last Testament of Oscar Wilde*. London: Sphere Books, 1988 [1983].
——. *Hawksmoor*. London: Sphere Books, 1988 [1985].
——. *Chatterton*. London: Sphere Books, 1988 [1987].
——. *First Light*. London: Sphere Books, 1990 [1989].
——. *English Music*. Harmondsworth: Penguin, 1993 [1992].
——. *The House of Doctor Dee*. Harmondsworth: Penguin, 1994 [1993].
——. *Dan Leno and the Limehouse Golem*. London: Minerva, 1995 [1994].
——. *Milton in America*. London: Minerva, 1997 [1996].
——. *The Plato Papers*. London: Vintage, 2000 [1999].
——. *London: The Biography*. London: Vintage, 2001 [2000].
——. *The Clerkenwell Tales*. London: Vintage, 2004 [2003].
——. *The Lambs of London*. London: Vintage, 2004.
de Certeau, Michel. 'Walking in the City', in *The Practice of Everyday Life*. Berkeley, CA: University of California Press, 1988: 91–113.
Derrida, Jacques. *Specters of Marx*. Trans. Peggy Kamur. New York and London: Routledge, 1994.
Finney, Brian. 'Peter Ackroyd, Postmodernist Play and *Chatterton*.' *Twentieth Century Literature*, 38: 2, Summer 1992: 240–61.
Gibson, Jeremy, and Julian Wolfreys. *Peter Ackroyd: the Ludic and Labyrinthine Text*. Basingstoke: Macmillan, 2000.
Head, Dominic. *The Cambridge Introduction to Modern British Fiction, 1950–2000*. Cambridge: Cambridge University Press, 2002: 202–4.
Heidegger, Martin: 'Building Dwelling Thinking', in *Poetry, Language, Thought*. New York: Harper & Row, 1967: 145–61.
Hutcheon, Linda. *Poetics of Postmodernism*. London: Routledge, 1989.
Lee, Alison. *Realism and Power: Postmodern British Fiction*. London: Routledge, 1990: 66–73, 83–7.
Lefebvre, Henri. *The Production of Space*. Oxford: Blackwell, 1991.
Nietzsche, Friedrich. *The Use and Abuse of History*. Indianapolis, IN: Liberal Arts Press, 1957.
Onega, Susana. *Metafiction and Myth in the Novels of Peter Ackroyd*. Columbia, SC: Camden House, 1999.
Todd, Richard. 'Fantasies of London: Past and Present', in *Consuming Fictions: the Booker Prize and Fiction in Britain Today*. London: Bloomsbury, 1996: 165–88.

CHAPTER SIX

Jenny Diski's Millennial Imagination 1997–2004

PHILIP TEW

Martin Buber, in 'People Today and the Jewish Bible: From a Lecture Series', writes of the *Old Testament*, 'The book has since its beginning encountered one generation after another. Confrontation and reconciliation with it have taken place in every generation. Sometimes it is met with obedience and offered dominion; sometimes with offense and rebellion. But each generation engages it vitally, and faces it in the realm of reality' (4–5). In a vein of both interrogation and irreverence, Jenny Diski completed two post-millennial novels, *Only Human: a Divine Comedy* (2000) and *After These Things* (2004), which focus on part of the scriptures that Buber finds eternally productive of response, that rework the narrative of Genesis, first book of the Pentateuch, the 'Five Books of Moses' that preface the *Old Testament*. God permeates the biblical accounts as an occasional, often off-stage presence, as a force shaping events. Ineluctably there is a suggestion of the parental, with his periods of sulky abandonment of his progeny, a theme typical of Diski's earlier writing.

This essay seeks to explore the context of Diski's adaptation and regeneration of this familiar cultural narrative, quite why her last two novels focus upon what Jacques Derrida in *The Gift of Death* (1992) describes as, 'the still Jewish experience of a secret, hidden, separate, absent, or mysterious God, the one who decides, without revealing his reasons, to demand of Abraham that most cruel, impossible, and untenable gesture: to offer his son Isaac as a sacrifice. All that goes on in secret' (57–8). In Diski's versions, God is a self-doubting figure; and as the initial narrator of *Only Human* he reflects, '——— And then I made my great error. I made sentience. I made self-consciousness. I made *I am*. Whatever anyone might say, I did not know what the consequences would be. Until I made the world, there had been no consequence, only inconsequential eternity. How could I have known? There was no distinction between eternity and the fact of my existence, not until the stirring of consciousness that separated me from it. The First separation' (10–11). Other key themes recur that are found in the scriptural account, especially in Genesis whose emphasis is not so much Creation, but primarily parenthood, lineage, family, betrayal.

In the scriptures, and both Diski's reworkings and her previous writings, such relations, although dysfunctional, are nevertheless central to the narrative impulse and to interrogating notions of identity.

Her immediately antecedent book, *Skating to Antarctica* (1997), represents a transformative moment in Diski's career. It represents the apotheosis of the autobiographical themes of loss and abandonment that characterize her early novels, where she compulsively rearticulates her own traumatic pre-adult experiences. Biographical details have explicitly subtended most of her characterizations; however, in *Skating to Antarctica* towards the millennium she appears to foreswear the indirection of fiction and decides to hybridize its form with variously that of the autobiography, the journal and the travel narrative. The text opens with her obsession with whiteness, not so much a symbol of unachievable purity within, as an externalizing of the wish for a *tabula rasa*, a longing for renewal and recovery, appropriate since its theme is estrangement and effacement of a lacunary loss. However, she admits her limitations in blanking out her life. 'In the morning, if I arrange myself carefully when I wake, I can open my eyes to nothing but whiteness. ... Eventually, I'll have to let colours in to my day, but for a while I can wallow in a seemingly boundless expanse of white' (*Skating* 1–2). Moreover, her epigraph, taken from Beckett's *Malone Dies*, appears to gesture towards her previous fictions, and the inevitable re-emergence of her self-obsession breaching the whiteness. 'I wonder if I am not talking yet again about myself. Shall I be incapable, to the end, of lying on any other subject?' (n. pag.).

According to Gunnthórum Gudmundsdóttir,

> Diski tells the story of her difficult childhood, her problems with depression from an early age, and how she became estranged from her mother at the age of fourteen, and had not seen or heard from her since. It was Diski's daughter who in her late teens decided to search for her grandmother, to at least find out whether she was still alive. That story is intertwined with a tale of a trip Diski made to Antarctica during her daughter's search. (92)

As Gudmundsdóttir indicates, in the first chapter, 'Schrödinger's Mother', Diski justifies the suspension of her mother's existence, whose lacunary presence, amorphous and negative, becomes not simply the engine for the narrative, but by Diski's own admission the informing dialectic of her life. Although un-godlike, the mother's petulant, protracted absence comes after a suitably portentous incident. Diski recalls a dramatic moment, her final encounter with her mother after her father's death (already long divorced from her mother), screaming at her in a library on Camden High Street:

> I sat in silence while she shrieked and wept, noisily enumerating my faults, not the least of which was being just like him: a liar, deceitful, treacherous, heartless. All true in this context. ... Then she departed, her aria over, leaving the library

in a silence it rarely achieved in the normal course of the day. I watched her disappear past the window in the direction of Camden Town underground, and then, I supposed, back to Hove, after her day out in London. I never saw her again. (*Skating* 26–7)

The confrontation is archetypal, of the sort deeply embedded in the account of the female rage of Sarah that Diski incorporates in her later books. Nevertheless, as it transpires, finding her mother might well have been an easy task, and on one occasion she recalls taking her young daughter to Brighton and passing very near to where her mother lived. Diski explores her own apparent indifference, her need to avoid the traumatic patterns of the past. As Gudmundsdóttir says, 'The reality of easy access to information and Diski's own reluctance to find out, to open the lid, is a constant theme in this text' (93). For Gudmundsdóttir the ending suggests a dialogue between Diski as mother and her daughter, the very kind of dialogue implicitly denied to Diski in her relations with her own mother. Intriguingly, Diski's own status as a parent haunts the text, potentially echoing her own mother, given her absence that allows the separate retrieval of the past by Diski and her daughter. The ending resolves the central issue of her uncertain identity, and works not so much through provisionality, but rather by diminishing the significance of narrative endings themselves.

The religious, cultural identity of Diski's mother might be regarded as an unexpected and inconclusive terminus of the text. Nevertheless, midway through the narrative Diski reflects explicitly upon both her familial lineage and her sense of the ethno-cultural origins that have hybridized her own identity, and that of the small migrant, diasporic community in which she lived. This new sensibility emerges conversationally, and is forced upon her by both her family and more aggressively her school-friends, shattering her naïve state of innocence:

There was almost nothing in the way of religious practice in my family, though when I was young my mother lit candles on Friday nights, and my family would take me to the local synagogue on the last night of Yom Kippur to hear the ram's horn being blown. But our Jewishness was constantly being reiterated: by my parents in their everyday conversation – bits of Yiddish from their East End immigrant families; whether famous people in the news were or were not Jewish; in what we ate – fried fish on Fridays, chicken soup with knedleich, bagels, soured cream, lockshen pudding; being Jewish was in the air. It was also evident from the outside world. At school the other kids told me I was not English, but Jewish. Killing Christ was still something – just a few years after the Second World War – I was held responsible for in the playground. Helen Levine, who, oddly, went to a Catholic school nearby the flats, was told to go home and look at her mother's feet by one of the nuns to see if they didn't have demonic hooves. She went to school somewhere else not long after. Nor, being Jewish, could I ever fit myself into the English class system. We weren't middle class, or exactly working class; it was *different*. (*Skating* 104–5)

As with her almost wilful lack of knowledge of her mother, there is something similarly lacunary in Diski's Jewish identity, although it does recur momentarily, resurfacing symbolically with her grandfather's signature which is inscribed in Hebrew on her father's birth certificate that awaits her on her return from Antarctica and its 'sublime empty landscape ...' (232), where she has decided she may retrieve her past and origins, rather than the fantasies and conflicts of her parents' lives. 'It's hard for me to assess what kind of journey it was from Israel Zimmerman, Sam Zimmerman's son, to James Simmonds, but it doesn't seem to have been one worth making' (238). In his absences between occasional communications, much like her mother in later life, her father seems retrospectively like the God she characterizes in her two Pentateuchal novels, increasingly withdrawn and reluctant to communicate with humankind, the archetype for the neglectful parent, although congruent somehow with Diski herself in her role of omniscient narrator. Perhaps finally in *Skating to Antarctica* she senses a need to exorcize and negate once and for all the explicitly auto-biographical framework, retrieving from the depths of her rather secular Jewish upbringing a different framing structure, that of a key story from the Pentateuch, adapting the story of Abraham and Isaac from Genesis, drawing upon its often innate themes of estrangement, dislocation, problematic relationships with parents and between spouses, and the repressed issues of gender, of female rebellion and identity. She bridges what Buber calls the 'abyss' between the scriptural and contemporaneity (8, 10), acknowledging his maxim explaining part of the process that leads to revelation, for 'we have sometimes a small experience that because it is of the same sort as the great experiences can provide us access to them' (11).

Pivotal to the dynamics of both of Diski's Pentateuchal novels (and Genesis itself) is Abraham's binding of Isaac for sacrifice on Mount Morah described in Genesis 22, which has long been both controversial and fascinating. This event is described in Jewish tradition, as Carol Delaney explains in *Abraham on Trial: the Social Legacy of Biblical Myth* (1998) as the *Akedah*, which word refers to Isaac (111). Delaney sees the *Akedah* as constituting and sustaining the essence of patriarchy. It is intriguing that Diski chooses this central focus around which all else in her two novels revolves, since she responds (whether knowingly or not) to Søren Kierkegaard's commentary in *Fear and Trembling* (1843), where he says 'And to think that there is no poet who could bring himself to prefer situations such as this [the *Akedah*] to the nonsense and trumpery with which comedies and novels are stuffed! The comic and the tragic make contact here in absolute infinitude' (29). He concludes, 'If faith is taken away ... all that remains is the brutal fact that Abraham meant to murder Isaac ... ' (30). Initially, Diski appears to concur, given Sarah's negative view of her husband hinted at the end of the first novel. However, in *After These Things* the narrator comments: 'A great long lordly sulk there was after Abraham bound his boy, challenging and defeating God-the-narrator with the threat of the premature end of His own story. God clammed up' (1). Nevertheless, as Isaac confronts in old age the inevitability of his own death, his response seems predicated on both an underlying notion of betrayal and a self-doubt deriving from the very moment of the *Akedah*. 'Once, in that first encounter with death, he might have run for it, but he didn't. A stupefied boy. A stupid boy. Not to protest at going to his own execution. Obedient, paralysed, disbelieving, suicidal; whatever his state, it was unforgivable, he now saw, to volunteer himself for death. And death had been with him ever since' (10).

Even though Diski attributes a deviousness to Abraham, at least conceptually and ethically, Diski's manner of exegetical reading is very specific and consistent with the literalism of Kierkegaard rather than Emanuel Swedenborg's reading of the *Akedah* in *Arcana Caelestia* (1985) as symbolic and allegorical. More immediately, Delaney's account appears to have prompted Diski's creative train of thought after her review, 'The Daddy of All Patriarchs', in the *London Review of Books* (8). Diski complains, 'Says Carol Delaney, *Genesis* we're lumbered with, deep in our psyche and social structure. She says we need "a new moral vision, a new myth to live by". This is to accept that we are helpless victims rather than interpreters of myth, and that our consciousness is solely conditioned by it. It is a bleak view of humanity's capacity for analytical thought, and an even bleaker view of the consequences of feminist criticism of patriarchal stories' (68). She continues: 'No one in Genesis asks to live for ever, but everyone is concerned with having children who will survive them' (73), which concurs with T. Desmond Alexander's outline in *Abraham in the Negev: a Source: Critical Investigation of Genesis 20: 1–22: 19* (1997) of Abraham's narrative representing an ' "heir" plot' (105), which itself results from the barrenness of Sarah and God's promise of an heir to Abraham, later repeated to Sarah (104). 'Finally, chap. 22 also focuses on Abraham's heir. On this occasion Isaac's life is threatened by the divine command that Abraham should sacrifice his "only son". Coming after Isaac's confirmation as sole heir in chap. 21, the account in chap. 22 provides a dramatic climax to the entire story' (104–5). Diski structures her narrative along similar lines, situating the *Akedah* as the culmination of the first novel, which largely concerns Abram (later Abraham) and God's relation to man, and the second novel considers the traumatic aftermath, the perhaps unexpected effects upon Isaac and the tribe of Israel. The consequences are played out in the life of the women as much as the men.

Both plots are too complex to summarize here effectively, but suffice to say they are almost entirely consistent with the scriptural accounts, except in matters of emphases, occasional analeptic and proleptic repositioning of certain aspects to allow comparison of different moments stressing interconnected causality, and the supplementary expansions of dialogue, recollections, motivations and the emotional framework of actions and events. Diski's exegetical understanding of scripture is informed not only by the Authorized King James Bible, but recent prose translations by Robert Alter and Everett Fox, as evidenced in her review of Delaney where

Diski alludes to such versions (*Human* 72). Diski chooses to foreground very self-consciously the notion of man's usurpation of an aspect of God which comes to represent one of mankind's most innate characteristics, that which appears to separate him from the rest of creation, that which includes the very act of narrative undertaken by Diski herself. She has God-the-narrator reflect in *After These Things*:

> And more like an affliction than a triumph, humanity's stories, the narrations humans had wrenched from the deity, came and came. Counterpointing, contradicting, refining, refuting, relating, distorting, destroying, deceiving, denying, explaining, excusing, blaming, boasting. Depending on who was doing the telling and who the listening. As if anyone ever stops telling for long enough to listen. And, we might wonder, is the telling really intended for another to listen to, so often is it done in silence and alone? Who could have made such consciousnesses up? Creatures like all others that creep and crawl and pad and thunder over the earth, with all their needs and functions, but who uniquely weld together bits of stuff − memory, fantasy and dream − into *stories. Homo fabulans.* (2)

This both undermines and sustains the various narratives and humanizes them. It serves as a multilayered comment, evoking variously the stories internal to the characters of the two novels, those internal to the characters within Genesis itself, Diski's own narrative ambition, and crucially even that of the writers or editors of the scriptures themselves. It allows Diski to reflect upon the retellings, repetitions and final futility of such stories (2–3). She articulates her own role as that of an editor, seeing in contrast the story-less world as 'unchoreographed', as a 'cacophony', whereas 'Editors are as obsessed about structure as the individual storyteller is obsessed about his or her *moments.* Editors patch and refit the various stories, each stuck in their various moments, into an order of some kind, so as to come to a conclusion. Where would humanity be without conclusions?' (4). This apparent antinomy is really more complex, since the editorship is part of a lineage associated with scriptural textual revision, allowing her to reconcile the fragments in a revised, feminized formation while still reflecting upon an essentially patriarchal text.

Interestingly, Diski gradually and subtly reorientates many of the biblical events towards first the consciousness of Sarah in the first novel and that of Rebekah in the second, rendering a gendered narrative that extends rather than simply objects to such a patriarchal myth or narrative. In her review of Delaney she offers clues as to her later development of the narrative in her novel: 'After God tried and gave up on the children of Adam and Eve, drowning the lot of them, and then scattered the offspring of Noah, he narrowed his sights to Abraham, a more manageable single individual of whom he would make a nation. It could be argued that Sarah was a necessary part of the package. She was already married to Abraham, and is claimed by all three religions as their matriarch' (69). She admits the gender bias in the Pentateuch, but regards Delaney's explication concerning the focus on male seed as insufficient, especially as Jewish identity is matrilineal (71–2), noting that the Pentateuch offers no afterlife, only posterity (72). Diski identifies the possibility of rereading such narratives 'differently, more carefully, less reverentially' (73), which response is the core of the two novels under scrutiny here. The first of these opens with a prelude that describes the deathbed of Sarah, an episode offstage in the biblical narrative, who responds enigmatically to questions concerning the significance of her life.

> 'It was all endings. Always. Endings, starting and ending, but no conclusion.'
> She looks directly at me with the hint of a question in her eyes, then lifts one tiny scrawny shoulder in a shrug that is no more than perplexed.
> 'Nothing else . . . ' (*Human* 4)

From the demise of the founding matriarch, Diski's narrative moves to its version of creation and God, who reflects on a theme that obsesses him, 'In the formlessness and the void, yes, and before it – I was. Before the incoherence, before the unity, before the separation – I was. Before the narrator, before the narrative, before the end implied in the beginning, before the beginning set in motion by the end – I was. Before the story, before the account, before the clarification, before the alibi, before all motivation to explain, before because – I was!' (6). The first section of the novel describes the emergence of otherness, of desire, of love, and of defiance. 'From them I learned of deception: that gardens could be hiding-places, that words could be lies, that thoughts and intentions were not actions. From them I learned about contingency. Humankind invented contingency' (13).

God is depicted as a slightly petulant figure aware of the absurdity of his position, of being drawn into the anthropomorphic world of his creations. His relationship with Abraham expresses a central ambivalence for both parties, demythologizes it. As Kierkegaard comments of Abraham:

> During all this time he had faith, he had faith that God would not demand Isaac of him, and yet he was willing to sacrifice him if it was demanded. He had faith by virtue of the absurd, for human calculation was out of the question, and it certainly was absurd that God, who required it of him, should in the next moment rescind the requirement. (Kierkegaard 35–6)

This is very similar to the paradox perceived and represented by Diski, which animates not only the responses of the more mature Sarah in the novel, but those of God in the triangular relationship that emerges to fuel the ironic comedy of the interactions and reflections. God analyses Abraham's divisions of his lands, sending Lot to the plain of the Jordan river, leaving his uncle in Canaan:

> ——— *Her* love. Her lifelong knowledge of her beloved. Only now did she begin to see a glimpse of Abram's deviousness. And she did not know the half of it. I knew him through and through, and yet, omniscient as I am, he still surprised me, still, so politely, challenged me. Challenged *me*. Such is the deluding power of love: knowing everything isn't enough. (*Human* 160)

According to Derrida, Abraham's morality is equally ambivalent: 'Abraham doesn't speak in figures, fables, parables, metaphors, ellipses or enigmas. His irony is meta-rhetorical' (77). Derrida adds, 'Whereas the tragic hero is great, admired, and legendary from generation to generation, Abraham, in remaining faithful to his singular love for the wholly other, is never considered a hero' (79). As Avivah Gottlieb Zornberg makes clear in *Genesis: the Beginnings of Desire* (1995), ambivalence permeates the *Akedah*, with its sense of meaning reached through encountering the universe's underlying vertiginous babble (118–19).

In her revisions, Diski crucially sees less of the heroic achievement in Abraham that Zornberg identifies (122), but throughout both novels she allows and emphasizes very human qualities: motivation, emotional depth and rivalry, passion and even terror of an existential kind. How she does so can be better demonstrated by considering closely one specific exemplary case, the period after Jacob's deception of Esau, after his flight from Canaan and his arrival in Haran. Here Jacob meets two women, both to become his brides, both eventually bearing him children. In Everett Fox's translation, *The Five Books of Moses* (1995), 'Leah's eyes were delicate, but Rachel was fair of form and fair to look at' (137), and the entire narrative describing Abraham's attraction to Rachel, the first wedding, the agreement to serve seven more years and the second wedding is given in Genesis 29: 15–30, not quite two full pages (329 words). Diski expands this to pages 102–28 of her second Pentateuchal novel; her method is to delve into the implicit aspects that potentially lie beneath the surface of the original, activating the interstitial possibilities, creating memories of past events, and thus evoking a supplementariness. Thereby she explores the possibilities that explain both the logistics and the psychological motivations that might be involved. Diski adds a recollection of Leah's solitary moments as a child, her childish desire to feel beautiful, and the reponse of her female relatives to the two sisters. ' "Well, not ugly. She isn't ugly, but plain, let's say." They tried to find out the right definition for her deficiencies. "It isn't that Rachel is beautiful ... no, she *is* lovely, in fact beautiful, but it's not that Leah isn't beautiful ... lots of girls aren't beautiful ... but she isn't ... *striking*." They would test all manner of descriptions to explain what it was about Leah that made it a pity she wasn't a boy, but it was hard to put a finger on it' (*After These Things* 93). Diski's Leah does take the initiative, refusing to be passive. This exchange is recalled as part of the domestic ritual and memory, part of the way women constrain themselves and are judged. For Diski, Leah rebels in her responses to Jacob. First, Jacob confesses his deception to Leah, his betrayal of Esau, to the sister to whom he is not attracted. Ironically Jacob does so to dampen Leah's ardour for him, by revealing his shame. The outcome is unpredictable.

> So he told her about Esau, about his boorish brother selling his birthright, about his mother's plan to take Esau's paternal blessing. Then he stopped and started again. He told her about tricking his dim and hungry brother out of his

birthright and how he had only worried he would be caught by blind and bedridden and despised Isaac impersonating his brother. With the telling of both versions, a passably accurate tale was told. ... In Leah's mind, Jacob's fineness thickened, his texture roughened. He was still all the things she knew him to be, but he had other aspects, wants, greeds and resentments. He became more human and less beyond her reach. (112)

Leah uses this knowledge to persuade her father, Laban, as a justification for deceiving Jacob into drunkenly marrying Leah herself as part of a bed-trick, allowing Laban a moment of amusement at the reception and satisfying the young woman, giving her preference over her prettier sister. The series of interactions is comic and explicit, and crucially in all scriptural accounts the determining mind appears to be that of Laban. In Alter's *Genesis* (1996), one reads after Jacob's demand for his marriage has been agreed, 'Laban gathered all the men of the place and made a feast. And when evening came, he took Leah his daughter and brought her to Jacob, and he came to bed with her' (154). The laconic brevity almost invites elaboration; the male emphasis demands revision. Diski does so, diminishing Laban and accentuating Leah's agency and her intervention.

Underlying the entire novel, as arguably it does the scripture – given that Isaac's narrative emerges in books named for his father, son and grandson – is Abraham's son's traumatic response to his near sacrifice, exhibiting weakness and secondariness. Diski emphasizes the dissatisfactions surrounding him, as with his bride, for 'The war began inside Rebekah and never reached a conclusion. It started at the moment her husband-to-be laid his coarse, blind hands on her, and it raged in her for the rest of her life. She would never know peace again, not if peace comprised a sense of clarity, a final choice as to how she should proceed in the world of her life' (48). Diski refuses to fundamentally distort the narrative, but by engaging with emotional depth and uncertainty, the struggles within, she extends the significance of her female characters, thus re-coordinating the narrative. Some implied visceral reaction is evident in the scriptural sources, such as in the rivalry of the two sisters, and in Jacob's unease, which Alter's *Genesis* conveys: 'And Rachel saw that she had borne no children to Jacob, and Rachel was jealous of her sister, and she said to Jacob. "Give me sons, for if you don't, I'm a dead woman!" And Jacob was incensed with Rachel, and he said, "Am I instead God, Who has denied you fruit of the womb?" And she said, "Here is my slavegirl, Bilhah. Come to bed with her, that she may give birth on my knees, so that I, too, shall be built up through her." And she gave him Bilhah her slavegirl as a wife, and Jacob came to bed with her. And Bilhah conceived and bore Jacob a son' (158–9).

For Derrida, the moment of the *Akedah* is central to ethics:

The account of Isaac's sacrifice can be read as a narrative development of the paradox constituting the concept of duty and absolute responsibility. This concept puts us into relation (but without relating to it, a double secret) with the

absolute other, whose name is here God. ... Absolute duty demands that one
behave in an irresponsible manner (by means of treachery or betrayal), while
still recognizing, confirming, and reaffirming the very thing one sacrifices,
namely, the order of human ethics and responsibility. In a word, ethics must be
sacrificed in the name of duty. (66–7)

Of course, such a concept is irredeemably human, which Diski reflects
through her God in *Only Human* who ruminates on the challenge and
strangeness to him of his creation, its difference. God recalls that from
prohibition man discovers opposition (12–13), and subsequently the
narrative switches to detailing the early relationship of Abram and Sarai,
interspersed with the other details of the early biblical narrative that so
exasperate God before the story of the flood, characterized by Diski as
almost a despairing afterthought. 'And if in choosing Noah I was to
populate the world with dullness, well, so much the better. I had seen
enough of the results of autonomy and imagination. Now I wanted
obedience' (67). Even such articulations of God's ambivalence expand and
emphasize scriptural elements. As Buber concludes from references in the
early books, 'God is assigned neither to the realm of nature nor to the realm
of the spirit, that God is not nature and is not spirit either, but that both
have their origin in him' (Buber 15).

By the end of the novel the aftermath of the *Akedah* becomes almost
a footnote to Sarah's rebellion against Abraham and inferentially the
patriarchal God himself, whereas one can infer from the Bible that she mocks
his promise: 'Sarai gasped with rage at the impertinence of this stranger who
mocked her ancient sterile body. Then, outraged, she began to laugh. "How
delightful," she rasped through her laughter. "Shrivelled with age, I am to
become an object of desire to my equally shrivelled husband, and a breeder
at last"' (*Human* 197). Rather than the original's parable of an underlying necessity for faith and obedience, in Diski Sarah acquires a more
transcendent dignity and stature, although certainly even in the original
women are pivotal to the narrative. Diski's perspective echoes that of
Zornberg who notes that even scripturally Sarah has doubts about her aged
procreation, responding with an inner as well as outer laughter. He notes
her 'grim realism', and that 'Sarah's experience is direct, physical, definitive.
Matter is intractable and encloses her' (113). Diski perceives a positivity in
Sarah for this stoical consistency. By this time one senses her character
might well concur with Kierkegaard regarding her spouse when he says,
'I am constantly aware of the prodigious paradox that is the content of
Abraham's life, I am constantly repelled, and, despite all its passion, my
thought cannot penetrate it, cannot get ahead by a hairsbreadth' (33).

By the end of the second book, the parental loss of Joseph is a dialectical
reversal of Diski's own abandonment, that event or series of moments
so repeatedly narrated and characterized in her earlier fiction, where there
is no single identifiable betrayal, no personal equivalent of the *Akedah*.
Jacob mourns the son he thinks he has lost; Abraham and Isaac are

dead, 'And from God, the Dreamed One, the great Redactor, the Editor in Chief, there was only silence. What are a handful of generations to him? Just original material gone its own way, good for nothing more than providing the means to pass the time with a little dreaming and a little interim editing' (216).

Bibliography and further reading

Diski, Jenny. *Skating to Antarctica*. London: Granta Books, 1997.
——. 'The Daddy of All Patriarchs.' *London Review of Books*, 10 December 1998. Reprinted in *A View from the Bed*. London: Virago, 2003.
——. *Only Human: a Divine Comedy*. London: Virago, 2000.
——. *After These Things*. London: Little, Brown, 2004.
Alexander, T. Desmond. *Abraham in the Negev: a Source-Critical Investigation of Genesis 20: 1–22: 19*. Carlisle, Cumbria: Paternoster Press, 1997.
Alter, Robert. *Genesis: Translation and Commentary*. New York and London: W. W. Norton, 1996.
Buber, Martin. 'People Today and the Jewish Bible: From a Lecture Series', in *Scripture and Translation*. Martin Buber and Franz Rosenzweig (eds), Bloomington and Indianapolis, IN: Indiana University Press, 1994: 4–26. Trans. Lawrence Rosenwald with Everett Fox.
Delaney, Carol. *Abraham on Trial: the Social Legacy of Biblical Myth*. Princeton, NJ: Princeton University Press, 1998.
Derrida, Jacques. *The Gift of Death*. Chicago, IL and London: University of Chicago Press, 1995 [1992]. Trans. David Wills.
Fox, Everett. *The Five Books of Moses*. London: Harvill Press, 1995.
Gudmundsdóttir, Gunnthórum. *Borderlines: Autobiography and Fiction in Postmodern Life Writing*. Amsterdam and New York: Rodopi, 2003.
Kierkegaard, Søren. *Fear and Trembling/Repetition*. Princeton, NJ: Princeton University Press, 1984 [*Fear and Trembling* 1843]. Trans. Howard V. Hong and Edna H. Hong.
Swedenborg, Emanuel. *Arcana Caelestia: Principally a Revelation of the Inner or Spiritual Meaning of Genesis and Exodus*, Vol. III. London: Swedenborg Society, 1985. Trans. [from Latin] John Elliott.
Zornberg, Avivah Gottlieb. *Genesis: the Beginnings of Desire*. Philadelphia, PA and Jerusalem: The Jewish Publication Society, 1995.

CHAPTER SEVEN

Assessing Ben Okri's Fiction 1995–2005

CHRISTOPHER RINGROSE

At the climax of *The Famished Road* (1991), Ben Okri's most celebrated novel, the father of the spirit child Azaro returns from a period of unconsciousness and dreaming. Dad, who has been a boxer, an exhausted manual worker, a winner and a loser, brings back from his dreaming a denunciation of the contemporary state of Nigeria alongside a visionary account of a glorious future:

> Dad was redreaming the world as he slept. ... He saw our people drowning in poverty, in famine, in drought, in divisiveness and the blood of war. He saw our people always preyed upon by other powers, manipulated by the Western World, our history and achievements rigged out of existence. (492)

In his address to his wife and son, resonant with postcolonial issues, Dad expresses a vision of imaginative and political renewal:

> 'We must look at the world with new eyes. We must look at ourselves differently. We are freer than we think. We haven't begun to live yet. The man whose light has come on in his head, in his dormant sun, can never be kept down or defeated. We can redream this world and make the dream real. Human beings are gods hidden from themselves.' (498)

This inspiring rhetoric comes from the man who had, earlier, been seen at work by a half-ashamed Azaro as a degraded load carrier at the transport depot, 'his hair ... white and his face ... mask-like with engrained cement ... almost naked except for a disgusting pair of tattered shorts' (148). Azaro and his family are indeed the glory, jest and riddle of the world, and *The Famished Road* itself is an unusual, even unique, book, the product of a major talent in contemporary fiction: a book of books that can be read as a series of reflections, a cyclical (or a-temporal) narrative (Quayson 129), realist, fantastic, magic realist (Faris 10), inspiring, political. It is indeed *sui generis*, but in the mass of distinguished criticism that has traced its meanings and provenance, many have been at pains to explore its connections to other writings and traditions. For Ato Quayson, these are its complex renegotiations with Nigerian 'orality, cultural nationalism, mythopoeia and liminality' (9). Quayson argues that these concepts may have been made available by Yoruba writers, but are no longer limited to them. (Okri's father is Urhobo, his mother Igbo [Fraser xii].) For Jo Dandy, it is the book's blend of the oral tradition, 'postmodern and pluralist form, resisting the closure of realism' and magic-realist narrative strategies that give it its distinctive richness (61). It has figured as an exemplary text in books on magic realism (Faris), and on religion in postcolonial writing (Housley and Scott). Both attributions are accurate up to a point, except that, like Toni Morrison, Okri does not need to look to South American literary traditions to produce a narrative where the other-worldly and supernatural rub up alongside the material world, the political and the quotidian.

This essay examines Okri's fiction since 1995, and the surprising and challenging ways in which it has developed since *The Famished Road*. Okri's three most recent novels, *Dangerous Love, Astonishing the Gods* and *In Arcadia*, represent a sustained imaginative project which in some ways sets itself up against a postmodernism whose explanatory power Andreas Huyssen has recently described as partial rather than totalizing: 'Post-modernism thought itself global, but was perhaps nothing more than the belated attempt to assert a US international against the European inter-national style of high modernism of the interwar period' (16). At the risk of enlisting Ben Okri in the service of yet another competing tradition or 'ism', I propose that the most useful way to look at his work of the last decade is through the lens of Romanticism — for example, the work of Samuel Taylor Coleridge. The European Romantic tradition is at least as important to Okri as those of postmodern fiction, postcolonial thought, magic realism or African writing, within which he has rightly been discussed. To hold Romanticism in view allows one to perceive his unfashionable devotion, pursued through a number of literary experiments from *The Famished Road* onwards, to balancing the demands of the material and spiritual worlds. Within that enterprise, the importance of concepts of space, and of inner and outer geographies must be taken into account. The conceptual vocabulary of Michel de Certeau and Gaston Bachelard can help to situate Okri's persistent preoccupation with domestic space (the compounds and the rooms in *Dangerous Love*), public space (Eurostar, the Channel Tunnel and the Louvre in *In Arcadia*, the ocean-side public park in Lagos in *Dangerous Love*) and space as an integral part of thinking, personal devel-opment, self-imaging and artistic creation, as in Omovo's artistic vision in *Dangerous Love*, the fantastic city in *Astonishing the Gods* and the tunnels, galleries and paintings in *In Arcadia*.

Such a preoccupation with space and geography, which is coming to be seen as central to the understanding of modernism, should not surprise us in an African writer. As Tim Woods points out, in Africa 'nation space has frequently been a troubled issue, often the legacy of colonial state bureaucracy and arbitrary map-making ... . Furthermore, linguistic and cultural spaces overlie national boundaries, leading in recent decades to some terrible civil wars and acts of racial genocide ...' (126). But are Okri's recent books the product of an African writer *tout court*? He has certainly continued to use African settings in some novels. However, his interesting decision to return to *The Landscapes Within,* and rewrite that powerful story of doomed love and family and social tensions as *Dangerous Love,* now looks like the beginning of a project to explore different literary forms, from realism to imaginative fable to metafiction and symbolism. Just as *The Famished Road* had conceived the natural and supernatural in spatial terms (the compound and family and community life on the one hand, and on the other the lurking spirit world calling back Azaro to walk back into its seductive diversity) so Okri's more recent themes are presented in terms of what Gaston Bachelard has called 'the poetics of space'.

Dangerous Love (1996) was in some ways a surprising enterprise to follow *The Famished Road* and its sequels (such as *Songs of Enchantment).* Nevertheless, it is a significant work in the context of its author's meditations on space and mental geographies. One way of approaching this dimension of the book is through de Certeau's distinction in *The Practice of Everyday Life* between space and place, with the former being seen as 'a practiced place', where 'users reappropriate the space organized by techniques of sociocultural production' (xiv). In *Moving Through Modernity,* Andrew Thacker has used this distinction to suggest the difference between modernism and nineteenth-century realism in their representation of place and space:

> Stories constantly oscillate around these two poles, transforming spaces into places, and places into spaces. For example, place becomes space when an inert object, 'a table, a forest, a person that plays a certain role in the environment (*PE*, p.118), emerges from a stable location and transforms it by narrative action into a space. De Certeau is careful to suggest that these are not unchanging binary terms, since places and spaces are constantly being transfigured into one another in the play of narrative. He also argues that it might be possible to produce a typology of the ways in which stories enact either *'an identification of places'* or an *'actualization of spaces'* (118). (Thacker 31–2)

Thacker contrasts the use of place in Thomas Hardy's *Tess of the D'Urbervilles* and James Joyce's 'actualisation of space' in *Ulysses* to suggest the difference between realism and modernism in this respect (32–4). The reference to *Tess* transfers neatly in some respects to *Dangerous Love,* which is, similarly, a novel of spatial restrictions. Like a Tess or a Jude Fawley, the hero Omovo exists in a 'mapped' world of restricted places, which in turn restrict his human development. His first action in the book is to have his head shaved by the barber's apprentice – a symbol of mourning and a vulnerable baring of himself, which persists throughout the novel. The Lagos compound in which he lives is both familial and communal, with its 'twin strips of bungalows ... airless trapped heat, the stuffy smells and the bustling noises .... The cement ground was grey, dirty and full of potholes. Above, the sky could be seen through the corrugated eaves' (6). Here, as later in the novel, the communal bathroom with its 'overpowering' stench and 'scum that had collected around the drain' (7) represents unwanted spatial intimacy, abject communion, that is persistent in the text.

Quickly, at the start, Okri sketches in alternatives. Omovo's love for Ifeyiwa, the young wife of an older neighbour, exists in an imaginative space of written notes, recounted dreams and yearning. But Omovo is also an artist, within whom love and desire have rekindled the urge to draw and paint. The first fruit of this is a drawing of children playing around an amputated tree, beneath a threatening, moribund sky. Like a number of key objects and persons in the novel, this picture will vanish, when it is stolen from Omovo's room. It still exists somewhere, presumably, out there in Lagos, or sold on by the boy who, suspiciously, thought it saleable to Europeans (8). The body of the young girl whose desecrated corpse Keme and Omovo find in the park similarly vanishes before a proper investigation can be made (57); Omovo's brothers have slipped away from the family home, and exist only in the form of cryptic brooding poems (396); Omovo's political painting vanishes, confiscated by the military authorities. Ifeyiwa herself disappears out of his life and then out of life itself into death (347). But none of these invisible elements of the text lose their power. They continue to exist, instead, in a kind of alternative imaginative space. In the confusion when Ifeyiwa returns home, only to be fired upon as she approached her own village, her attackers articulate a significant confusion between the realms of spirits, bodily existence and politics:

> She heard rapid voices.
> 'It's a spirit.'
> 'An animal.'
> 'An enemy.'
> Then a shot was fired. (347)

We are not so far here from the material, spiritual and ideological components of *The Famished Road*. *Dangerous Love* may be the more realist text of the two, but its realism gains its power from its ability to engage with the spiritual and artistic, as well as the material.

Okri's realist mapping of place is powerful. Omovo's first drawing, for example, is quickly absorbed into the community. The inhabitants of the compound (like the outraged member of the military, later) act as impromptu art critics. Omovo's plaintive response – 'Why don't you people just go away and leave me alone!' (8) strikes a *leitmotiv* for the novel, for the opinions and bodies of others which surround the central love story represent a force of social reaction, of jealous levelling. Nevertheless, Okri's method is not simplistic, for he evokes a creativity and vivacity in everyday life – qualities that cannot be suppressed.

It is primarily against a sense of enclosure, however, that the novel's love story unfolds. Omovo is drawn to Ifeyiwa, the wife of an older husband. She is his muse, and eventually becomes his lover in a single sexual encounter of startling immediacy and power. But their love-making is stolen in the stifling room of a friend of Ifeyiwa's, and concludes with the invasive hammering on the door of their 'place' by Takpo, Ifeyiwa's husband: 'Come out! I know you are both in there' (264). Where could they go, where can they meet, the novel asks, in a space outside the places owned by family or community? Okri brilliantly sets a number of their trysts on the Badagry road, with its potholes and traffic. She tells her dreams; they share a kiss. The notion of private space hardly exists, and Omovo finds when he exhibits his political painting of a 'national scumpool' that the dominant political forces can also invade the private and imaginative realms through confiscation. In a nation where the author Ken Saro-Wiwa was to be executed for treason in 1995, despite the protests and representations of the international literary community, art's space within place can become extremely dangerous for its creator. In Okri's fiction, as in Coleridge's conversation poems, reflections on a repressive regime coexist with a celebration of the liberties of the imagination. In 1797, the Wordsworths, Dorothy and William, visited Coleridge at Nether Stowey and came to live at Alfoxden, nearby. As Coleridge was to say later in *Biographia Literaria*, 'our conversations turned frequently on the two cardinal points of poetry, the power of exciting the sympathy of the reader by a faithful adherence to the truth of nature, and the power of giving the interest of novelty by the modifying colours of imagination' (376). Coleridge's conversation poems, according to Kelvin Everest in *Coleridge's Secret Ministry: the Context of the Conversation Poems, 1795–98*, grew from a situation in which radical writers like Coleridge had found themselves cut off from public life as British politics became more repressive:

> Volunteer movements and loyalty oaths were details in the pattern of Coleridge's social experience in Somerset from 1794 to 1798, and this pattern, of barely muted hostility in the quotidian life of intercourse with neighbours and a local rural population, of distressing persecutions endured by friends, emerges with, if anything, increased clarity even after Coleridge's attitudes change and his radicalism dissolves after 1796. (119)

The poems explore the nature of the imagination, and its ability to transcend any physical limitations – a theme also central to Okri's work. As Azaro's father said in *The Famished Road*, 'the man whose light has come on in his head, in his dormant sun, can never be kept down or defeated. We can redream this world and make the dream real' (498). In *Astonishing the Gods* and *In Arcadia*, Okri's Romantic affinities become even more pronounced. In 'This Lime Tree Bower my Prison' (1797), Coleridge had cleverly worked together inner and outer space, imaginatively accompanying his friends on a walk while confined at home by an injury. He had also espoused the relationship between art and nature, which would preoccupy Okri in *In Arcadia*:

> Nature ne'er deserts the wise and pure;
> No plot so narrow, be but Nature there,
> No waste so vacant, but may well employ
> Each faculty of sense, and keep the heart
> Awake to Love and Beauty!

'Fears in Solitude' (1798) situates Liberty within a personal quest through Nature, as Coleridge looks out across the sea:

> Yes, while I stood and gazed, my temples bare,
> And shot my being through earth, sea and air,
> Possessing all things with intensest love,
> O Liberty! My spirit felt thee there.

Similarly, Omovo, meditating by the ocean in his provincial retreat, experiences 'the wonder that had awoken in him' (361), crystallizes his historical sense of the oppression of Africans, and links this to inner energies: 'understand things slowly – digest thoroughly – act swiftly – redream the world – restructure self' (363). Like Coleridge, too, Okri expresses the difficulty in holding on to moments of vision and acting upon them, for 'the wonder was soon gone' (364).

How could such moments of wonder be dramatized and sustained? Few critics reviewing Okri's work of the early 1990s could have been prepared for *Astonishing the Gods*, which appeared in 1995. For many he was viewed primarily as a 'magic realist', who had been undertaking the task of defamiliarization neatly defined by Wendy B. Faris in *Ordinary Enchantments* (2004):

> In magic realism, reality's outrageousness is often underscored because ordinary people react to magical events in recognizable and sometimes also in disturbing ways, a circumstance that normalizes the magical event but also defamiliarizes, underlines, or critiques extraordinary aspects of the real. (13)

In *Astonishing the Gods*, however, the spiritual dimension of existence takes over the novel to such an extent as to suggest that Okri's commitment to 'the real' in its common-sense version had always been more ambiguous. There is little doubt that in this book, 'the real' is the world of the imagination, the spirit or soul. The novel's nameless hero engages in a quest for spiritual knowledge, and completes it. Admittedly, the opening of the narrative is grounded in metaphors relating to nationality and ethnicity, since the central character is an invisible man:

> He was born invisible. His mother was invisible too, and that was why she could see him. His people lived contented lives, working on the farms, under the familiar sunlight. ... It was in books that he first learnt of his invisibility. He searched for himself and his people in all the history books he read and discovered to his youthful astonishment that he didn't exist. (3)

Robert Fraser (88) and Ralph Pordzik (49) are surely right to see this trope as connected to Ralph Ellison's novel *Invisible Man*, where the African-American lives the paradox of being both defined by appearance (by 'a different sun', as Okri was to put it in *In Arcadia*), and invisible in the sense suggested above. But when Okri's hero arrives by ship in an apparently deserted city, the trope of invisibility modulates, for the city is populated and created by The Invisibles, philosopher-citizens whose dream is to create the first universal civilization of justice and love (155). Their values are founded on the concepts of creativity and grace, and their invisibility and devotion to spiritual values and civic virtues is fostered by their invisibility. As we learn at the end of the text, the purpose of invisibility is perfection (155).

Astonishing the Gods is the story of a quest for enlightenment, carried out through a series of visions, tests, guides and interrogations. In keeping with Okri's fictional methods, that quest takes place within a detailed geography: in this case that of a beautiful city of palaces, halls, bridges, libraries, towers, gates and piazzas. Throughout Okri's work, inner and outer space have been held in counterpoint, and this remains true here, except that this fabulous, poetic narrative is the closest Okri has come to an other-worldly fiction, a Blakean evocation of untrammelled human vision: 'A horse in the distance became a mist when he got there. Fountains dissolved into fragrances. Palaces became empty spaces where trees dwelt in solitude. Cathedrals became vacant places where harmonies were sweetest in the air' (40).

In one sense *Astonishing the Gods* is a very unfashionable book. If we think of the postmodern as putting sceptical inverted commas round those great abstractions and ideals ('truth', 'perfection', 'beauty', 'nature') which had preoccupied the Romantics, then Okri's determination to reinstate and use them without irony is courageous and independent-minded. On the other hand, the Invisibles' teachings about consciousness and intuition: 'Don't try to understand ... Understanding comes beyond trying' (15) ... 'The first law of our city ... is that what you think is what becomes real' (46) have been seen by some, like Bruce King in his review of *In Arcadia*, as modish new age slogans (86). Such a dismissal would be unfair to Okri's enterprise, which is to work through, in an imaginary landscape, what a relentless devotion to justice, beauty and learning might mean. As often with his more recent work, multiple intertexts suggest themselves, from Blake's 'Jerusalem' — as noted by Robert Fraser (92–3) — to *Zen in the Art of Archery*, the paradoxes of *The Marriage of Heaven and Hell* and the Utopian literary tradition in Africa as well as Europe (Pordzik 45). *Astonishing the Gods* is an inspirational text that counsels trust in intuition, respect for learning, the need to take artistic creativity seriously, the need to avoid cynicism and easy scepticism, and the renunciation of ego. At the end of his trials, the hero is addressed by the voice of an invisible speaker, 'sweet and primeval':

'Because your heart is pure you have found without seeking, overcome without knowing that you overcame, and arrived here when all who have tried have failed. You were born invisible. For anyone to get here they must, one way or another, come through your condition. There is no other way.' (157)

The insistent, poetic narrative voice, the predilection for abstractions, and the innovative use of symbolic space make *Astonishing the Gods* an admirable but exhausting experience for the reader. For the duration of this text, Okri opts for space over place, and sets aside his realism – his skilful evocation of how material and spiritual worlds can collide. In his next novel he was to re-establish a material location (European, in this case) and interweave it with metaphysical speculation.

In Arcadia (2002) marks out Okri as transnational writer, in the sense in which the term has been proposed by Andreas Huyssen, who sees the concept of transnationalism as a way of overcoming the false dichotomy between the local and the global, counteracting and complicating the 'argument that only local culture or culture *as* local is good, authentic and resistant, whereas global cultural forms must be condemned as manifestations of cultural imperialism, i.e., Americanization' (13). In this, Okri's most recent novel, Lao, an intellectual, celebrity presenter and a black human being (112), narrates part of the story of the making of a documentary film about the idea of Arcadia; at other times he is the Jamesian 'reflector' of a third-person narrative.

The search for this elusive world of pastoral innocence and fulfilment involves eight people: Lao himself, the struggling film director Jim, sound man Propr, researcher Husk, garrulous chief cameraman Sam, assistant camera-person Riley ('Strangest creature I ever saw. Don't know how to describe her' [12]), administrator and accountant Jute, and Lao's companion Mistletoe. The filming journey is scheduled to end, appropriately enough, in Greece, where the original mythical and/or geographical Arcadia is said to have existed, but in fact the novel ends before Greece is reached, with the characters bound for Switzerland, as 'the train bore them towards Arcadia' (230). The *mise-en-scène* of the novel thus bears some relation to Ben Okri's participation in the 1996 television series *Great Railway Journeys* (Fraser xvii), though Okri is at pains to point out that the characters and events are fictional.

In Arcadia is an unusual and experimental fiction that in some ways appears inconclusive. Bruce King, in an interesting review that acknowledged the interesting formal properties of the book, compared it unfavourably to *The Famished Road* and Okri's early fiction (86). Yet this novel-as-compendium, which blends the novel, travel writing, art criticism, allegory, meditation, aphorisms, autobiographical fiction, dialogue and inspirational text, reminds one of Bakhtin's insight that the early novel was made up from a blend of many textual genres and sources. Indeed, the structure of Laurence Sterne's *A Sentimental Journey* might provide an instructive parallel. The structure of *In Arcadia* also reminds readers that, however different the forms of Okri's fictions may be, certain enduring preoccupations exist which are central to *Dangerous Love* and *Astonishing the Gods* as well as to *The Famished Road*. Among these are his Romantic project to reinstate the concept of spirituality in modern life, outside the institutions of organized religion; his sense of the importance of race and ethnicity; his questioning of the relationship between the spiritual and political health of individuals and nations; and his testing of spatial and geographical parameters, both metaphorically and literally.

Given these concerns, it is possible to see why the notion of Arcadia, established in classical culture by the *Idyls* of Theocritus and the *Eclogues* of Virgil, might be a potent one for Ben Okri. It has persisted through different literary traditions, even when, as in the case of Wordsworth, writers protested their own distance from the notion of rural innocence. Wordsworth retained a sense of the magical and restorative nature of the rural environment, while writing in 'Michael', a highly original pastoral about contemporary shepherds. He himself pointed out the difference between his shepherds and those of Virgil, Shakespeare and Spenser:

> [They are] not such as in Arcadian fastnesses
> Sequester'd, handed down among themselves,
> So ancient Poets sing, the Golden Age;
> Nor such, a second race, allied to these,
> As Shakespeare in the Wood of Arden plac'd
> Where Phoebe sighed for the false Ganymede ...
> Nor such as Spenser fabled ... (Book VIII, 183–8, 191)

What is ordinary, what is strange? In a way, Wordsworth wants to make Arcadia 'ordinary'. In the late 1980s, the South African writer Njabulo Ndebele, dismayed by what he saw as the preoccupation of his national literature with the 'spectacle' of political propaganda and the representation of violence, called for a 'rediscovery of the ordinary', whereby politics could be traced through the everyday lives of ordinary Africans. For Okri, on the other hand, the issue is more the rediscovery of the marvellous and the spiritual in a materialistic age, and his narrator Lao is drawn to the notion of Arcadia precisely because of its apparently absurd idealism and other-worldliness. A self-confessed cynic, loathing 'everything in life' and swaggeringly enjoying 'this acidic perception, this delicious jaundice' (10), Lao nevertheless turns from an iterative tirade against twenty-first-century injustices to allow space to the idea of an alternative reality, half imaginative, half geographical:

> All over the world, presidents are deaf, prime ministers are out of touch, the young stumble towards rude awakenings, the aged stumble towards the long dream of reckonings, those in between are weighed down with the apparent pointlessness of it all. And I, in my heart, where no poison or cynicism ever

reaches, I seemingly with a band of fools, who might well be a band of seekers too, I am travelling in disguise towards the place where Hades is averted, turned away, transformed into something else: a hint of paradise lurking in this great universal wound of living. (58)

In Arcadia is a meditation on the way modern spaces such as the city, the gallery, the train, 'the narrower spaces of the intimate relations between people when travelling' (Thacker 84), and the space of the Imagination (such as Arcadia) are inter-dependent. This juxtaposition had been present in *Dangerous Love*, where Omovo's skill in gaining a place on the heaving, infrequent, blue danfo Lagos buses (217–24) is a counterpoint to his painting and his ecstatic, space-annihilating meditations by the sea (361–4).

In *The Poetics of Space*, Bachelard deals intriguingly with the space within the houses and rooms within which we grow up and live, as well as with national variations in the experience of living space: 'In Paris there are no houses, and the inhabitants of the big city live in superimposed boxes' (26). Bachelard's ninth chapter, 'The Dialectics of Outside and Inside', considers the importance of spatial experience and metaphors to our thinking and metaphysics: 'an implicit geometry which – whether we will or no – confers spatiality on thought' (212). It is this insight that Okri shares, and which provides the ground-plan upon which his fiction, however various in other ways, is conceived.

Astonishing the Gods had been a fable of self-discovery and enlightenment set in an incandescent, timeless urban space, a monument to human creativity and collaborative endeavour. Every location in *In Arcadia* has symbolic resonance. The 'closed world' within the Channel Tunnel, for example, 'makes us see inward, against our will' in a place where 'thoughts become stiller' (69), and the daylight world becomes suddenly more purely inscribed when we emerge into it. A commonplace customs barrier in Paris becomes for Lao a boundary, inducing what Camus called 'humiliated consciousness' (106). 'Society has invisible lines and nets', says Lao to the film director Jim as they approach the barrier, 'points of interrogation' (107–8) which hardly exist for the white European traveller like Jim himself. For all his outward confidence, Lao dreads the possibility that he, as a black human being, will not be allowed into the country 'because of a different sun' (107).

Jim's empathetic response to this different sense of space marks a different phase in Lao's relationship to him, and initiates an almost *Canterbury Tales* phase of the text, a series of monologues in a Parisian café where each of these supporting characters, who has hitherto been seen in grotesque terms, is given narrative licence to develop a brief personal manifesto. Even when these are antithetical to what one has come to see as Okri's own world view – like Sam's affirmation of appearances ('I trust the camera' [141]) or Jute's impatience with 'life beyond death, intangibles, the miraculous, invisibles' (78) – they are given dialogic space in the text in a way that Bakhtin saw as characteristic of the novel's generous hospitableness as a literary form. This dialogism is one of the more disarming qualities of Okri's fiction; Omovo may be the central consciousness of *Dangerous Love*, but his father is given space in which to represent himself in dialogue, and, as Robert Fraser has pointed out, one of the most moving scenes in the book is when Ifeyiwa's apparently brutish husband Takpo takes his young wife to the bush and pleads with her to respect him (286–90; Fraser 35).

At the end of *In Arcadia*, Okri has his film-makers visit the Louvre to view Nicolas Poussin's beautiful, haunting painting *Et in Arcadia Ego* (c. 1637) and to discuss it with the gallery's director. In Virgil's fifth eclogue, two shepherds come across the tomb of the poet Daphnis – who, in Okri's words 'was famous, gifted and beautiful and . . . died young' (208). In Poussin's painting, three shepherds and a shepherdess walking in the Arcadian landscape have come across a tomb, and are trying to decipher its inscription '*Et in Arcadia Ego*' – 'I too have lived in Arcadia'.

Lao and Okri ponder this painting, and the inscription, at length. It provides the springboard for the rhetoric which, in a characteristic Okri strategy, ends the novel (one thinks of Dad's speech at the end of *The Famished Road*, the culmination of *Astonishing the Gods*, and Omovo's epiphany, 'THE MOMENT' towards the end of *Dangerous Love*). It is a development, more initially severe than some of his earlier versions, of the Romantic paradox: repressive politics and the brutal inevitability of death (even citizenship of Arcadia was no refuge from death for the Everyman beneath the tomb), set against beauty, art and the possibility of imaginative transcendence. Okri makes the painting's challenge explicit through Lao's formulations:

> There is transcendence in Virgil, the poet.
> There is no transcendence in Poussin.
> There is just the bare statement of fact, an impenetrable fact: 'I too lived in Arcadia'.
> This fact is a labyrinth without any exit. It is closed.
> The mind either learns to live within the closed labyrinth of the conjoining of death and life;
> Or the mind develops wings, and soars. (209)

Based on this homage to the imagination, the book concludes with a more general theme: the enigma of revolution and social change, and whether it will come from within or without. Like *Astonishing the Gods*, which moves from the opening anger at African 'invisibility' to develop its glorification of the power of thought, emotion, imagination and self-actualization, *In Arcadia* ends with an extended spiritual testament, the conclusion of which is a counsel against despair, melancholy and cynicism: 'living is the place where gods play within mortal flesh' (229–30). Few other contemporary writers would risk such an open-hearted, vulnerable, inspiring, resoundingly un-ironic conclusion.

Bibliography and further reading

Okri, Ben. *The Famished Road*. London: Vintage, 1992 [1991].

——. *Astonishing the Gods*. London: Phoenix House, 1996 [1995].

——. *Dangerous Love*. London: Phoenix House, 1997 [1996].

——. *In Arcadia*. London: Phoenix House, 2003 [2002].

Bachelard, Gaston. *The Poetics of Space*. Trans. Maria Jolas. Boston, MA: Beacon Press, 1969.

Bakhtin, Mikhail. *The Bakhtin Reader: Selected Writings of Bakhtin, Medvedvev, Voloshinov*. Pam Morris (ed.). Oxford: Blackwell, 1994.

Coleridge, Samuel Taylor. *Poetical Works*. Oxford: Oxford University Press, 1912.

——. *Biographia Literaria. Criticism: the Major Texts*. Walter Jackson Bate (ed.). New York: Harcourt Brace, 1952.

Dandy, Jo. 'Magic and Realism in Ben Okri's *The Famished Road, Songs of Enchantment* and *Astonishing the Gods*: an Examination of Conflicting Cultural Influences and Narrative Traditions', in *Kiss and Quarrel: Yoruba/English, Strategies of Mediation*. Birmingham University African Studies Series No. 5. Birmingham: Centre of West African Studies, 2000: 45–63.

de Certeau, Michel. *The Practice of Everyday Life*. Trans. Steven Randall. Berkeley, CA: University of California Press, 1984.

Ellison, Ralph. *Invisible Man*. London: Victor Gollancz, 1953.

Everest, Kelvin. *Coleridge's Secret Ministry: the Context of the Conversation Poems, 1795–98*. Brighton: Harvester, 1979.

Faris, Wendy B. *Ordinary Enchantments: Magic Realism and the Remystification of Narrative*. Nashville, TN: Vanderbilt University Press, 2004.

Fraser, Robert. *Ben Okri*. Tavistock, Devon: Northcote House, 2002.

Herrigel, Eugen. *Zen in the Art of Archery*. New York: Vintage, 2000.

Housley, Paul Simpson and Jamie S. Scott (eds). *Mapping the Sacred: Religion, Geography and Postcolonial Literatures*. Amsterdam: Rodopi, 2001.

Huyssen, Andreas. 'Geographies of Modernism in a Globalizing World', in *Geographies of Modernism: Literatures, Cultures, Spaces*. Peter Brooker and Andrew Thacker (eds). London, Routledge, 2005: 6–18.

King, Bruce. Review of Ben Okri, *In Arcadia*. *World Literature Today*, 77:1, 2003: 86.

Ndebele, Njabulo. *South African Literature and Culture: Rediscovery of the Ordinary*. Manchester: Manchester University Press, 1994.

Pordzik, Ralph. 'An African Utopographer: Ben Okri's *Astonishing the Gods* and the Quest for Postcolonial Utopia.' *Zeitschrift für Anglistik und Americanistik*, 48:1, 2000: 44–56.

Quayson, Ato. *Strategic Transformations in Nigerian Writing: Orality and History in the Work of Rev. Samuel Johnson, Amos Tutuola, Wole Soyinka and Ben Okri*. Oxford and Bloomington & Indianapolis, IN: James Currey and Indiana University Press, 1997.

Sterne, Laurence. *A Sentimental Journey*. Paul Goring (ed.). London: Penguin Classics, 2001.

Thacker, Andrew. *Moving Through Modernity: Space and Geography in Modernism*. Manchester: Manchester University Press, 2003.

Woods, Tim. 'Memory, Geography, Identity: African Writing and Modernity', in *Geographies of Modernism: Literatures, Cultures, Spaces*. Peter Brooker and Andrew Thacker (eds). London, Routledge, 2005: 126–35.

Wordsworth, William. *The Prelude or, Growth of a Poet's Mind*. Stephen Gill (ed.). Oxford: Oxford University Press, 1990 [1888].

CHAPTER EIGHT

Salman Rushdie: Paradox and Truth

ROBERT EAGLESTONE

The creative process is rather like the processes of a free society. Many attitudes, many views of the world jostle and conflict within the artist, and from these frictions the spark, the work of art, is born. This inner multiplicity is frequently very difficult for the artist to bear, let alone explain.

(*Step Across This Line* 232)

You can either break your heart trying to work it all out, or you can go sit on a mountain, because that's where all the truth went ... it just upped and ran away from these cities where even the stuff under our feet is all made up, a lie, and it hid up there in the thin thin air where the liars don't dare come after it in case their brains explode.

(*The Satanic Verses* 313)

Take away the paradox from a thinker and you have a professor.

(Kierkegaard 406)

As befits the work of one of the world's great writers, Rushdie's novels stir up controversy: most significantly, of course, in relation to the *fatwa* of 14 February 1989, and in various lawsuits in India and Pakistan. But his work has also been controversial in the academic world. While some praise his 'unbridled talent' (Ravi 7), others judge that he presents his

compatriots ... as mindless, illogical, brutal, bloody and boorish. There is hardly any attempt to communicate understanding to the reader. The figures are violent, picturesque; their motives cannot be shared; they are not 'equals' of the writer or reader.

(Goonetilleke 149)

Tim Parnell argues for the 'political limitations of Rushdie's attempts to harness postmodern poetics to a postcolonial political agenda' (257), a complaint echoed in accusations over his 'failure to construct a viable alternative ideology for himself or for postcolonial society in general' (Khan 143). Some praise Rushdie's focus on migrancy as 'an agent for sustaining life' (Sanga 44) and find hope in this mixing and hybridity: 'How Newness enters the world' as Homi Bhabha, citing Rushdie, argues. In contrast, Aijaz

Ahmad attacks the term 'migrant': he judges that because Rushdie makes this term universally applicable to all humanity, the term becomes meaningless and disconnected from any reality. Instead, Rushdie is a 'vagrant': quoting Orwell, Ahmad argues that ' "it is unlikely that he [the vagrant] will understand, in any depth, the life about which he is writing ...", rather he simply ' "report[s] upon the curious or the exotic ..." ' (157). Timothy Brennan, who offers a more nuanced view of Rushdie, argues that his work is not addressed to 'the people' (Brennan 1989: 58) and that, despite its benefits, 'Rushdie's "cosmopolitanism" tends to obscure the conflicting interests between, say, non-English-speaking guest workers and Cambridge educated novelists within a blurry "postcolonialism"; and [has a] tendency to ridicule, without homage or fairness, the extraordinary heritage of the anti-colonial liberation movements' (Brennan 1992: 274). And if some critics found his most recent novel *Shalimar the Clown* 'calmer, more compassionate, wiser ... [his] most engaging since *Midnight's Children* ... grappling imaginatively with the shock of 11 September 2001' (Cowley 17), others found it 'confused' (Roth 19), with an 'increasingly absurd plot and a style that is more and more mannered' (Walter 21).

In the light of these criticisms I want to defend Rushdie, on the grounds that his books are, at the very least, paradoxical, and are simply not reducible to positions: they are the opposite of what Adorno and Horkheimer call 'ticket thinking' (Adorno and Horkheimer 206), their term for the ways in which judgement and complexity – experience, in fact – are overridden by both virtuous and vicious political demands. It's not his books that are absurd and confused but experience itself, and the books represent this. This is to build on Deepika Bahri's Adorno-inflected argument against the current state of postcolonial criticism and theory. Burdened by the demand of 'native informancy' which 'ethnographically and ideologically' saturates texts and creates a 'disinterest in aesthetic mimesis', she argues that a return to an

> attention to the aesthetic innovation, plural origins and formal commitments of postcolonial works uncovers their complex and uneven relationship to ideology, revivifying their potential to make radical contributions to the larger project of social liberation, a potential that issues from the very historical conditions that irreducibly limit and define it. (Bahri 4–6)

The aim, then, is to attend to postcolonial writing aesthetically – in a renewed sense, as I discuss below – rather than through the straitjacket of rigid political frameworks and expectations. This is not to suggest that Rushdie's novels are simply 'art for art's sake', but rather to find in his art other forms of knowledge and other sorts of power. Rushdie is a thinker, in the sense of being a public intellectual (on the magazine *Prospect*'s list of the world's top 100 intellectuals, for example) and more importantly, as Michael Wood argues, because literature 'thinks'. Stimulated by Peter de Bolla's question of a Barnett Newman painting, 'what does this painting know?', Wood writes that 'every poem and novel' holds a 'decisive (but speculative) thought ... in a unique and unalterable form, every reading or rereading [is] another moment among the essays of our life' (Wood 189–90). Literature 'thinks' precisely in a manner that encourages paradox, complexity, lack of conclusion, and productive confusion. In the case of Rushdie, as epitomized in the case of the inconclusive conclusion to *Shalimar the Clown*, it is precisely the decisive lack of decisiveness, the paradoxical confusion and contradiction of 'many views of the world' and 'inner multiplicity' that forms his oeuvre. 'Take away the paradox from a thinker and you have a professor', wrote Kierkegaard: being a 'professor' means ironing out paradoxes, establishing positions, proffering the (not an) answer from the fobbed belly of time and, whatever else he might be, Salman Rushdie is not a professor.

Migrancy and paradox

As the critical comments touched on above suggest, one of the most significant areas in which Rushdie's work is paradoxical, and powerfully and rewardingly self-contradictory, is over the nexus of ideas around hybridity, diaspora and migrancy. On the one hand, and in no small part stemming from Homi Bhabha's groundbreaking criticism, Rushdie's work is taken as the epitome of the celebration of hybridity and diaspora, almost to the point of cliché: J. M. Coetzee, in his review of *The Moor's Last Sigh*, writes of the 'by-now-familiar Rushdian celebration of bastardy, mongrelhood, and hybridity' (178). Rushdie's novels are seen to revel in the mixing of cultures in a postcolonial or globalized world, whether as 'chutnification' in *Midnight's Children*, or, in *The Moor's Last Sigh*, 'weaving'; 'or more accurately an interweaving ... these were polemical pictures ... an attempt to create a romantic myth of a plural, hybrid nation' (227). This idea of intermixing, taken from its original context in Rushdie's work which refers clearly and explicitly to India, has been expanded to model the whole contemporary world. Rushdie as critic endorses this line of thought: writing of what I consider to be his greatest novel to date, Rushdie argues that those

> who oppose the novel most vociferously today are of the opinion that intermingling with a different culture will inevitably weaken and ruin their own. I am of the opposite opinion. *The Satanic Verses* celebrates hybridity, impurity, intermingling, the transformation that comes of new and unexpected combinations of human beings, cultures, ideas, politics, movies, songs. It rejoices in mongrelisation and fears the absolutism of the Pure. Melange, hotchpotch, a bit of this and a bit of that is *how newness enters the world*. It is the great possibility that mass migration gives to the world, and I have tried to embrace it. ... It is a love song to our mongrel selves. (*Imaginary Homelands* 394)

On the other hand, this sort of celebration of hybridity is also attacked: Rushdie is a first world court jester offering exotic jokes in a palatable Western form; hybridity leads to abstraction rather than 'the contingencies of an actual "homeland"' (Smith 256). As 'vagrant' work, *pace* Ahmad, Rushdie and his novels are disconnected from the real non-Western communities they claim to represent.

However, both camps — the 'pro' and 'anti' hybridity in Rushdie as it were — ignore the counter-vision in his actual paradoxical, complex novels. There is a chthonic Rushdie, too, who coexists with the hybrid, migrant Rushdie. This vision, which lies within all his novels but which becomes both increasingly clear and bleak in his later writing, finds intermingling destructive: it castigates and ridicules hybridity and finds in new and unexpected combinations only disaster, rage potent and impotent, hate, killing, abuse of power, child murder and mass slaughter, racism, corruptible seed, suicide, 'tyranny, forced conversions, temple-smashing, iconoclasm, persecution and genocide' (*Shalimar* 239): in short, the great, vicious train wreck of a world gone wrong unstoppably. If Timothy Brennan could write in 1989 that staring 'in the face of misery, and with serious doubts about the future of the human race, Rushdie insists on the comic' (Brennan 151), this is no longer the case: even when, in human misery, the comic seems to emerge — say, in the huge list of apologies offered by the doctor in the makeshift hospital towards the end of *Shalimar the Clown* — these fragile moments are simply smashed: the people die, there 'were no relatives on hand to collect the bodies and no facility existed for returning the five dancers to their home village and they were burned on the municipal pyre, even the three Jews' (*Shalimar* 304). The negative — always there in Rushdie — has been accentuated.

But is this simply what Ahmad would call Rushdie's 'aesthetic of despair' (155)? No, because hybridity not only brings disaster for this rooted Rushdie: the lack of hybridity, a sense of rooted identity and behaviour is also offered as positive. It isn't only sinister clerics and racist Thatcherite business people who distrust mixing: this distrust is also shared by crucial figures that represent salvation and are clearly admirable. In *The Satanic Verses*, Otto Cone, Holocaust survivor and Levi-like suicide, font of wisdom, believes that the 'world is incompatible ... Ghosts, Nazis, saints, all alive at the same time' (295) and that if these lives 'that have no business mingling with one another ... meet ... It's uranium and plutonium, each makes the other decompose, boom!' (314). Tai, the boatman, from *Midnight's Children* is the 'living antithesis of Oskar-Ilse-Ingrid's belief in the inevitability of change ... a quirky, enduring spirit of the valley' (15), a mystical, peaceful figure. Similarly, in *The Ground Beneath Her Feet*, the saintly Patangbaz Kalamanja, widower and generous spirit, blazes out at Vina — the martyred symbol of hybridity, 'never big ... on authenticity which she held to be a pernicious notion that needed "deconstruction"' (338) — shouting:

'Who are you to speak of old learning? . . . this same ayurveda you praise is expressly opposed diametrically and inalienably opposed – to your brand of debauched activities . . . You have the cheek to speak of vegetables when your whole life is an abomination? . . . Leaves India's sacred knowledge within India's national boundaries!' (334)

Vina's ragbag of philosophies (frequently ridiculed in the text) are shown up for the slight, vagrant and (paradoxically) inauthentic fancies they are. Balasubramanyam Venkataraghavan, the 'important banker' (*Fury* 222) who ends Malik Solanka's sexual abuse by his stepfather, is presented (indeed, almost magically invoked by the repetition of his 'magnificent' [80] name) as an authentic figure, giving up his world to become a *sanyasi*, seeking knowledge and peace in the approach to death (though, as Rushdie lets his abandoned son Chandra comment, 'I hate knowledge! And peace, too. I really hate peace *a lot*') (81). Even in *The Satanic Verses*, we are invited, in fact, to admire the Prophet, in his steadfastness and as a model for living: the returned and redeemed Salahuddin reflects that after his father's death he lives an 'orphaned life, like Muhammad's, like everyone's' (534). Indeed, the Prophet's death in Gibreel's dream is told with such beautiful simplicity (393–4) that even the diabolic narrator can't corrupt it.

But even more than this, roots and location are a path for redemption. Aleid Fokkema writes of *The Satanic Verses* that

> in the end the multiple self gives way either to death (Farista) or to a re-established community (Chamcha). The author who once wrote that the idea of roots is a conservative myth now redeems one of his protagonists by letting him return to India, giving him 'another chance'. (Fokkema 62–3)

And even the odd, but melancholically joyful ending of *Fury* invokes a return to family roots with (paradoxically) Malik Solanka bouncing up and down to attract his son's attention. (Indeed, was there ever a better symbol of both rootedness and movement than a *bouncy* – inflatable, soft, trans-portable, encouraging movement, child's play – *castle* – solid, immutable, with a long heritage, a grim affirmation of adult power?) The 'good' characters and the sense of salvation show that this chthonic Rushdie is not only a rhetorical or narrative ploy, a straw, 'pure' figure against which the 'mongrel goodie' can win: it embodies real and potent forces, offers real possibilities. As Anuradha Dingwaney Needham argues, the multiplicity of 'ideological mediations, of all accounts, assertions and positions' (70) in Rushdie's fiction is not simply a deconstructive trick but constitutive of the work itself, even when critics – and even the author as critic – find them unpalatable, 'difficult to bear'.

The contrasting positions in Rushdie (and this issue of migrancy and roots is only the leading one from many) are also enacted in the plots and structure of the novels through the constant appearances of less and less resolved or resolvable combative dualities and doublings, one of the recurring tropes — like beneficial sicknesses or handicaps — that structure his work. Moreover, and this is the key point, these contrasting positions, these oppositions, say, between a bleak rooted conservative Rushdie and a hopeful hybridity liberal Rushdie, never reach a satisfactory *aufhebung*: there is no synthesis or conclusion. The ends are not tied up. This is to say, of course, that reading either version of Rushdie as right is a wrong reading and that precisely what makes him such a great and important writer is lost in the critical 'professorization' of paradox and complexity.

... and truth

This discussion of migrancy and identity, of roots and movement is even more important because of the constant link that Rushdie makes between these issues and all the other 'big questions': the 'question of origins is one of the two great questions ... the second great question [is] the question of ethics' (*Shalimar* 211), says Peggy Ophuls. One of Rushdie's great strengths as a writer is to approach existential questions head on. It is, in a secular vein, to engage with what are often thought to be religious experiences but are perhaps equally well understood as existential experiences: anxiety, doubt, fear, conscience, death, figuring out who one is and what one should do, to which story one belongs, how one fits, or refuses to fit that shape and shaping: issues of truth and ethics. That is to say that Rushdie has an interest in religion, not only because much of his writing is about 'reality as it is experienced by religious people' (*Imaginary Homelands* 376), but also because it wishes to 'fill up that emptied God-chamber with other dreams' (377). This is what Rushdie means when he writes that the novel offers the 'elevation of the quest for the Grail over the Grail itself' (a transformation of the Arthurian myth into the Simurg myth, that lies behind *Grimus*): it is a way of 'fulfilling our unaltered spiritual requirements' (422) not by providing, for example, consolation and escapism but, more importantly, by working through problems in life: aesthetic existential thinking. That is, in contrast to Ahmad finding migrancy an empty and in the end narcissistic metaphor, for Rushdie, it is the experience of migrancy, the 'very experience of uprooting, disjuncture and metamorphosis (slow or rapid, painful or pleasurable) that is the migrant condition' (394) which allows consideration of Ophul's second question, the question of ethics, of how to live.

This inextricable interlinking of migrancy with ethics, and so with truth, occurs most clearly at the core of *The Satanic Verses*. The *locus classicus* for this in the novel is the contrast between Lucretius and Ovid: Lucretius is taken to show that change (migration, or here, more literally, turning into a devil) means the death of the old self and the birth of the new, while Ovid is taken to mean that underneath a superficial manifestation of change, a real essence remains immutable. As Salahuddin comments, this is pretty cold comfort ... Either I accept Lucretius and conclude that some demonic and irreversible mutation is taking place in my inmost depths, or I go with Ovid and concede that everything new emerging is no more than a manifestation of what was already there. (277)

Of course, with typical Rushdie complexity, as the implied author of the novel is, in fact, the Devil, we are at liberty to doubt or question the very premise that offers these two alternatives. Moreover, it would be nice and neat if these two contrasts could be easily mapped onto the various doubles that structure the book: if, for example, the Prophet could be seen as Lucretian – championing the death of one world, Jahilia, and the birth of another, Islam – and Baal the poet as Ovidian maintaining an internal consistency; or if Gibreel were Ovidian, wishing a continuity despite his 'stage names and performing' (427) and Salahuddin intentionally Lucretian, with 'selected discontinuities' and 'willing reinvention' (ibid.). But (again, of course ...) Rushdie denies us this simplicity. The diabolic narrator rejects these distinctions 'resting as they must on an idea of the self as being (ideally) homogenous, non-hybrid, "pure", – an utterly fantastical notion!' This rejection, with '(ideally)' and the hyperbole of the 'utterly fantastical' placed so as to render the sentence ambiguous, is typical 'Devil talk': fine-sounding, but totally confusing when we try to work out what it might actually mean. Are we to conclude that self is *actually* (i.e. not *ideally*) homogenous, non-hybrid, 'pure'? Is this notion in fact 'fantastical' (in a story, told by the Devil, in a novel)? Or do we (we can if we wish) agree with the Devil narrator? The next step in the passage makes the leap to the second question of truth and ethics. Justified by the suggestion that willing reinvention is false and inauthentic, and that we can 'call this "evil" (ibid.), the Devil narrator suggests a deeper (and more conservative) thesis, that 'evil may not be so far from our surfaces as we like to say it is. – That in fact, we fall towards it naturally, that is not against our natures ... the true appeal of evil being the seductive ease with which one may embark upon that road' (ibid.). This reminds and warns us that Salahuddin, the survivor and in some sense the core protagonist and focalizer of the novel, is morally a double murderer, his choice of 'thirty nine' (443) voices driving Gibreel to murder and suicide. And this is the (open) secret at the heart of the novel, the (as it happens, false) syllogism of which the narrator is trying to convince: *the Devil is a migrant* (Defoe in the preface speaks of his 'vagabond, wandering, unsettled condition'); *we are all migrants* (a metaphor for humanity); *therefore, we are all devils*. (It is false because being a migrant is a set into which both 'we' and the 'Devil' fit, but do not necessarily, whatever the narrator would like us to believe, share any other characteristics save being a migrant.)

If this discussion, which structures *The Satanic Verses*, reveals how migrancy is interwoven with the discussion of ethics and truth, 2005's *Shalimar the Clown* marks another step in Rushdie's existential and aesthetic thinking. Roger Clark, in his brilliant book on Rushdie, argues that *The Satanic Versus* exhibits the same ideal as *Haroun, Grimus, Midnight's Children* and *Shame*, summed up in the figure of Everest which 'stands for a meaning which lies beyond the arguments and manipulations of the satanic narrator' (Clark 132). Rushdie's novels are about struggling to come to terms with an absent truth. Consider Alleluia Cone's view, when drunk, in *The Satanic Verses*:

> You can either break your heart trying to work it all out, or you can go sit on a mountain, because that's where all the truth went ... it just upped and ran away from these cities where even the stuff under our feet is all made up, a lie, and it hid up there in the thin thin air where the liars don't dare come after it in case their brains explode. (313)

By truth, Alleluia here, and Rushdie in general, clearly don't mean what most philosophers mean by truth, which is roughly, 'some sort of correspondence relation between words or thought-signs and external things and sets of things' (Putnam 126). Instead, truth is being invoked as something that 'confronts us with the deepest questions about our self-understanding' (Bowie 165). Wittgenstein remarks that 'If I have exhausted the justification' for my actions 'I have reached bedrock, and my spade is turned. Then I am inclined to say: "This is simply what I do"' (Wittgenstein 85). In this sense truth is 'bedrock', the answer to the repeated question of *The Satanic Verses* 'What kind of idea are you?' (335 *inter alia*) and of *Shalimar the Clown*; Max's father says, 'one never knows the answers to the questions of life until one is asked' (143). This is in part the renewed sense of aesthetics I referred to above, the sense that an art work can be 'more truthful than empirical truth' (Bernstein 2), and has a unique capacity to think or to show the world: only in art, perhaps, can the answers to these questions be represented.

This bedrock of truth (who one is, what one does) for Rushdie, is uncovered at moments of *kairos*. Frank Kermode, developing a usage from the German theologian Paul Tillich, writes that 'kairos' is a ' "moment of time" or ... "the fate of time" ... firmly associated ... with a specifically modern sense of living in a epoch when the "foundations of life quake beneath our feet"' (Kermode 47). In contrast to *chronos*, 'passing time' or 'waiting time', *kairos* is 'the season, a point in time filled with significance, charged with a meaning' (47). As Kermode writes, this is 'the time of the novelist, a transformation of mere successiveness which has been likened ... to the experience of love, the erotic consciousness which makes divinely satisfactory sense out of the common place person' (46). Rushdie consistently links the kairos of the individual with the kairos of the world: Saleem and India in *Midnight's Children*; Saladin and Gibreel and the birth of Islam and the moment of the emergence of a fundamentalist Islam in *The Satanic Verses*; the collapse of Indian secularism in *The Moor's Last Sigh* ('a principle had been eroded; a pebble bounced down a hill: plink, plonk, plank' (233); in *The Ground Beneath Her Feet*, the birth of modernity and globalization as or in rock and roll; in *Fury*, the fear and fury of the world

('America ... fears the fury of the world and renames it envy' (114), the 'whole world was burning on a shorter fuse ... Human life was now lived in the moment before the fury ... or the moment during ... or in the ruined aftermath' (129). In *Shalimar*, this is even clearer: the 'age of reason is over ... as was the age of love. The irrational was coming into its own' (226); an 'age of fury was dawning and only the enraged could shape it' (272); the 'time of demons had begun' (89). These moments ask of us who we are, and form a repeated trope in the novel: Max's father cited above, but also Sardar Harbans Singh: 'You never know the answer to the questions of life until you're asked' (284), Shalimar's deceptive forgiving 'to bring matters to a head ... to force him to choose between oaths, so that he could find out what sort of a man he really was' (237).

And it is clarity of the depiction of this answer to the question, the plunge into this fury, which marks the step taken in *Shalimar the Clown*: Shalimar actually does go up into the mountains and finds there not the mystical insight for which Alleluia Cone hopes, but a hard and frightening bedrock. A truth is uncovered: not ignored, prevaricated and got on with, bluffed away, redeemed by a return, or given to someone else (as, for example, the suicidal act of redemption in *Fury* is given to Neela Mahendra). But the truth that Shalimar finds at Forward Camp 22, his bedrock, is not pleasant. As ever with Rushdie, the story is complex: Shalimar's goals are 'personal as well as national' (258): not terroristic religious ideology but personal revenge and honour, which ranks 'above everything else, above the sacred vows of matrimony, above the divine injunction against cold blooded murder, above decency, above culture, above life itself' (258) — more than a shadow here of Rushdie's account of the daughter murdered by her father in *Shame* (115). Shalimar, in a contrapuntal litany on truth — 'only the truth can be my father ... my mother ... my wife' (266) — pretends to be converted to the Islamist 'truth' and tears his clothes in a performance of such skill he convinces the Mullah and almost himself. However, Moro sees through him and sees that the truth that Shalimar has discovered is not the Mullah's, save in its certainty, but that he has become a killer, 'death' (298). 'All he knew now was slaughter' (323). But if this offers some hope (this terrorist assassin at least is motivated by personal not religious motives) the terrorist context clearly does not. The virtues of the edenic Kashmir of tolerance — 'We're all of a jumble here in Pachigam' (103); 'The words Hindu and Muslim had no place in their story, he told himself' (57) — and change: 'A rope could become air. A boy could become a bird. Metamorphosis was the secret heart of life' (56) are swept away to leave only the harsh immutable truth. There is truth up in the mountains: the iron mullah preaches that the

> infidel believes in the immutability of the soul ... But we believe that all living things can be transformed in the service of truth. The infidel says that a man's character will decide his fate; we say that a man's fate will forge his character anew. (267)

This interplay of choice and fate echoes throughout the novel: Shalimar's defender, William Tillerman, argues that 'character is destiny' (382), taking a leaf from Heraclitus ('the lost poet of broken wisdom, part philosopher, part fortune cookie' [343]). In contrast, the victims of the attack on Pachigam – 'we are no longer protagonists, only agonists' (295) – die in a failed hospital and, as the narrator writes, their 'characters were not their destinies' (304). How might this opposition into which the characters fall like sleep-walkers – character is destiny, destiny is character – be resolved? Is it a West–East dichotomy? If there has been resolution, or redemption, in Rushdie's work before, there is none here: the truth has been seized, not simply glimpsed as streaks of light in a dark time but in this new, furious world and there is no longer hybridity: only an incommensurable opposition, an aporia, between, on the one hand, character and choice and, on the other, inexorable fate, no resolution even in death. This is why the novel does not end. Kashmira lets her arrow fly at Shalimar, but we do not see it hit, or its consequence: perhaps Shalimar will catch the arrow, or perhaps, mortally wounded, he can kill her too. The aporia is too terrible to be seen clearly. 'There are things that must be looked at indirectly because they would blind you if you looked at them in the face, like the face of the sun. So, to repeat, there was no Pachigam anymore. Pachigam was destroyed. Imagine it for yourself' (*Shalimar* 309).

Conclusion

Much recent criticism on Rushdie seems to replay a dichotomy between a critical desire for rooted history and political programmes against an equal desire for abstracted thought and existential queries. However, I have argued that Rushdie's work is simply too lacking in unity, too paradoxical and continually shifting for any firm view which relies on a single position properly to embody it. That is, for Rushdie, attitudes and views of the world 'jostle and conflict', and – however hard it is to bear – it is this that makes up the text, not a facile sort of tidying up. This is clearly the case with the issue of hybridity in his novels (even if it is not a view shared by Rushdie as a critic of his own work). In relation to a critical conflict between those who favour existential questions and those who turn to historical particulars, two mutually reflective questions arise: where could existential issues be aired, save in particular histories? How can particular histories be reflected upon, except through a wider, existential mirror? These two are inextricably woven into each other, and woven through Rushdie's work (with, perhaps, the exception of *Grimus*). To choose any side is to betray the other. It is not the case that, despite his length and prodigality, Rushdie includes everything. Instead, it is the case that Rushdie's novels offer conflicting and irresolvable oppositions and difficulties, just as difficulties in the real world seem, or are, perhaps, hard and intractable. This in itself is a manner of thinking, an unending working through, even if (as in the case of

Shalimar the Clown) we are not at all reassured by the lack of conclusion. Jean-François Lyotard would call this paralogical thinking: the generation of ideas without the aim of consensus, without following the strict rules of logic, the sort of thinking that also applies to 'dream reasoning'. It does not rule out truth, or self-revelation. Unless we attend to his work as this sort of thinking, Rushdie's work will continue to elude us.

Bibliography and further reading

Rushdie, Salman, *Grimus*. London: Gollancz, 1975.

———. *Midnight's Children*. London: Jonathan Cape, 1981.

———. *Shame*. London: Picador, 1983.

———. *The Satanic Verses*. London: Viking, 1988.

———. *Haroun and the Sea of Stories*. London: Granta, 1990.

———. *Imaginary Homelands: Essays and Criticism, 1981–91*. London: Penguin Books/Granta, 1992.

———. *The Moor's Last Sigh*. London: Vintage, 1995.

———. *The Ground Beneath Her Feet*. London: Jonathan Cape, 1999.

———. *Fury*. London: Jonathan Cape, 2001.

———. *Step Across This Line: Essays 1992–2002*. London: Vintage, 2002.

———. *Shalimar the Clown*. London: Jonathan Cape, 2005.

Adorno, Theodor W., and Max Horkheimer. *The Dialectic of Enlightenment*. Trans. John Cumming. London: Verso, 1997.

Ahmad, Aijaz. *In Theory: Classes, Nations, Literatures*. London and New York: Verso, 1993.

Bahri, Deepika. *Native Intelligence: Aesthetics, Politics and Post-Colonial Literature*. London: University of Minnesota Press, 2003.

Bernstein, J. M. *The Fate of Art*. London: Polity, 1992.

Bhabha, Homi. *The Location of Culture*. London: Routledge, 1994.

Bowie, Andrew. *From Romanticism to Critical Theory*. London: Routledge, 1997.

Brennan, Timothy. *Salman Rushdie and the Third World*. London: Macmillan, 1989.

Brennan, Timothy. 'Rushdie, Islam, and Postcolonial Criticism.' *Social Text*, 31/32, 1992: 271–6.

Clark, Roger Y. *Stranger Gods: Salman Rushdie's Other Worlds*. London: McGill-Queens University Press, 2001.

Coetzee, J. M. 'Palimpsest Regained.' *New York Review of Books*, 43:5, 21 March 1996: 13–16.

———. 'The Moor's Last Sigh.' *Stranger Shores: Literary Essays 1986–1999*. New York: Viking, 2001: 169–78.

Cowley, Jason. The *Observer*, 11 September 2005: 17.

Fokkema, Aleid. 'Postmodern Fragmentation or Authentic Essence? Character in *The Satanic Verses*', in *Shades of Empire in Colonial and Post-Colonial Literatures*. C. Barfoot and Theo D'haen (eds). Amsterdam: Rodopi, 1992: 51–63.

Goodheart, Eugene. *Does Literary Studies Have a Future?* London: University of Wisconsin Press, 1999.

Goonetilleke, D. C. R. A. *Salman Rushdie*. London: Macmillan, 1997.

Kermode, Frank. *The Sense of an Ending*. Oxford: Oxford University Press, 1966.

Khan, Fawzia Afzal. *Cultural Imperialism and the Indo-English Novel*. University Park, PA: Pennsylvania University Press, 1993.

Kierkegaard, Søren. *Papers and Journals: a Selection*. Trans. Alastair Hannay. London: Penguin, 1996.

Lyotard, Jean-François. *The Postmodern Condition*. Trans. Geoff Bennington and Brian Massumi. Manchester: Manchester University Press, 1984.

Needham, Anuradha Dingwaney. *Using the Master's Tools. Resistance and the Literature of the African and South-Asian Diasporas*. London: Macmillan, 2000.

Parnell, Tim. 'Salman Rushdie: from Colonial Politics to Postmodern Poetics', in *Writing India, 1757–1990*. Bart Moore-Gilbert (ed.). Manchester: Manchester University Press, 1996: 236–62.

Putnam, Hilary. *Reason, Truth and History*. Cambridge: Cambridge University Press, 1981.

Ravi, P. S. *Modern Indian Fiction*. New Delhi: Prestige, 2003.

Reader, Michael (ed.). *Conversations with Salman Rushdie*. Jackson, MS: University Press of Mississippi, 2000.

Roth, Marco. 'Salman Rushdie's Many-Ringed Circus'. *The Times Literary Supplement*, 9 September 2005: 19–20.

Sanga, Jaina C. *Salman Rushdie's Postcolonial Metaphors: migration, translation, hybridity, blasphemy, and globalization*. London: Greenwood Press, 2001.

Smith, Andrew. 'Migrancy, Hybridity, and Postcolonial Literary Study', in *The Cambridge Companion to Postcolonial Literary Studies*. Neil Lazarus (ed.), Cambridge: Cambridge University Press, 2004: 241–61.

Spivak, Gayatri Chakravorty. 'Reading *The Satanic Verses*', in *What is an Author?* Maurice Biriotti and Nicola Miller (eds), Manchester: Manchester University Press, 1993: 104–34.

Walter, Natasha. The *Guardian*, 3 September 2005: 21.

Wittgenstein, Ludwig. *Philosophical Investigations*. Trans. G. E. M. Anscombe. Oxford: Blackwell, 1963.

Wood, Michael. *Literature and the Taste of Knowledge*. Cambridge: Cambridge University Press, 2005.

Section Three: States of Identity

Introduction

ROD MENGHAM AND PHILIP TEW

The politics of identity was one of the most frequent and conspicuous items on the agenda of 1970s and 1980s fiction, and the critical and theoretical discoveries of that period – variously Marxist, poststructuralist, Commonwealth, feminist and queer – were concerned with establishing strong positions within a contested field. The fiction of the 1990s inaugurated a different trend, much more interested in hybridity, mobility and in broaching the possibilities of imagination and experience beyond the confines of given identities. The work of writers like Jeanette Winterson seemed to be fuelled by the desire to exceed the limits imposed by given subject positions. Fiction embraced a kind of supplementarity. Sonya Andermahr's chapter in this volume demonstrates the systematic nature of this turn towards multiplicity, towards an indefinability of sexual and social relations.

Winterson's fiction has always been elaborated from the work already done by other texts in questioning the reproduction in culture of existing ideologies of gender, race and class. But Andermahr's chapter underlines the dynamic nature of this intertextuality, and points towards the shift of emphasis found in the work of writers like Toby Litt and Zadie Smith, for whom the performance of identity is not simply reported in fiction but enacted through a practice of reading, listening, opening up to a work of art.

The questioning of the reader's identity is in fact the focus of most of the essays in this section. Leigh Wilson's chapter is especially graphic in its characterization and analysis of the way in which fiction embroils its readers. She offers an account of a text based in large part on a representation of her own life, a novel by her partner, Toby Litt. If identification with the text is inevitable in this instance, the experience of recognition and emotional projection amplifies an aspect of reading that is always present in our initial response to fiction, but which is always left out of academic criticism. Wilson's recovery of this fundamental dimension in our relationship to literary writing owns up to an important part of our motivation in reading it, and lays the foundations for a new account of the phenomenology of reading. Her essay incorporates the subjective approach of the amateur reading group (and these are gaining in popularity) within the professional discourse of the academic critic in order to develop a third, different method of reading.

There is a similar anxiety about the limitations of professional reading methods behind the choice of subject matter in Zadie Smith's third novel, *On Beauty*. The routine suppression of affect in academic responses to art is a preoccupation of Smith's both within the plot and characterization of the novel, and outside it in the scope of her activities as essayist and public speaker. In conversation, she has found common cause with the non-academic critic James Wood in perceiving the role of academic discourse to be a form of telling lies, insofar as it is silent about the subjective and emotional benefits of interaction with art. This interrogating of the adequacy of criticism derives ultimately from an awareness of the responsibilities of writer and reader, whose identities are realized through mutual definition.

Lynn Wells's examination of Ian McEwan's constant rehearsals of identity crisis, in scenarios that revolve around the dilemmas of the self wrestling with its social obligations, reaches back over the entirety of McEwan's career, and so gives a longer perspective on fiction's changing relationship to issues of identity, confirming what the other contributors to this section have suspected is a major shift towards the foregrounding of readerly competence, not of the technical, structuralist variety, but with regard to its moral scope, its adaptability to an ethics of reading.

CHAPTER NINE

Possessing Toby Litt's *Ghost Story*

LEIGH WILSON

Toby Litt and the possessed reader

Toby Litt's work to date has been possessed by the experience and dynamics of possession. In *Finding Myself* (2003a), a young girl, Edith, is possessed by the spirit of another young girl, the late occupant of Edith's holiday bedroom. Edith dresses in the dead girl's clothes, making herself 'a girl-ghost dressed as a ghost-girl' (192). In *deadkidsongs* (2001), Matthew dies of meningitis, and later enters the body of his friend Paul to act out revenge. 'I didn't know what possessed me', says Paul (384). In 'Moriarty', two teen-age girls, overcome by secrets, grief and longing, 'become' Sherlock Holmes and Dr Watson (*Adventures in Capitalism*). In possession, the relationality of haunting (I see a ghost, the ghost haunts me) collapses, and the two, haunter and haunted, become one. This collapse brings not sameness and identity, though, but the internalized alterity suggested by Paul's clichéd phrase.

Such spooky goings-on would suggest both a writer tuned in to the 'hauntological' as set out and provoked by Derrida's *Specters of Marx* (1994) and a writing committed to the anachronology and lack of linearity Derrida suggests is enacted by the spectre's presence; Hamlet's 'The time is out of joint' is epigraph and chorus in *Specters*. However, Litt is a writer dedicated to the pleasures of plot and as such his work is committed to a temporal coherence and progression at odds with Derrida's account. Indeed, Litt's work so far seems characterized by an exploration of genre, in part as a way of constructing gripping and seductive plots. In different ways, each of his novels has taken the form of and rewritten a particular genre. *Beatniks* (1997) transfers the youthful road novel from the US to provincial England; *Corpsing* (2000) is a crime thriller that both uses and eviscerates the seductions of the genre; *deadkidsongs* uses the familiar form of revenge tragedy and draws on the cultural status of *The Lord of the Flies*, as well as on the less familiar echoes of the *Kindertotenlieder*; the narrator of *Finding Myself* is a chick-lit novelist; *Ghost Story* (2004) makes its borrowings clear in its title.

In each of these novels, the first effect of these borrowings is to put in place a narrative momentum through the privileging of plot. The reader is clearly supposed to read quickly, breathlessly, eager for the next turn of the page. Indeed, in this way Litt's work is possessed by possession beyond character and theme. The familiar gestures and idiosyncrasies of genre seduce the reader; the use of ends-directed plot (revenge, love story, whodunit) privileges possession over cognition in the reading experience. Litt's novels want to possess their reader. Certainly, in interview, Litt clearly articulates an awareness of the page-by-page experience of the reader. Speaking of *Finding Myself*, which has handwritten 'editorial notes' in its margins, he says: 'By having the handwriting in the margins by the editor, I was hoping that the readers would feel they were reading things they shouldn't, that they'd see behind the curtain' (Dwyer Hogg 22). In an interview about the problems of writing for online reading, he says that: 'People may return to a site for news, but they don't come back to follow a narrative story. Being engrossed, totally involved, and turning the pages, is not the same experience as clicking with a mouse' (Stevenson 2002). For Litt, the ideal reader, the reader he wants his novels to create, is the reader possessed, who cannot put the book down, whose fingers reach early for the turn of the page, who is breathless with expectation as that page turns.

If Derridean hauntings cannot fully account for this central aspect of Litt's work, neither can the reading of it as 'postmodern'. Litt's work is most often characterized as such by critics inside and outside the academy (see Dwyer Hogg; Bradbury 537–8), and the use of genre motifs and conventions has indeed been seen as a central feature of the 'postmodern novel'. However, what distinguishes Litt's use of genre from other novels identified as postmodern is indeed a commitment to a certain kind of readerly pleasure. In Rushdie or Carter, for example, popular forms such as music hall, Bollywood film, or rock music are either borrowed thematically rather than formally, or are taken up for only part of the narrative, creating the stitched, fragmented form so often focused on by critics. Litt's borrowings, however, are not partial or fragmentary in effect. Each one permeates an entire narrative. While they are always knowing, and irony is very often created through the first-person narrator's relation to the conventions of genre, his novels always involve what Lowe has called a 'classical plot'. This Lowe defines as a particular kind of narrative structure, as:

> an impression of elegance, economy, and efficiency in the deployment of narrative resources. There is a strong sense of unity and closure to the narrative structure, with particular importance attached to a firm and satisfying ending. At the same time, the audience and reader is teased with guessing-games over what is to happen: twists, surprises, mischievously thwarted expectations. (Lowe x)

To read Litt as 'postmodern' ignores not just the centrality of such plots in his novels, but more crucially the readerly experience created by them (Tew 185–6). Such plots in themselves have had little interest for 'postmodernist' critics, and, as Lowe remarks, have been almost completely ignored by narratologists, because they force the consideration of that which is beyond the textual, that is, of readerly pleasure and of the relation between the novel and a real, experiential world (3). In contrast to postmodernism's focus on the text, the reader's position is absolutely crucial to Lowe's understanding of the functioning of plot: 'Plot, then, is something texts do inside our heads in the action of reading' (Lowe 33). He argues that the reader reads with two stories in mind: one is revealed through time, and one exists as a timeless whole, although unknown in its detail until the denouement:

> the *tension* between our twin internal models of the story is the source of the dynamic and affective element in plot. What we, as readers, want is for our temporal and atemporal models of the story to coincide; and all the while we read, we are actively on the lookout for ways in which they will ultimately converge ... our desire for harmony between our two dissonant and incomplete story models makes us vulnerable to *sustained and purposeful affective manipulation*. It is this, I would argue, that accounts for the power of plot. (33; emphasis in original)

This model is clearly based on a first reading. Lowe sees second readings, once both stories are fully known, as more complex but not qualitatively different from the first (24). This is comforting for the critic, but doesn't seem sustainable in terms of the considerable emphasis Lowe puts on the gap between the two 'stories' in the construction of plot. The German literary critic Michael Maar sees first and second reading as profoundly different. For him, 'With a first reading alone do we watch a world being made; on every later one it lies there finished.' He does assert that 'Nothing is so underestimated by academic critics as the epistemological value of the first reading of a novel' (Maar 100), but doesn't follow up any of the implications of this for critical practice. If this underestimation is the case, how much more absent from academic critical discourse is the emotional or corporeal value of the first reading. Indeed, in Maar's subsequent account of a first reading, it is those more than the epistemological that dominate. In Maar's schema, the first reading is the novel's 'ordeal by fire', the second is its 'ordeal by water' (102); these metaphors of warmth and coolness betray the extent to which the first reading is bodily and affective, and the second intellectual. It is during the first reading that the reader is possessed by the novel.

How can Toby Litt be read critically in a way that does not underestimate the experience of the first reading, nor the extent to which his work, in its commitment to plot, makes readerly possession necessary for its central effects?

Disappearing books: first readings and the problem of identification

Literary culture in Britain since the early 1990s has been shaped to a great extent by a particularly lively and active reading culture, most obvious in the proliferation of reading groups. While this has attracted a certain kind of critical attention, as with Jenny Hartley's *Reading Groups* (2001), literary critical work which acknowledges such practices has been outside the academy, for example in broadsheet newspapers and in material supplied by publishers. Indeed such reading practices are often constructed and defined *against* what are thought to be critical or academic readings (Hartley 5, 62, 75–6, 90 and *passim*). The split between academic and non-academic criticism has recently been articulated as a problem by the latter, due in part to increased lay-readerly confidence. For the lay reader, the denial of affect by academic criticism constitutes its major offence. Recently, a *London Review of Books*-sponsored debate between critics Terry Eagleton, Frank Kermode, James Wood and novelist Zadie Smith discussed the possibilities for a 'new criticism' which would speak to and for the lay reader without compromising intellectual standards. An 'in conversation' between Smith and Wood following this debate is typical in its characterization of academic writing. Smith is of course one of few contemporary novelists to have received both critical and popular acclaim, and she also writes criticism; Wood is probably the most important British non-academic literary critic. The two agree on what it is that they don't want to do in their criticism. Discussing the possible pedagogical aims of her criticism, Smith says 'I can't lie. Certainly I used to when I was a student and I would lie about the reasons I came to fiction. But I don't have to do that any more.' About this, Wood agrees. He goes on: 'it's sad to me that that should be the experience of the formal study of literature at university .... [T]o go back to our earlier question, it's how to do some essential renovation on academic criticism, so you don't feel you're lying when you write' (Smith and Wood n. pag.).

What the lying consists of is a denial of affect. Writing elsewhere, Smith summarizes the movement of the passionate pre-adolescent reader to the serious student of the novel: 'A peculiar thing happens at this point. We find that our initial affective responses are no longer of interest to the literary community in which we find ourselves' (Smith n. pag.). For Smith, the opposite of a criticism that lies is a criticism that admits love. While many of the criticisms levelled against academic reading can be rightly challenged, I want to argue here that it is the charge of the denial of affect that makes academic critics most uncomfortable. The novel as a form demands possession of the reader. The contemporary novels bought and read by the largest numbers of readers attest to this. This is not a failure of these readers, it is their partial success. Partial because the affects produced by such possession do not represent the full spectrum, but nevertheless we do not read novels without boredom, offence, fear, love, lust, pity, anger, excitement and nausea.

Over the last few decades it is true that a number of critical practices have challenged, from different perspectives, literary criticism which assumes itself to be predicated on distance, a primarily rational, intellectual activity. Feminist, poststructuralist and New Historicist readings have all attempted to bring back into account that which is excluded by such a definition – the body, the other, indeterminacy, marginalized voices and identities. However, crucially none of these challenges have fully acknowledged the effect produced by their own reading. Andrew Gibson's call for a reading in which sensibility is not subordinate to 'cognition and critique' (Gibson 164) recognizes the extent to which criticism, from Leavis to contemporary theory, constructs itself as 'a movement out towards an object, rather than susceptibility or openness to the event' (*ibid.*). However, while his readings locate and illuminate the dynamics of such a sensibility within texts, they are not themselves given up to such a possession. In *Thinking Through the Body* (1988), Jane Gallop comments: 'In graduate school I read Rousseau's *Julie*, noting in the margin each time I cried. I imagined that some day I could do a reading based on understanding when I cried and why. This fantasy was kin to the project of writing on Sade, a text which moved me to masturbate' (18). This is the only occasion I can recall such an admission in academic writing. Tellingly, though, Gallop's marginalia remain just that; such fantastical readings are not considered as appropriate critical discourse. Indeed, the practice of academic literary criticism was founded on the banishment of affect. Richards' 'practical criticism' was in part an attempt to eliminate the unpredictable, emotional response to a work, and the critic's social function was dependent on a judgement made possible through distance, precision and 'scientific' objectivity. If the general reader's emotions had to be stopped from getting out of hand, neither could the critic be allowed to be overcome. Walter Raleigh, the first exclusively 'literary' Professor of English at Oxford, and the bête noir of Richards, Leavis *et al.*, believed the job of the critic to be 'to raise the dead ... It is by the creative power of this art [criticism] that the living man is reconstructed from the letters of blurred and fragmenting paper documents that he has left to posterity' (128–9). Such an admission of possession – the body of the dead writer is resurrected through the mediumship of the critic – undermined English literature's claims to be a serious discipline in far too many ways.

However, while the explicit criticisms of Smith and Wood, and those implicit in the practices of reading groups, are useful for the problematics they reveal, the alternatives they offer are not the answer. Indeed, they threaten the novel and criticism with becoming moribund. It is identification rather than possession which is central to this practice of reading. The privileging of 'sympathy' so crucial to Smith and to Hartley's reading groups (Hartley 132–3) risks reconfirmation of everything the reader already knew, an objectification of the other in a denial of difference, and a readerly self-satisfaction that would make novel reading and criticism arising from it deeply conservative (Gibson 26–7). While the criticisms of academic reading outlined above focus on the denial of affect, in its place is not a reading that admits the potential strange transformations of possession (I am myself but not myself), but the recognition of sameness and the assumption of commonality. For Smith, the good that novels do is that 'When we read with fine attention, we find ourselves caring about people who are various, muddled, uncertain and not quite like us' (Smith n. pag.), but like enough for love to be the privileged affective response. This does not, as Smith claims, recognize the otherness of the other, but assumes its identity. Identification is antithetical to possession as it negates the disturbance consequent on the presence of the other as other. In an essay on 'Reading' published in *Poetry Review*, Litt sets out what an enraptured reading might be. This is contrasted with professionalized reading, a danger for the writer, a deathly obsession for a certain kind of academic. This latter criticism is hyperbolic – 'the statistical verbal analysis practised by, say, Shakespeare scholars ... is reading done by a low-grade computer' ('Reading' 56) – but low-grade reading is certainly seen as an effect of distance. The desirable effects of proximity are set out at the opening of the essay:

> One reviewer of J. K. Rowling's fourth book asked their child what they thought of it. The child said, 'It took a while for the book to disappear, but after that it was great'. This is the best description I have come across of enraptured reading. The second best comes from Wallace Stevens' poem 'The House Was Quiet and the World Was Calm': 'The words were spoken as if there was no book'. Very strangely, this follows rather than leads up to the more extreme statement that, 'The reader became the book'. Which, surely, is the most enraptured of all imaginable readings – when the boundaries of personal identity are felt to have dissolved. (56)

This quotation contains two very different effects, but the differences are rather buried. To read a book as if it were not a book but an experience that is actually happening to you is a very different proposition from the dissolution of self. The latter is not just a more extreme version of the first, it is its opposition. The enthusiastic reader of J. K. Rowling experiences identification; Wallace Stevens' poem speaks of possession. However, Litt acknowledges in his companion essay, 'Writing', 'Writers lie to themselves consistently about how they work – about how their work works' (42), and if he smooths the differences in the essay, the demands of his novels suggest a more nuanced and less comfortable sense of reading as possession. In the final part of this chapter, I want to attempt to reread a first reading such that identification is transformed into the possibilities of possession.

Toby Litt, *Ghost Story* and a first reading

Toby Litt is my partner. We have a son, Henry, who was born in November 2004. In 2002 I had three miscarriages. In October 2004 Litt published a novel, *Ghost Story*, which was a response to, and an explicit memorializing of, these three lost pregnancies. The novel is split into two quite discrete parts, 'Story' and 'Ghost Story'. The latter is a novel about a couple, Agatha and Paddy, whose second child dies *in utero* during the last weeks of pregnancy. Soon after, they move into a new house. Agatha becomes unable to leave the house, or to have her first child with her. As she haunts the house during her long days and nights alone, she starts to hear the house breathe. The former, 'Story', a long preface, presents itself in part as autobiography. 'Story' is in the first person, and sections of it recount episodes of the narrator's life — a family holiday to Wales when he was young, visits to friends, domestic routine, the three miscarriages. The following is an excerpt from the account of the third:

> After the first burst of our grief, which I'll describe in a little while, she picked the baby and its accoutrements out of the water and put it into a plastic freezer bag that I'd fetched at her request from the kitchen. I did not see this retrieval, she closed the bathroom door whilst I stood crying in the living room — through there. I also sat, I think, on the arm of the sofa — which is blue, cheap and which we have been meaning to get rid of for about a year. Leigh didn't want me to see what had come out of her. 'It won't help,' she said. I told her I wanted to see it. I said that I felt left out — I meant that *otherwise* I would feel left out. I didn't want that door closed upon me, too; I felt a need to see everything. She showed me, or rather let me look: the freezer bag was lying there, on the window sill. (*Ghost Story* xxviii–xxix, xlv)

I quote this section at length, despite not wanting to quote it at all. Not so much because the memory is painful, but because in typing it here I feel shame. I do not think it is appropriate. But as a first-time reader, my reading was without the distance necessary for such a judgement. Now, I bring this passage into a different discourse, a discourse of second reading. It is the incongruence of this passage within my discourse of second reading that makes the difference, that provokes disgust and shame. Disgust is a consequence of abjection. In feeling disgust, the subject rebels against the abject not because it is an alien object, but because it is 'something rejected from which one does not part' (Kristeva 4). The abject is not the other so much as challenging the whole idea of self and other. If affect produces disgust within academic discourse it is because the very discourse is constructed through and defines itself by affect's absence. However, in the attempt to disavow affect, it paradoxically returns as disgust. Abjection attempts to disavow but also crucially marks the reader's possession by the text. What my experience of disgust in a second reading of a novel with which I cannot help but identify makes clear is the way that abjection marks the movement from identification to possession. It is the attempt at a second reading of a novel of which the first reading remains so insistent that opens out the possibilities of an affective academic criticism. Such a reading of *Ghost Story* could reveal a novel itself struggling with the relations between the rational and the affective, between the dangers and possibilities of possession. Academic discourse open to affect, then, can produce a sense of critic and novel engaged in the same tensions, with the power of influence and determination not wholly on one side or the other, but rather productively fluid.

The final section of the 'Story', 'Foxes', comes immediately after the most autobiographical sections. The realism of those – the use of actual names and places, a recognizable world, a coherent and trustworthy narrator – disappears. 'Foxes' is a strange, fairy-tale-like piece. An unnamed first-person narrator flees his home when his wife gives birth to three foxcubs. Coming after those sections where I found myself easily identified, the attempt to do so here, and its affective consequences, suggest that the novel too is trying to contain a conflict. In 'Foxes' I seemed to have disappeared; both this and the possibility that I was still there in a displaced way were disturbing. 'Foxes' seems to be the attempt of the 'Story' part of *Ghost Story* to ward off its own possession.

Explaining his flight, the narrator tells us that the foxcubs, moments after birth, immediately started to destroy the order of the house: '[they] had been tearing at the books on the lower shelves, some of them my own' (*Ghost Story* lv). As the narrator begins to tell the story of his wife's pregnancy, though, it becomes clear that such challenges to order preceded the strange birth. His pregnant wife, he says, 'became convinced of a series of abominations, concerning myself and our children-to-be' (lvii). After the birth, however, she shows no signs of shock that she has given birth to animals, whereas the narrator tells us that he 'at this juncture, was retching as if trying to dislodge a turd coated in stomach acid that had fought its way up into my oesophagus' (lviii). As he continues to remember the preg-nancy, language fails: 'I set myself to thinking of the weight and the wait of the third trimester ... I couldn't' (lviii). The silent horror indicated by the ellipses is immediately rationalized: 'This was intolerable: I would have to return to the house and find out how my fox-children were faring; how many books had they destroyed?' (lviii). After a strange encounter with a dog-walker, the narrator returns home, 'Quietly, so as to be able to escape if I saw anything disgusting.' He looks through a window, and sees his children eating the cooked body of a man laid out on the kitchen table:

> The foxes were talking as they ate, and this is what they said: 'One, two, three!' 'One.' 'One two three.' 'One-two.' 'Three. One.' 'One.' 'One!' 'One.' 'Two.' 'One.' 'One two three one two three one two three.' 'Two.' 'Three.' (lix)

So the preface ends. We are not told if this vision is disgusting enough to provoke another flight. What does happen in these last words, though, is the assertion of a relation between things which is crucial to the novel's own rhetoric of possession. The repeated counting brings together the miscarriages described in the previous sections, the fairy-tale grotesque of the narrator's experience, and the horrific glee as the foxcubs devour human flesh. What 'Foxes' speaks is a horror of reproduction, and its antithetical relation to intellect and culture (all those chewed books).

A number of reviews of *Ghost Story* have remarked on the 'Jamesian' qualities of the 'Ghost Story' part of the novel, Joanna Briscoe identifying its 'formal and expositional Jamesian dialogue' (n. pag.). This is indeed a second reading, privileging textuality over attention to the experience that such textuality provokes. It is not a misreading, but it mistakes the extent to which such devices are themselves an attempt to write a second reading to contain the pain of the first. Without this, the novel threatens to collapse into abjection. To any discourse which denies its own first reading, the novel's own 'first reading', its struggle with affect and abjection, and with the contaminating dynamics of possession remain subordinate to its attempts to control them. There is almost what could be called a 'first writing' here, and a second writing which finds the contents of the first abject. The surreal subject matter of 'Foxes' makes opaque the extent to which disgust and horror are direct responses to reproduction. Maternity and its failures are of course the epitome of many kinds of horrors in many discourses (from the gothic to 'celebrity' culture's obsession with the post-pregnant body), but contemporary culture utterly represses this with a sentimental totalizing of feelings of familiarity and love associated with childbirth. The more 'autobiographical' sections of 'Story' do, however, contain clues as to the not-quite-written-out presence of the abject. The section immediately before 'Foxes', still recounting the third miscarriage, opens with a question: 'writing about the subject, the incident, at all: isn't this merely grotesque and absurd?' (li). This question is not explicitly answered, but an earlier section gives a clue as to the answer:

> I think bad things, I write them, and sometimes after I've written them they happen. I am terrified not only of a baby carried to term but of a baby born deformed. During pregnancy, one attracts horror stories; tragedies seem to have occurred just to be brought to your attention. I heard recently of a woman who at six or seven months learnt that her foetus had died, and yet there was nothing for her to do at such a late stage but carry it dead to full term .... . Perhaps this didn't happen, was just an urban myth. (xxxiv)

The horror that *all* reproduction provokes is revealed in the second sentence. It is the deformed baby which provides the momentum and subject for the rest of the paragraph; but any baby carried to term is horrific. Crucially, too, here is an origin for the 'Ghost Story' that follows; an originary story that provokes such horror that its reality is questioned. However, the link given earlier between horror and reality is writing: 'I think bad things, I write them, and sometimes after I've written them they happen.' Writing, too, is a kind of reproduction that produces abjection because it, as much as critical reading, forces a split between possession and control.

In 'Ghost Story', after the death of her child, Agatha becomes both agoraphobic and convinced that she can hear the house breathing. As suggested earlier, the very title 'Ghost Story' tells us which genre has been chosen this time, and certainly the novel could be read for its use of the conventions of the ghost story. This novel too draws on the conventions of the 'classical plot'; the narrative is not fractured by Agatha's grief, but is rather a tightly controlled exercise in slow revelation and suspense. However, unlike *Corpsing*, where chapters and paragraphs are often very short as the reader is rushed along, the pages of the novel section of *Ghost Story* are dense with text. Often a paragraph will last for several pages, as the omniscient, seemingly detached narrator tells in painful detail the movement of Agatha's thoughts as she sits in the house, listens to, and tries to make sense of what has happened to her and her baby, and of her response to it. Indeed, this 'making sense' is crucial, for what Agatha does as she sits in her house full of absences is think. She is not haunted by her dead child, she is possessed by thought and by the house. The house is affect and corporeality so that she does not have to be: 'In the security of the breathing house, Agatha tried, systematically, to think herself to the bottom of her thought' (109). Agatha and the narrator of 'Foxes' are both implicated in this displacement of feeling. For both, thought exorcizes horror.

Quite late on in 'Ghost Story', after two-year-old Max has returned to live with his parents, Agatha is forced to cope with the proximity of her elder child, while still working out how to mourn the death of her second. Again, her attitude to her situation is rational, she does not repress her difficult response to her son: 'She formulated it: "Because Rose died, part of me wants Max to die, too. It would tidy the world up, if he were gone; if he were gone, I could be done with the whole thing"' (203). At the same time, because of losing Rose, Agatha's usual parental anxieties over Max's well-being are vastly increased. The complexity of her fears is outlined in dense prose. Agatha thinks about Max, about her fear of him dying, so central is he to her life, and she decides to kill him:

> Max went beyond being a reason for living, he was a lived life. It was hard, without him, to see how there might be life at all. And his death, his glorious variety of possible deaths, preoccupied her more even than it had done immediately following his birth. Agatha thought up ways and ways he might just. And as the afternoon turned darker, Agatha began to think of killing Max. (207)

Agatha takes Max into the bathroom for his evening bath, and fills the tub almost to the overflow. She places the little boy in the bath and places her hand on the crown of his head, as if ready to push him under. What Agatha desires at this moment is to identify with Max, to respond to his self in such a way that would force her to save him. However, Agatha is no longer able to respond to Max appropriately. 'She wanted Max to convince her of the worth of living, and in himself, by being himself, he just couldn't do that any more' (214). Agatha sees Max from too great a distance, and from that distance, it seems obvious that she must kill him. The tension here for both Agatha and reader is terrible. Here both Agatha and the reader desire the same thing. At the final moment the narrative cries out in Agatha's voice: 'Oh, she wanted Paddy to come through the front door and stop her stupid experiment ...' (214). The reader too is desperate for this, but of course we know that such identification is silly and naïve, and such a way of saving Max would be a clumsy *deus ex machina*. We know this, but we cannot bear the alternative. The sentence continues:

> and this was exactly what happened. Now he was coming through the door, not the front door but the bathroom door, and she hadn't heard him in the hall, or on the stairs. She had no time to pull Max from the cruelly cold bath, to calm him and normalize him. Now he was close beside her and now, together, they were lifting Max from the water, up in their arms, water going everywhere, not mattering. He knew – he must know. She helped him carry Max into their bedroom, where they wrapped him in one of their huge white towels. It was strange: Max wasn't shivering or crying, he was laughing – and Paddy, perhaps, was magically turning the whole thing into a fun game. They weren't tickling Max but he was laughing as if they were: laughing with a tensed stomach, laughing against. 'You came back early,' said Aggie. 'Why?' But Paddy didn't answer because Paddy wasn't there, and the hands which had saved Max seemed to have been hers alone. (214–15)

Agatha here experiences a possession, the dissolution of the self, the collapse of the self into an other, which saves. In her state of breakdown, identification is not enough; it will not save Max. This moment of possession begins Agatha's regeneration. Crucially, too, what this possession saves is the reader's ability to be possessed. Paddy's return both does and doesn't happen. What we are forced to desire both does and doesn't happen. Our identification is dissolved into the strange disunities of possession.

Bibliography and further reading

Litt, Toby. *Adventures in Capitalism*. London: Secker and Warburg, 1996.
——. *Beatniks*. London: Secker and Warburg, 1997.
——. *Corpsing*. London: Hamish Hamilton, 2000.
——. *deadkidsongs*. London: Penguin, 2001.
——. *Finding Myself*. London: Hamish Hamilton, 2003a.
——. 'Reading.' *Poetry Review*, 93:2, Summer 2003b: 56–9.
——. 'Writing.' *Poetry Review*, 93:3, Autumn 2003c: 42–8.
——. *Ghost Story*. London: Penguin, 2005 [2004].
Bradbury, Malcolm. *The Modern British Novel: 1878–2001*, 2nd edn. London: Penguin, 2001 [1993].
Briscoe, Joanna. 'Ghost Lit', http://books.guardian.co.uk/reviews/generalfiction/0,61211317674,00.html, n. pag. Accessed 1 November 2005. First published in the *Guardian*, 2 October 2004.
Derrida, Jacques. *Specters of Marx*. Trans. Peggy Kamuf. New York and London: Routledge, 1994 [original French edition 1993].

Dwyer Hogg, Clare. 'Adventures in Postmodernism.' *The Independent Magazine*, 21 June 2003: 22.

Gallop, Jane. *Thinking Through the Body*, New York: Columbia University Press, 1988.

Gibson, Andrew. *Postmodernity, Ethics and the Novel: From Leavis to Levinas*. London and New York: Routledge, 1999.

Hartley, Jenny. *Reading Groups*. Oxford: Oxford University Press, 2001.

Kristeva, Julia. *Powers of Horror: an Essay in Abjection*. Trans. Leon S. Roudiez. New York: Columbia University Press, 1982.

Lowe, N. J. *The Classical Plot and the Invention of Western Narrative*. Cambridge: Cambridge University Press, 2000.

Maar, Michael. 'The Ordeals of Fire and Water.' *New Left Review*, 2, March/April 2000: 97–103.

Raleigh, Walter. *Style*. London and New York: Edward Arnold, 1897.

Smith, Zadie. 'Love, Actually', www.books.guardian.co.uk/review/story/0,12084, 1074217,00.html, n. pag. Accessed 1 August 2005. First published in the *Guardian*, 1 November 2003.

——, and James Wood. In conversation with Jonathan Derbyshire, 22 December 2004. Transcript of interview via personal communication. Shortened version: *Time Out*, 26 January 2005.

Stevenson, Val. 'deadkidsongs', www.nthposition.com/deadkidsongs.php, 2002, n. pag. Accessed 24 August 2005.

Tew, Philip. *The Contemporary British Novel*. London: Continuum, 2004.

CHAPTER TEN

The Ethical Otherworld: Ian McEwan's Fiction

LYNN WELLS

Ian McEwan's growth as a fiction writer runs parallel to shifts in his characterization and themes: while his often macabre early work centres on issues of childhood, adolescence and initiation, his later novels deal increasingly with the adult world of sexuality, violence, history and politics. Reviewers have hailed the best-selling *Atonement* and *Saturday* as signs of McEwan's artistic maturity, with the *Times Literary Supplement* declaring him 'the most admired English writer of his generation' (Tait 4). This narrative of McEwan's development away from the insular grotesqueries of his early fiction towards a broader, more morally relevant vision closer to the tradition of the great English novelists was articulated by Kiernan Ryan as early as 1994 in his study *Ian McEwan*, and it had become the 'received wisdom' (Ryan 2) about McEwan's work well before his current celebrity.

Yet the assumption that his later fiction is superior to his earlier texts is one that I wish to scrutinize, especially in terms of his depiction of ethical relationships. At the heart of McEwan's work (and indeed most fiction) is the encounter between the self and other, whether the latter implies other individuals or society at large; this encounter is frequently mirrored in, and complicated by, the characters' mostly urban and often alienating environments, located within cultures (primarily English and late twentieth century) of waning moral affect. While the early texts tend to focus on psychosexual development and gender conflict, in his fiction from the 1980s onwards he broadens his scope beyond sexual dynamics (with their larger social implications) to include staged scenes of ethical confrontation that call into question the individual's true ability to deal compassionately with the other. As we shall see, the reader's response to these scenes becomes complicated by McEwan's evolving aesthetic in his most recent work towards greater textual self-consciousness and generic manipulation.

In an early story such as 'Conversation with a Cupboard Man' (from *First Love, Last Rites*), for example, the individual's engagement with the outside world fails, as the traumatized title character attempts to seclude himself entirely and regress to the narcissistic state of infancy. Most of the stories as well as McEwan's first novel *The Cement Garden*, however, reveal individuals attempting to negotiate the tricky passage into sexual and social maturity, figured in psychoanalytic terms as the Oedipal conflict. In some cases, these negotiations take the form of sexual role-playing, as characters try on various aspects of conventional masculinity and femininity. The boy Henry in 'Disguises' (*First Love, Last Rites*), for example, is forced by his aunt to dress as a girl; Jack, the narrator of *The Cement Garden*, and his sister Julie assume parental roles after the deaths of their tyrannical father and weak mother in a modern English urban wasteland. In some instances, characters successfully forge sexual or filial relationships, such as the lovers in 'First Love, Last Rites' or Stephen Cooke and his daughter Miranda in 'In Between the Sheets', both from the collections of the same names.

Much of the early work, however, revolves around acts of sexual domination. Jessica Benjamin suggests in *The Bonds of Love* that structures of domination are engrained in the Oedipal drama, with 'woman's subordination to man ... taken for granted' (7). The little girl Jane in 'Butterflies' (*First Love, Last Rites*) is merely a possession to be left behind in a fetid London canal by the paedophile who kills her, much like the plastic doll he purchases for her and is forgotten by her moments later. In 'Dead as They Come' (*In Between the Sheets*), we see the absolute subjugation of woman as other, as a rich man purchases a mannequin to serve as his completely objectified lover; in 'Pornography', from the same collection, McEwan reverses the polarity by having the callous pornography salesman O'Byrne dominated and finally emasculated by his neglected girlfriends. These depictions, in keeping with McEwan's acknowledged interest in feminism, set the stage for the scenes of sexual coercion and violence in later texts such as *The Innocent*, in which Leonard Marnham, an English technician stationed in Berlin in the 1950s, presumes that his German lover Maria shares his fantasies of violent sexual humiliation, which in fact remind her of atrocities against women during the Second World War.

While *The Innocent* uses sexual domination as a form of political allegory – with the relationship of Leonard and Maria symbolizing the power of the British military over defeated Germany – *The Comfort of Strangers* also provides a wider social critique. The mysterious Robert uses sexual violence in order to shore up his phallic power, damaged by his oppressive father and undermined by his inability to sire children. As Judith Seaboyer points out, Robert's 'personal trauma' reinscribes 'the trauma faced by patriarchal culture at the end of the twentieth century' (979) with the rise of feminism. Yet despite this 'disruption of the "dominant fiction"' (*ibid.*), McEwan makes clear, the patriarchal world view persists; as a character in 'Psychopolis' (*In Between the Sheets*) suggests, 'There will always be problems between men and women and everyone suffers in some way' (145). One of the reasons for the durability of patriarchy that is enacted in *The Comfort of Strangers* is complicity, the willingness of both women and men to reproduce structures of dominance and participate in their own objectification. The English tourists Colin and Mary allow themselves to be led astray in a labyrinthine city reminiscent of Venice, and seduced by Robert and his wife Caroline.

All three of Robert's 'victims' entertain violent fantasies of their own, in which they brutalize or are brutalized by their lovers: Mary, for instance, imagines 'amputat[ing] Colin's arms and legs' and 'us[ing] him exclusively for sex', while he dreams of a machine that would immobilize her so that he could 'fuck her, not just for hours or weeks, but for years ... till she was dead and on even after that' (63). In both cases, as well as Caroline's confessed enjoyment of being hurt during intercourse, sex entails the complete degradation of one party by the other; this desire to dominate the other is manifested in conventional gender terms regardless of the characters' actual sex, with the feminized Colin as the ultimate object of Robert's sadistic tendencies. McEwan captures the image of the still-inevitable reification of gender roles in the image of two dummies on a bed in a department store window, which, like the often twin-like Mary and Colin, are 'from the same mould' (11), yet have gender-specific night-wear and different accessories on their respective sides of the headboard: a 'make-up cabinet' and a 'nursery intercom' for the female versus a 'drinks cabinet' (11).

Jessica Benjamin notes that this kind of persistent 'gender polarity . . . creates a painful division within the self and between self and other; it constantly frustrates our efforts to recognize ourselves in the world and in each other' (172). McEwan captures the failure to recognize the other in *The Comfort of Strangers* through Mary's belated realization that the photo she is shown by Robert in his apartment is in fact a picture of Colin. Scenes of failed or mistaken recognition are prevalent in McEwan's fiction, such as in *The Cement Garden*, with Jack's supposed sighting of his mother on a bridge some time after her death: 'Great relief and recognition swept through me and I laughed out loud. It was not Mother of course, it was Julie, wearing a coat I had never seen before' (75). In this case, the misrecognized body is a projection of repressed fear; like the badly entombed maternal corpse that obtrudes from its cement casing in the family's basement, the figure on the bridge represents a challenge to Jack's new paternal authority and his incestuous desire for his sister.

In other cases, characters find in the world around them projected images of their own desires, which they misrecognize temporarily as reality. Stephen Lewis, the main character in *The Child in Time*, whose three-year-old daughter Kate is abducted, constantly searches for his child in the dystopian, Thatcherite London in which he lives. In his desperate need to see what he wishes to see, he falsely recognizes Kate first in one of the beggars licensed by the state, and then in a girl skipping outside a school. When he enters the school in pursuit of this girl, he becomes caught up in a narcissistic fantasy of regression to childhood, similar to that of his friend Charles Darke; he enters a classroom, behaves like a student, and then acts out a 'schoolboy daydream' (171) of leaving his seat without permission.

Bernard in *Black Dogs* indulges a different kind of fantasy: he imagines, at times, that his wife June, a spiritualist, is trying to communicate with him after her death by appearing in the faces of young women. When two girls pass him and his son-in-law Jeremy, the novel's narrator, in Berlin, Bernard is certain for a moment that one of them has 'June's mouth and something of her cheekbones', and is therefore a 'message' (61) to him from his wife. Yet Bernard the rationalist cannot sustain this illusion for long, and refuses to accept Jeremy's view that the woman, who saves Bernard from being seriously hurt when he tries to stop a group of skinheads from beating a young communist to death, is actually 'his guardian angel, the incarnation of June' (76). McEwan contrasts Bernard's temporary treatment of the other as the image of his own desire with his willingness to put himself in mortal danger to protect a total stranger. Witnessing this benevolent act becomes part of Jeremy's development from a state as a literal orphan to being the Tremaines' de facto son. The one 'enduring principle' (xx) that Jeremy takes away from his experiences with June and Bernard is the 'possibility of love transforming and redeeming a life' (xxii); while he refers specifically to the romantic love between him and his wife Jenny as well as between his in-laws, Jeremy also finds that non-erotic love for the other can be redemptive. From June, he learns compassion for 'all life' (56), even a dragonfly that Bernard once killed for his entomological studies; from Bernard, he gains the courage to sacrifice himself on behalf of the less powerful.

In a scene that parallels Bernard's confrontation with the skinheads, Jeremy acts to save a boy being brutalized by his parents in a Paris restaurant. Although Jeremy recognizes his own suffering as an orphan in the boy's plight, his identification is not self-serving but rather moral. When he challenges the boy's father and mistakenly says in French, 'Are you frightened of fighting someone your own size, because I would love to smash my jaw' (107), he figuratively takes the boy's punishment onto himself. As his violent impulses overcome his urge simply to help the boy, however, Jeremy has to be prevented from 'stomp[ing]' the father 'to death' (108) just as the skinheads planned to do to Bernard. At that violent extreme, Jeremy becomes associated with the novel's central metaphor of malignant power, the black Gestapo dogs that attacked June on a hiking expedition with Bernard in France in 1946.

McEwan's depictions of the effects of Nazi Germany in *Black Dogs*, *The Innocent* and, as we shall see, *Atonement* stress what Tim Woods, citing the ideas of Emmanuel Levinas, calls the 'absolute denial of the other as Other' (54), which is the basis of totalitarianism. In his critique of thinkers such as Martin Heidegger, Levinas shifts the emphasis away from the individualism inherent in existential ontology, with Being at its centre, to the ethical relationship that beings bear to one another. For that relation-ship to be 'founded not on violence but on love' (Woods 55), Levinas asserts, people must acknowledge others in the world in their individual and distinct being; his image for this point of acknowledgement is the face: 'To be in relation with the other face to face — is to be unable to kill' (*Entre Nous* 10). What the face represents is not the power implied by various social roles, but the utter vulnerability of the being in the world: 'The absolute nakedness of a face, the absolutely defenseless face, without covering, clothing or mask, is what opposes my power over it, my violence' (*Collected Philosophical Papers* 21). In the truly ethical relationship, the other's weakness 'summons' (*Entre Nous* 147) us to responsibility and caring, without expectation of reciprocation; despite the fact that one dominates over the other, 'this power is the complete opposite of power' (9). As we saw in the restaurant scene in *Black Dogs*, the recognition of the boy's defencelessness compels Jeremy to act protectively on his behalf; it is only when Jeremy loses sight of the father's humanity, his 'face', and treats him like an 'animal' (107) to be killed that he replicates the violence he rightly seeks to end.

Similarly, *The Child in Time* thematizes the importance of acknowledging the other's suffering and acting compassionately in response. Stephen grows beyond his need to imagine others as projections of his own hopeless desire for his daughter, so that when he encounters the beggar girl for the second time, he sees in her face only herself: 'He tried to remember how he had seen Kate in this girl' (228). Touched by her destitution, he covers her exposed body, huddled on a street vent, only to discover that she is already dead. Stephen's sympathetic identification is fostered by his peculiar experience, as an adult, of observing his parents in a pub many years before discussing the possibility of aborting him. This temporal aberration takes place shortly after Stephen's wife Julie has left him in her despair over their missing child, and the episode leaves him feeling 'a bitter sense of exclusion and longing' (65). Yet when Stephen tests his story against his mother's recollection, he finds that his wave of acknow-ledgement towards the young woman in the pub had been noticed, and became his mother's main motivation for continuing her pregnancy. Although Claire later assumed that the face at the window must be a local boy, she was convinced at the time that she was looking at her own child, and immediately thought of her foetus as 'a separate individual . . . a life that she must defend with her own' (207). Like Claire with her acceptance of her son's claim on her protection, Stephen eventually moves beyond his self-absorbed grief to empathize with Julie, who had been 'right in front' (242) of him all the time, and recognize her love as the means of his reintegration with the world. Their second baby, born in the novel's final pages, makes its own demand for recognition − '*Did you not realize it was me all along? I am here*' (261) − and leads Stephen to an understanding of the connected-ness of humankind.

McEwan makes the choice of whether to sacrifice oneself to help the other in need the focal point of highly dramatic scenes that implicate the reader in the characters' ethical dilemmas in *Enduring Love* and *Amsterdam*. The former begins with a daring rescue attempt by six men trying to save a boy trapped in a drifting hot-air balloon. While all of the men are holding onto the balloon's ropes, the effort has some chance of success; but when one of them lets go to save himself, all but one of the others follow suit and the boy is practically left to his fate. Joe Rose, one of the would-be rescuers, draws readers into his reflections on the justifiability of their actions:

So can we accept that it was right, every man for himself? . . . We never had that comfort, for there was a deeper covenant, ancient, automatic, written in our nature. Co-operation — the basis of our evolving capacity for language, the glue of our social cohesion. . . . But letting go was in our nature too. Selfishness is also written on our hearts. (14)

Joe first rationalizes his opting for self-preservation on the grounds that he was not the first to give up: 'Someone said *me*, and then there was nothing to be gained by saying *us*' (15). Second, as the husband in a childless marriage, he convinces himself that he should not have to die to save someone else's child. The rightness of his decision is, on the one hand, confirmed by the death of John Logan, the young doctor who hangs onto the balloon and then falls, a needless tragedy given the eventual safe landing of the boy with no adult help. On the other hand, Joe cannot help but feel the contrast between his own choice and Logan's heroism, as well as guilt over the doctor's death, for which he is partially responsible. In his memory of approaching Logan's body, Joe recalls his initial thoughts as being centred on 'a kind of self-love': '*that man is dead . . . and I am alive*' (19), yet he is haunted by the image of Logan's 'shattered' face, with its 'radical, Picassoesque violation of perspective' (23).

The choice of self over other is horribly parodied in the erotomania of Jed Parry, one of the rescuers, who pursues Joe with no regard for his independent desires. Despite Joe's categorization, as a writer of popular scientific journalism, of Jed's obsession as de Clérambault's syndrome, he finds himself acting irrationally in parallel with his victimizer, concealing information from his wife Clarisse and erasing phone messages. Joe's self-isolation with his fears leaves him feeling like 'a mental patient at the end of visiting hours' (58); gradually, Clarisse, who is disturbed by Joe's odd behaviour, becomes isolated as well, and she cites his refusal to share his thinking with her as one of the primary factors in the nearly tragic outcome of Jed's homicidal fantasies. So immured is Joe in his egocentricity that he fails to recognize Jed in the restaurant where his hired assassins attempt to murder the object of his desire.

In *Amsterdam*, the central ethical quandary involves the composer Clive Linley, who puts his selfish ambitions ahead of another's welfare. As a white, middle-class male of established artistic talent, Clive prospers in the text's debased English society, in which a Thatcherite government, similar to that in *The Child in Time*, has laid the foundation for rampant commercialism, environmental degradation and political opportunism. One mark of Clive's privileged status in this fallen world is his commission to compose a symphony celebrating the turn of the millennium, and like William Wordsworth and his contemporaries he seeks his inspiration away in the natural beauty of the Lake District. Though he claims to 'loathe' the 'arrogance' of artists who play 'the genius card' (62), he nonetheless subscribes to a Romantic sense of his own superiority. When he finally manages to separate himself from the irritating 'human meaning' (78) of the city and the other tourists in the District, Clive finds the creative stimulus that he has sought for months in the call of a bird. Faced with the decision at that very point of whether to go to the aid of a woman being assaulted down the cliff, he immediately places a higher value on his composition and turns away: 'It was as if he wasn't there. He wasn't there. He was in his music. His fate, their fate, separate paths' (88–9). Yet Clive's decision does not go unpunished: his inspirational moment is spoiled by his inner voice of 'self-justification' (88), and his best friend, the tabloid newspaper editor Vernon Halliday, takes him to task for his lack of 'moral duty' (119).

Vernon's outrage is largely hypocritical, however, when seen in context of his intention to publish scandalous photos of the politician Julian Garmony as a transvestite. Despite Vernon's protestations that his reason for doing so is to prevent Garmony from furthering his right-wing agenda by becoming Prime Minister, his real motivations of profit and fame are as self-serving as Clive's. Vernon's plan is foiled by Julian's genuinely humane yet media-savvy wife Rose, who calls a press conference, Hillary Clinton-style, to announce that she accepts her husband as he is and predicts the downfall of his attackers, since 'love was a greater force than spite' (124).

These collisions of moral values set in motion the book's denouement, in which Clive and Vernon plan each other's murder-as-apparent-suicide in Holland, where euthanasia is legal. Like the Siamese twins in the story covered by Vernon's tabloid, who cannot be separated but who bite each other's faces, Vernon and Clive carry out a series of mutual betrayals that lead inexorably to their accidental deaths at their own hands. The novel's clearly visible structure, which McEwan has described in others of his texts as being 'architectur[al]' (Noakes and Reynolds 13), along with its overt meditations on the act of contemporary artistic creation, contribute to *Amsterdam*'s self-consciousness, an aspect of McEwan's work that has grown more pronounced over his career (Malcolm 9–12). Passages such as Clive's encounter with the woman and the rapist on the cliff, described as being like 'actors striking up a tableau whose meaning he was supposed to guess' (85), are clearly staged scenes that enjoin readers to reflect on their own ethical practices.

In *Atonement*, this sense of deliberate theatricality is pervasive, particularly in Part One, which establishes Briony Tallis's 'crime' (156) — her false accusation of her family's charwoman's son Robbie Turner of raping Lola Quincey — for which she seeks expiation through writing. McEwan's novel opens as an ostensible third-person narration about a summer day in 1935, on which the adolescent Briony persuades her visiting cousins, Lola and her twin brothers Jackson and Pierrot, to perform in a melodrama she has written to attract the attention of her older brother Leon. In keeping with this incestuous motivation, the play itself becomes a re-enactment of the Oedipal drama, with the children trying on various parental and romantic roles, including some cross-dressing. As in *The Cement Garden*, the children's sexual role-playing is intensified by the virtual absence of parents, not only the cousins', who have recently separated, but also Briony's: her father, a shadowy figure of phallic authority, is off in London calculating the number of German casualties hoped for in the coming war, and her mother is an invalid protected by her offspring. But the play, with its potential to serve as an 'ego-ideal' (Benjamin 144) that will allow Briony to find her place in the Oedipal order, is cancelled by her in reaction to a scene she witnesses between her sister Cecilia and Robbie, in which the two struggle over filling a vase at the fountain. The complexities of this 'dumb show' (*Atonement* 41), which seems to encompass both a marriage proposal and an attempted drowning, show Briony 'how easy it was to get everything wrong' (39), and prompts her to abandon fantasy in favour of a more adult style of psychological realism.

This apparently sudden movement to maturity, however, is in fact only a sign of Briony's evolving narcissism; she begins to imagine herself (and subsequently reimagine herself) as increasingly powerful: a brilliant neophyte novelist, an Olympic flayer of nettles and so on. Her abrupt change in perspective has serious repercussions for the twins, who see her cancellation of the play as a further rejection by an uncaring family, and run away, though they are found unharmed. More damaging is Briony's assumption that she can henceforth understand the intricate world of adult behaviour. Having read without permission Robbie's erotic letter that he sends inadvertently (though with subconscious intent) to Cecilia, Briony becomes convinced that he is a 'maniac' (119). Despite her presumed literary sophistication, Briony is frequently confounded by language; she is unsure what 'cunt' (86, 114) refers to in Robbie's letter, and like the word 'divorce' (57) for the twins, 'maniac' takes on for her indeterminate evil dimensions, leading her to interpret Cecilia and Robbie's love-making as rape. This hermeneutic confusion is mirrored by the murky darkness in which Briony and the others search for the missing twins; she incorrectly perceives her mother's leg in the lighted window as 'disembodied' (161), then the crouching Lola and her assailant as a 'bush' (164). When Briony insistently misidentifies the attacker as Robbie despite Lola's evasive answers and evidence of his innocence, she is defending her new-found power of adult interpretation. She is also, we later discover, taking revenge for his rejection of her declaration of love when she was ten, a variant of the incestuous desire manifested by her play.

In *Atonement*, then, as in other novels, misrecognition involves the projection of self-centred desire; but does McEwan convert that egotism, as he does most clearly in *The Child in Time* and *Black Dogs*, into an ethical engagement with the other? Claudia Schemberg, in *Achieving 'At-one-ment'*, argues that Briony's total narrative, which McEwan's novel comprises, represents a legitimate effort to transcend narcissism: while 'Briony's youthful imagination ruthlessly and egoistically subordinated the world and other people to schemes and patterns ... such as fairy-tales', her more mature artistic conception, evident in the sections of the text relating Robbie and Cecilia's experiences during the Second World War and her own final days in 1999, 'furnishes a final proof that in her quest for atonement Briony has learned how to imaginatively put herself in the position of other people' (85). Schemberg locates this compassionate response in Briony's refusal to fabricate Robbie's forgiveness for her role in his incarceration for a crime he did not commit.

Yet all of Briony's narrative, including Part One, which we come to see as thinly disguised and self-aggrandizing autobiography, is characterized by a preference for fantasy resolution over realism. Despite the suffering of those retreating to Dunkirk in Part Two, Briony's rendition of Robbie's adventures in France tend towards the comic: he dreams of a 'paradise' (238) in the nearby woods to which he can escape; Mace stops angry soldiers from beating to death a myopic RAF officer by carrying him from the scene like 'Tarzan' (253); and Robbie survives to return to England. Briony's experiences as a nurse in a London hospital, detailed in Part Three, are clearly modelled on the self-sacrifice of Florence Nightingale, and her acts of contrition with the reunited Robbie and Cecilia, promising to set the record straight, show her in the best possible light. Though the final section suggests a shift to reality with the revelation of the 'true' fates of Robbie and Cecilia, both killed in 1940, even that note of verisimilitude is short-lived as Briony reverts to romance: 'As long as there is a single copy ... of my final draft, then my spontaneous, fortuitous sister and her medical prince survive to love' (371). Briony's entire narrative, therefore, up to her joyous reintegration into the family around the performance of her play, is constructed as a fantasy text that elevates her self-interest over genuine concern for the other.

Similarly, *Saturday* presents a dramatic ethical confrontation between two characters within an essentially comic textual structure that obfuscates the serious social implications of that encounter. McEwan's most recent novel is the story of one Saturday in the life of successful neurosurgeon Henry Perowne, a day that begins and ends with potential tragedy owing to the incursion of menacing elements into the doctor's comfortable world. He awakes early to see a flaming plane streaking across the London sky, renewing his fears of terrorism in the wake of the 11 September 2001 attacks in the United States. Although the burning plane turns out to be harmless, Perowne's anxiety is sustained by the massive protest against the imminent Iraq war going on in the city, as well as by his children's opposition to the invasion, which seems largely justifiable to him. In fact, the doctor is convinced of the need to protect his lifestyle from a number of different threats, some of which are closer at hand: from the window of his opulent townhouse with its elaborate security system, he watches the goings-on of the indigent and the drug-dealers in the city square with the 'remote possessiveness of a god' (13). With detectable irony, the narrator informs us that Perowne 'imagines himself as Saddam, surveying the crowd with satisfaction from some Baghdad ministry balcony' (62). Yet the implied authorial indictment of Perowne's alarming sense of superiority becomes harder to discern over the course of the character's interactions with the novel's villain.

The thug Baxter represents the ease with which the threatening other can infiltrate the privileged world of the predominantly white middle class. When Baxter's car smashes into Perowne's silver Mercedes, the doctor sees only 'a flash of red' (81), a clear association with the burning plane and international terrorism. But the true danger he symbolizes is the domestic presence of people of different cultures and backgrounds, such as the three women in 'black burkhas' (124) whom Perowne disapprovingly notes in his drive around London. While the narrator, through the doctor's focalized perspective, frequently identifies others by race or culture, the description of Baxter conspicuously avoids any such mention. Instead, he is characterized in animalistic terms:

> He's a fidgety, small-faced young man with thick eyebrows and dark brown hair razored close to the skull. The mouth is set bulbously, with the smoothly shaved shadow of a strong beard adding to the effect of a muzzle. The general simian air is compounded by sloping shoulders ... (87–8)

Perowne's immediate response to this face-to-face encounter is repulsion and fear, followed by growing confidence as he diagnoses Baxter's tremors as a symptom of Huntingdon's disease. With this medical knowledge, he gains the advantage over his attacker, rationalizing that he 'was obliged, or forced to abuse his own power' (111) to protect himself, just as Prime Minister Blair claims is the case with Iraq.

Perowne's entitlement to dominance is confirmed in his final conflict with his antagonist, when Baxter invades his home and threatens his family. The doctor's son and even his drunken father-in-law act chivalrously in defence of his wife and daughter, while Baxter's henchman ignobly deserts him. Incredibly, Baxter's mayhem is stopped in its tracks by a recitation of Matthew Arnold's 'Dover Beach', an emblem of English cultural superiority. Indeed, the entire scene in the Perowne's house takes on a sense of literary unreality: the monstrous invader ends up crumpled at the bottom of the stairs, while the family reunites in loving harmony. Like Briony, Perowne is able to contrive his own form of forgiveness by operating on his enemy, so that he feels 'he's been delivered into a pure present, free of the weight of the past or any anxieties about the future' (258). Yet this comic ending obscures the miserable fate of inevitable poverty and suffering awaiting Baxter, as well as the horrifying consequences of failing to recognize the needs of the alienated other in contemporary England. As Perowne thinks at the novel's end, 'London ... is waiting for its bomb' (276); yet the triumph of McEwan's hero provides no sense of the need for urgent cultural change to prevent the horrors of domestic terrorism that occurred, all too predictably, in July 2005.

In 'Two Fragments: March 199-' – (*In Between the Sheets*), another Henry perambulates on a Saturday in a futuristic, dystopian London landscape in which all sense of community has collapsed under extreme societal decline. The first 'fragment' relates Henry's efforts to comfort his young daughter Marie after she watches a young woman violently dominated by her father in a street-performance for money; in the second, Henry attempts to reconnect with a former lover Diane, before becoming involved in a chance encounter with a 'Chinaman' (67) who asks for his help in moving a heavy cupboard. Both parts of this early story point to McEwan's profound concern with the need for compassionate interaction among people in the difficult moral terrain of contemporary life, a concern that has remained central to his work throughout his career. David Malcolm concludes the first chapter of his 2002 study *Understanding Ian McEwan* by saying, 'One does not know what he will do next' (19). As admirers of McEwan's fiction, we can only wait to see whether his ethical agenda will continue to evolve in concert with his increasing literary sophistication and international renown.

Bibliography and further reading

McEwan, Ian. *First Love, Last Rites*. New York: Random House, 2003 [1975].

——. *In Between the Sheets*. New York: Random House, 2003 [1978].

——. *The Cement Garden*. London: Vintage, 1997 [1978].

——. *The Comfort of Strangers*. London: Vintage, 1997 [1981].

——. *The Child in Time*. Toronto: Lester & Orpen Dennys, 1987 [1987].

——. *The Innocent*. Toronto: Lester & Orpen Dennys, 2002 [1990].

——. *Black Dogs*. Toronto: Alfred A. Knopf, 1992 [1992].

——. *Enduring Love*. Toronto: Vintage, 1998 [1997].

——. *Amsterdam*. Toronto: Vintage, 1999 [1999].

——. *Atonement*. Toronto: Vintage, 2002 [2001].

——. *Saturday*. Toronto: Alfred A. Knopf, 2005 [2005].

Benjamin, Jessica. *The Bonds of Love: Psychoanalysis, Feminism, and the Problem of Domination*. New York: Pantheon, 1988.

Levinas, Emmanuel. *Collected Philosophical Papers*. Trans. Alphonso Lingis. Pittsburgh, PA: Duquesne University Press, 1987.

——. *Entre Nous*. New York: Columbia University Press, 1998.

Malcolm, David. *Understanding Ian McEwan*. Columbia, SC: University of South Carolina Press, 2002.

Noakes, Jonathan, and Margaret Reynolds (eds). *Ian McEwan*. London: Vintage, 2002.

Ryan, Kiernan. *Ian McEwan*. Plymouth: Northcote House, 1994.

Seaboyer, Judith. 'Sadism Demands a Story: Ian McEwan's *The Comfort of Strangers*.' *Modern Fiction Studies*, 45:4, 1999: 957–86.

Schemberg, Claudia. *Achieving 'At-one-ment': Storytelling and the Concept of the Self in Ian McEwan's 'The Child in Time,' 'Black Dogs,' 'Enduring Love,' and 'Atonement.'* Frankfurt: Peter Lang, 2004.

Tait, Theo. 'Ian McEwan's Longest Day.' *The Times Literary Supplement*. Online edition accessed 12 October 2005, www.the-tls.co.uk./this_week/story.aspx?story_id = 2109934, 9 February 2005, 4 pages.

Woods, Tim. 'The Ethical Subject: the Philosophy of Emmanuel Levinas', in *Ethics and the Subject*. Karl Simms (ed.). Amsterdam and Atlanta: Rodopi, 1997: 53–60.

CHAPTER ELEVEN

Identifying the Precious in Zadie Smith's *On Beauty*

FIONA TOLAN

Zadie Smith's third novel, *On Beauty* (2005), continues and develops much of the successful formula of her first, the widely celebrated *White Teeth* (2000). Both texts are founded on the interconnecting relationships of two families and both pose a multicultural family challenged by a father's infidelity. Despite striking similarities, however, *On Beauty* marks a shift in Smith's concerns, most superficially demonstrated by the relocation of her fiction from *White Teeth*'s north London setting to east coast America. This move is only the physical expression of a changing theoretical focus. In the earlier novel Smith wrote: 'it's about time people told the truth about beautiful women' (27). In this later text, aesthetic concerns predominate and inform an ongoing ethical enquiry.

In *On Beauty*, the Belsey family inhabit a large and beautiful New England house with mottled green windows, the historical and aesthetic import of which is undermined by the need to protect the increasingly commodified value of the past. The reader is informed that:

> They are not original these windows, but replacements, the originals being too precious to be used as windows. Heavily insured, they are kept in a large safe in the basement. A significant portion of the value of the Belsey house resides in windows that nobody may look through or open. (16)

The windows provide the monetary value of the home, but their true worth is primarily aesthetic, situated in their rarity and beauty. Beauty, at this early stage in the novel, is a commodity to be protected and hidden. Some time later, the Belsey daughter, Zora, rebuffs a friendly approach from Carl, a beautiful but poor young black man to whom she is attracted, because, the narrator tells us, 'Zora's paranoia got the better of her. She imagined for a moment that all these questions were a kind of verbal grooming that would later lead – by routes she didn't pause to imagine – to her family home and her mother's jewellery and the safe in the basement' (139). Again, the narrative turns back to the beautiful windows locked away in the basement safe. Seeing Carl walk away from her, 'Zora was filled with the sad sense that something precious had escaped' (139). In both instances, the appreciation of beauty is marred by fear, and throughout *On Beauty*, Smith examines the tensions surrounding beauty, including its aesthetic appreciation, its commodification and increasingly, its politicization. In each of these dialogues with beauty, the characters of the novel are forced to define and defend what is precious to them.

In her acknowledgements for *On Beauty*, Smith points the reader to two significant sources of inspiration:

> Thank you to Elaine Scarry for her wonderful essay 'On Beauty and Being Just', from which I borrowed a title, a chapter heading and a good deal of inspiration. It should be obvious from the first line that this is a novel inspired by a love of E. M. Forster, to whom all my fiction is indebted, one way or the other. This time I wanted to repay the debt with *hommage*. (N. pag.)

Much was made by the book's reviewers of Smith's reworking of Forster's *Howards End*. Some, such as Alex Clark of the *Daily Telegraph*, viewed the project as a failure, arguing that *On Beauty* 'labours, from its opening sentence, under the restrictive covenant of being substantially based, structurally and in spirit, on another novel, E M Forster's *Howards End*' (9). Others looked beyond the plot parallels to glimpse more fundamental sympathies between the two British writers. Jonathan Derbyshire, writing in the *Financial Times*, suggested that, while the book 'borrows its structure unapologetically' from *Howards End*, an evident appreciation of Forster has more broadly 'shaped Smith's notions about what the novel, as a form, can do' In support of this, he quotes Smith's own statement — given in her 2003 Orange World Lecture, and rewritten as an essay, 'Love, Actually' — that she learned from Forster that there is 'no bigger crime, in the English comic novel, than thinking you are right'; that his novels show us that our 'moral enthusiasms make us inflexible, one-dimensional, flat' (quoted in Derbyshire 32). For Derbyshire, the influence of Forster on Smith can be traced through all three of her novels, rather than simply in this, the most recent.

A similar point was made by Frank Kermode in the *London Review of Books*, although he diagnosed the influence not so much in Smith's feel for the comedy of the moralizer, but rather in her sense of the moral purpose of the novel. Kermode argued that:

> Zadie Smith's real debt may not lie in her echoes of *Howards End*, though she does insist on them ... . The main resemblance between the two books goes beyond the plot allusions everybody talks about. What lies behind both is an idea of the novel as what Lawrence called the one bright book of life — a source of truth and otherworldliness and prophecy. (13)

For Kermode, this sympathy is not necessarily a profitable one. Recalling the famous scene in which Forster's Schlegel sisters attend a performance of Beethoven's Fifth Symphony, he pronounces it a 'glaring failure ... altogether an embarrassing couple of pages' (13). Consequently, when

Smith rewrites the scene as a 'Mozart in the Park' event in middle-class Wellington, Kermode's verdict is dismissive:

> ... it seemed to both authors necessary to make more of the concert: to prophesy, philosophise, to hint that the music is an image of the universe; but to make the explanations facetious or trivial, mere metaphorical bombast. It is a fault completely out of character in this gifted novelist, and Forster has led her into it. (13–14)

Kermode identifies in *On Beauty* a self-conscious tendency towards ethereal philosophizing that conflicts with what he considers to be Smith's talent for 'being in the world, for knowing and loving its diversity' (13).

Yet despite the connections made between Smith and Forster in general, and between the literary philosophizing of both in particular, in comparison, little or nothing was said of the more evidently philosophical application of Scarry's work to the novel. By taking her title from Scarry's essay, which in turn takes its terms from the works of myriad other philosophers of ethics and aesthetics, from Plato to Immanuel Kant, Smith clearly points to a significant element of conscious philosophical investigation and analysis in her novel that has gone largely unremarked.

The section from Scarry's text that Smith takes as one of her epigraphs reads: 'To misstate, or even merely understate, the relation of the universities to beauty is one kind of error that can be made. A university is among the precious things that can be destroyed' (127). Again, Smith brings the reader into contact with the notion of the precious. Here, according to Scarry, the university is precious for its dual role in the perpetuation of beauty and the preservation of a dialogue on beauty. In *On Beauty and Being Just*, she argues that the 'willingness continually to revise one's own location in order to place oneself in the path of beauty is the basic impulse underlying education' (7). In Smith's *On Beauty*, Carl, taking the Leonard Bast role in the novel, offers his views on Mozart to Zora, and tells her 'That's college, right? That's what you paying all that money for – just so you get to talk to other people about that shit' (137). And in Howard Belsey's art history class, a nervous young student 'used to dream about one day attending a college class about Rembrandt with other intelligent people who loved Rembrandt and weren't ashamed to express this love' (250). But in Smith's novel, and particularly in Howard's classes, the university has moved beyond an appreciation of beauty and entered into the terminal phase of its deconstruction.

In a text full of opposites, one of the key pairings is the liberal Howard and his academic nemesis, the conservative Monty Kipps. Both Rembrandt scholars, their ideological differences are epitomized by their differing perceptions of art and beauty. Unable to call 'a rose a rose', Howard 'called it an accumulation of cultural and biological constructions circulating around the mutually attracting binary poles of nature/artifice' (225). In contrast, Howard's born-again-Christian son, Jerome, is relieved to learn from

Monty that 'Art was a gift from God, blessing only a handful of masters' (44). The text sets up an opposition between a transcendent and a culturally situated understanding of art and beauty. For Monty, motivated largely by his Christianity, beauty transcends the individual and points to a higher spiritual perfection.

This notion of transcendence corresponds with Scarry's view that 'Something beautiful fills the mind yet invites the search for something beyond itself, something larger or something of the same scale with which it needs to be brought into relation' (29). This view is shared by Jerome in *On Beauty*, for whom Howard's denial of beauty is tied to his denial of God:

> It's like he *knows* he's blessed, but he doesn't know where to put his gratitude because that makes him uncomfortable, because that would be dealing in transcendence – and we all know how he hates to do *that*. So by denying there are any gifts in the world, any essentially valuable things – that's how he shortcircuits the gratitude question. If there are no gifts, then he doesn't have to think about a God who might have given them. (237)

In *On Beauty and Being Just*, Scarry begins her discussion by positing that a primary response to the experience of beauty is the desire to replicate it. This desire has propelled art forward in a self-perpetuating series of readings and rereadings of natural and cultural icons of beauty. Consequently, artistic beauty inevitably points backwards to its precedents, as much as it points forwards to new acts of creation. In looking on beauty, the viewer seeks ever earlier precedents:

> ... and the mind keeps tripping backward until it at last reaches something that has no precedent, which may very well be the immortal. And one can see why beauty ... has been perceived to be bound up with truth. What is beautiful is in league with what is true because truth abides in the immortal sphere. (30–1)

This analysis is inimical to Howard's beliefs. He identifies the beauty of a work of art as existing simply as a product of its political and cultural matrices. Presenting a vision of Rembrandt as 'a merely competent artisan who painted whatever his wealthy patrons requested', Howard invites his students 'to imagine prettiness as the mask that power wears. To recast Aesthetics as a rarefied language of exclusion' (155).

Scarry, however, rebuts this argument. In accordance with Smith's vision, Scarry points to what she terms the 'banishing of beauty from the humanities in the last two decades', and suggests that, although much of the business of the humanities is to explore beautiful things – poetry, prose, paintings – 'Conversation about the beauty of these things has been banished' (57). In *On Beauty*, Smith envisions this censorship in comic form, as Monty's daughter Victoria informs Howard that his art history class 'is all about never *ever* saying *I like the tomato*' (312). Jerome diagnoses his father's refusal of beauty as 'a denial of *joy*' (236), but Zora, following

Howard, confronts her poetry tutor with a dismissal of the pastoral as 'depoliticized reification' – 'all this beauty stuff about landscape? Virgil, Pope, the Romantics. Why idealize?' (218). For Zora, as for her father, the purely aesthetic appreciation of artistic beauty is a reprehensible depoliticization of art's cultural and social expression.

Addressing this perceived intellectual refusal to engage with beauty, Scarry suggests that it is premised on the false belief that a dominating concern with beauty leads to 'lateral disregard' – 'the worry that inevitably follows in the wake of observing the beautiful: "something's receiving attention" seems to involve "something else's not receiving attention"' (80–1). That is, assuming a limited capacity for intellectual engagement, a preoccupation with beauty is a distraction from politics. Scarry counters this assertion by arguing that the cognition of beauty, which involves the perceiver in both a desire to replicate beauty and the 'impulse toward a distribution across perceivers' (6) in fact 'actually assists us in the work of addressing injustice ... by acquiring of us constant perceptual acuity – high dives of seeing, hearing, touching', which are then available to be employed elsewhere: 'The problem of lateral disregard is not, then, evidence of a weakness but of a strength: the moment we are enlisted into the first event [the cognition of beauty], we have already become eligible to carry out the second [the cognition of injustice]' (81). For Scarry then, beauty leads to a desire to create, to share and 'to locate what is true'. Consequently, 'beauty is a starting place for education' (31). Without this cognition, a person's capacity for these morally improving actions is diminished.

In *On Beauty*, Howard's intellectual choices are seen to impact on other areas of his life, most particularly, on his familial relations. In the first pages of the novel, a portrait of Howard's father – the only non-photographic portrait hanging in the Belsey house – is described: 'Howard himself hates it as he hates all representational painting – and his father' (18). Just as Jerome identifies the refusal of beauty as a refusal of joy, so Howard's hatred of the artistic representation of his father seems here indistinguishable from his hatred of the man himself. It is almost as though one enables the other.

Later in the novel, when fighting with his wife Kiki, Howard is depicted standing beneath an abstract painting:

> Its main feature was a piece of thick white plaster, made to look like linen, crumpled up like a rag someone had thrown away. This action of throwing had been caught, by the artist, in mid-flight, with the 'linen' frozen in space, framed by a white wooden box that thrust out from the wall. (206)

The painting is characterized by an absence of colour and an attempted exposure of the fallacy of naturalistic representation. The artificiality of both the natural fibre and the fluid movement that it appears to contain is highlighted by the white frame which encloses and freezes its contents. The painting interrogates connections between movement and stasis, between the artificial and the real. This latter binary is equally present in the division between the 'academic' and the 'emotional' language that, respectively, Howard and Kiki use in their argument, although Howard 'would never, *never* concede the point that Kiki's language was any more emotionally expressive than his own' (204–5). As Howard leaves the room, between his desire to slam the door and her desire to kick it shut, 'The force of it knocked the plaster picture to the floor' (208). The fall of the painting is obviously tied to the collapse of their relationship. But more precisely, it seems to point to a connection between Howard's ascetic intellectualism and the failing of communicative emotion within his marriage.

The intellectualizing of aesthetic discourse is countered in the novel by the instinctual and emotional response to art pursued by Carlene Kipps. Where Monty and Howard debate deconstructionist principles in public forums, in contrast, their wives enter into a parallel but notably intimate and anti-intellectual dialogue on art. Showing her friend a beautiful Haitian portrait of a goddess, Carlene dismisses its economic aspect, explaining, 'It's worth a great deal, I believe, but that's not why I love it.' When Kiki attempts to appropriate Howard's language in compensation for what she fears to be her critical incompetence, her friend sweeps away her pretensions: 'That's a very clever way to put it. I like her parrots' (175). For Carlene, in absolute contrast to Howard, and even in opposition to her husband, for whom art is informed by religious principles, the value of the painting rests solely in its beauty, which transcends all other aspects of its power, and it is the beauty of art that makes it transcendent.

Although Smith is obviously much indebted to Scarry for her analysis of beauty and its potential for transcendence in this novel, the subject is one that has also been addressed by Smith's other great influence, Forster. In *Aspects of the Novel*, he repeatedly speaks in terms of the construction of beauty by the novelist, and particularly of the potential for beauty in the pattern and rhythm of the well-structured plot. At one point, he describes beauty as an aesthetic quality 'at which a novelist should never aim, though he fails if he does not achieve it' (119). And for Forster, the fundamental element of the novel is the transcendent aspect of art.

At the start of *Aspects of the Novel*, he states: 'All through history writers while writing have felt more or less the same. They have entered a common state which it is convenient to call inspiration, and, having regard to that state, we may say that History develops, Art stands still' (34–5). In illustration of this view, he famously envisioned a room in which all the novelists of the last 200 years could be imagined working together, 'subject to the same emotions and putting the accidents of their age into the crucible of inspiration' (218). And in his conclusion, he develops this idea further:

> But we must visualize the novelists of the next two hundred years as also writing in the room. The change in their subject matter will be enormous; they will not change. We may harness the atom, we may land on the moon, we may

abolish or intensify warfare, the mental processes of animals may be understood; but all these are trifles, they belong to history not to art. History develops, art stands still. The new novelist will have to pass all the new facts through the old if variable mechanism of the creative mind. (218–19)

Forster makes a distinct though contentious division of art and history. In his discussion of Forster's work, Nicholas Royle points out that 'from today's perspective [this opposition] appears to combine a facile conservatism ("art stands still") with an absurd quietism (the bombing of Hiroshima and Nagasaki will be as a mere trifle)' (48). Forster himself admits that 'History develops, Art stands still is a crude motto' (35), but nevertheless, its assumption runs throughout his discussion.

Royle's accusation of the conservatism and quietism of Forster's motto is the same argument that Howard would put to Monty. And although Smith in *On Beauty* does betray much sympathy with Carlene's transcendent view of art, which, for one, cuts through the intellectual elitism of Howard's discourse, she also exposes the inability of this perspective to address the multifaceted cultural and political realities of the Haitian painting. And this despite the fact that Carlene herself points to a myriad of interpretations of the goddess: 'She represents love, beauty, purity, the ideal female and the moon ... and she's the *mystère* of jealousy, vengeance and discord, *and*, on the other hand, of love, perpetual help, goodwill, health, beauty and fortune'. Faced with such a plenitude, Kiki can only respond: 'Phew. That's a lot of symbolizing' (175).

Throughout the novel, this abstract symbolism takes on a literal aspect in various reactions to the painting. For Clotilde, the Haitian maid, the Voodoo goddess is the subject of superstitious fear. For Monty, the painting is ostensibly part of his mission 'to protect important black art' (113) while also being of evident financial import. For Kiki, the painting's significance is personal. Thinking of Howard's betrayal, she asks, 'So, does she avenge herself on men?' (175). And for Levi Belsey and his Haitian immigrant friends, the painting is an emblem of America's economic imperialism. When they steal it, Levi argues:

> ... *this painting is stolen anyway*. It don't even *belong* to that guy Kipps, not really – it was like twenty years ago and he just went to Haiti and got all these paintings by lying to poor people and buying them for a few dollars and now they be worth all this money and it ain't *his* money ... (428)

Like the windows hidden in the basement, the economic and political value of the painting prompts first Monty to hide it in his office, and then Levi to hide it under his bed.

Smith uses the painting to demonstrate the manner in which history impacts on art. It is a view shared by Umberto Eco in his 2004 art history text, also called *On Beauty*, in which he states: 'Beauty has never been absolute and immutable but has taken on different aspects depending on the historical period and the country' (14). The beauty of art is not, by this view, transcendent, and consequently, the history of America's intervention in Haiti changes Carlene's painting in a way that she may refuse to recognize but which nevertheless persists.

In her review of the novel, Stephanie Merritt suggests that Smith's characters are 'troubled by the question of the use or value of art and literature in a post-9/11 world where all established values seem to have been upended; neither the "high" culture of the academy, nor the "low" culture of the street escape this interrogation, while the notion of distinguishing between them is also dissected' (15). In *On Beauty*, Rembrandt emblemizes the cultural hegemony, typically shored up by the conservatism of Monty's 'hugely popular (and populist) brick designed to sit heavily atop the *New York Times* bestseller list for half a year, crushing every book beneath it' (29), and by the 'Rembrandt Appreciation Society', unsuspecting sponsors of a forthcoming lecture by Howard. In opposition to canonical art stands Carl, a Spoken Word poet, initially dismissed by Zora as not a '*poet* poet' (77). Smith, however, reads hip-hop as contemporary poetry and the poetic lineage is alluded to in a student's clumsy description of Carl as 'like Keats with a knapsack' (230). But the authenticity of Carl's marginal position is challenged by Levi, who labels him 'The kind of rapper white folk get excited about' (238), and contrasts him to the Haitian rappers who are poetically inarticulate but 'got the *suffering people* behind them' (238). Each of the Belsey children seeks something different from art, whether that is spiritual enlightenment, post-modern deconstruction or racial identity.

As the function of art is debated, the notion of genius is also dismantled. In his class, Howard asks his students to interrogate 'the mytheme of artist as autonomous individual with privileged insight into the human ... the quasi-mystical notion of genius' (252). Overhearing the Belseys debate Mozart's genius, Carl later explains to Zora that a large part of Mozart's *Lacrimosa* was in fact composed by the unrecognized Süssmayr:

> ... which is the *shit*, man, 'cos it's like the *best thing* in the Requiem, and it made me think *damn*, you can be so close to genius that it like lifts you up ... and all these people be trying to prove that it's Mozart 'cos that fits in with their idea of who can and who can't make music like this, but the *deal* is that this amazing sound was just by this guy Süssmayr, this average Joe Schmo guy. (137)

Here, historical and biographical knowledge changes the perception of both art and genius. But where Howard dismisses the concept of genius as an attempt to reify the liberal humanist self, Carl seeks to democratize genius. For him, the essence of the 'Christian sublime' (71) that Howard identifies and dismisses in Mozart exists, but not solely for the inspiration of a handful of blessed masters, as Monty would have it. Rather, genius for Carl, as beauty for Scarry, is generative, it 'seems to incite, even to require, the act of replication' (Scarry 3). So Smith, like Scarry and Forster, points to the belief that the connected principles of art, beauty and genius participate in more than aesthetic pleasure: that they can represent 'a Good in our lives' ('Love, Actually' 4).

In her essay on Forster, Smith argues that many novels share an Aristotelian ethical vocabulary, and explains that 'Central to the Aristotelian inquiry into the Good life is the idea that the training and refinement of feeling plays an essential role in our moral understanding' ('Love, Actually' 4). However, and as Merritt suggests, contemporary political instabilities mean that Smith's characters experience this notion of morality and ethics – as they experience aesthetics – as a complex and shifting construct. Smith epitomizes something of this instability by obliquely referring to the unfortunate falling of Howard and Kiki's wedding anniversary on 11 September. As Kiki invites a friend to a party to commemorate their 30th anniversary, she sees 'that tiny, involuntary shudder with which Kiki had, in recent years, become familiar' (68). Here politics can be seen to infiltrate even the most impenetrable of private spaces, rewriting and recoding them, so that what was once stable and fixed becomes open to movement and redefinition.

In response to confusing times, many of the characters of *On Beauty* undergo an interrogation of their values, from Jerome's affirmation of his Christianity and Levi's politicization, to Kiki and Howard's reassessment of their marriage. The difficulties that these examinations unearth are not always resolved, but Smith seems to be working within the parameters of Forster's vision of the novel when he writes in *Aspects of the Novel*: 'Expansion. This is the idea the novelist must cling to. Not completion. Not rounding off but opening out' (216). This refusal of certainty has exposed Forster to accusations of leaving his novels and his readers in a state of confusion, but Smith responds: 'What Forster's muddled style has to tell us is that there are some goods in the world that cannot be purely pursued rationally, we must also feel our way through them'. In her own novel, Smith rejects the absolutism of the many definitions of the Good offered by various characters, but she also nevertheless asserts her own understanding of what she considers to be 'the bond between the ethical realm and the narrative act', when she states that careful reading leads to 'caring about people who are various, muddled, uncertain and not quite like us (and this is good)' (4).

Smith's characters are left to negotiate contested ideas of beauty and truth in order that they might seek their own definition of the Good – in order that they might come to some understanding of what it is that is most precious to them. Despite the myriad obstacles placed by contemporary life in the path of this search, Smith offers one possible solution in the reconciliation of opposites, not into a homogenous whole, but into a system of harmony and equilibrium rather than one of irreconcilable differences. Racial and national identities, as well as class, politics and gender are all radically opposed by the novel. Informed by Scarry's opinion that beauty, 'in its symmetry and generous sensory availability' (Scarry 109), promotes justice, Smith turns to a recognition of beauty to resolve some of the imbalances within the text.

Scarry explains this connection between beauty and justice by arguing that beauty is democratic, that it is available to all. Historically, she points out, the overriding characteristic of beauty has been its balance and symmetry, and this aspect of its form is analogous to the notion of equality inherent in justice. Consequently, we can draw a parallel 'between beauty as "fairness" and justice as "fairness," using the widely accepted definition by John Rawls of fairness as a "symmetry of everyone's relations to each other"' (93). In *On Beauty*, Monty and Howard refuse to acknowledge any form of symmetry between their beliefs, whereas Kiki and Carlene, while maintaining great differences in their ideological positions, enter into a dialogue that enables an appreciation of what is shared as well as of what is opposed. It is this dialogue that prompts Carlene to bequeath her painting to Kiki, fulfilling Scarry's claim that 'beautiful things give rise to the notion of distribution, to a lifesaving reciprocity' (95).

Beauty also, ultimately, points Howard towards a cognition of true worth when it enables him finally to recognize the value of his wife and marriage. Scarry argues that, while the primary response to beauty is the desire to replicate it within art, 'the simplest manifestation of the phenomenon is the simple act of staring' (5). And so the very first glimpse of a bird does not lead to an immediate wish to photograph it, but rather a desire to simply keep watching it '[for] as long as the bird is there to be beheld' (6). In the concluding paragraphs of *On Beauty*, Howard sees Kiki as though for the first time, and the experience is described in terms of his entranced gazing on her: 'Howard looked at Kiki. In her face, his life . . . . He looked out into the audience once more and saw Kiki only' (442–3). This recognition of Kiki's beauty — her value and her preciousness — is, if we trace Smith's debt to Scarry's philosophy, a moment of epiphany for Howard. Scarry suggests that,

> At the moment we see something beautiful, we undergo a radical decentering . . . . It is not that we cease to stand at the center of the world, for we never stood there. It is that we cease to stand even at the center of our own world. We willingly cede our ground to the thing that stands before us. (111–12)

The recognition of the beauty of the other finally enables Howard to relinquish his selfishness. It prompts an act of generosity within him as he surrenders his centrality to his wife. It also directs him to the symmetry of their two lives as he sees himself in her aspect, and so, following Scarry, prompts a move towards an experience that is more just, more fair and more beautiful. Smith connects this affirmation of beauty with the capacity to relinquish the self and care about the other, which is, as she asserted previously, 'a good thing'.

Bibliography and further reading

Smith, Zadie. *White Teeth*. London: Penguin, 2001 [2000].

——. 'Love, Actually.' The *Guardian, Saturday Pages*, 1 November 2003: 4.

——. *On Beauty*. London: Hamish Hamilton, 2005.

Clark, Alex. 'Forster Family.' The *Daily Telegraph, Books*, 10 September 2005: 9.

Derbyshire, Jonathan. 'Truths and Beauty.' *Financial Times Weekend Magazine*, 17 September 2005: 32.

Eco, Umberto (ed.). *On Beauty*. Trans. Alastair McEwen. London: Secker and Warburg, 2004.

Forster, E. M. *Howards End*. London: Penguin, 2000 [1910].

——. *Aspects of the Novel*. London: Edward Arnold, 1927.

Kermode, Frank. 'Here She Is.' *London Review of Books*, 6 October 2005: 13–14.

Merritt, Stephanie. 'A Thing of Beauty.' The *Observer, Review Pages*, 4 September, 2005: 15.

Royle, Nicholas. *E. M. Forster*. Plymouth: Northcote House, 1999.

Scarry, Elaine. *On Beauty and Being Just*. London: Duckworth, 2000 [1999].

CHAPTER TWELVE

Jeanette Winterson's *Lighthousekeeping*

SONYA ANDERMAHR

I thus drew steadily nearer to that truth by whose partial discovery I have been doomed to such a dreadful shipwreck: that man is not truly one, but truly two. (Robert Louis Stevenson, *The Strange Case of Dr Jekyll and Mr Hyde* 48–9)

One can hardly tell which is the sea and which is the land. (Virginia Woolf, *To the Lighthouse* 119)

Introduction

Dating from her first novel, *Oranges Are Not the Only Fruit*, Jeanette Winterson has evinced a preoccupation with both the theme of storytelling and the fictional practice of reworking existing texts, known as intertextuality. These concerns are not of course unrelated; as many critics have argued storytelling involves the utilization and transformation of extant narratives. Narratological approaches, exemplified by Vladimir Propp's morphological analysis of the folktale, demonstrate that the telling of stories necessarily involves a reorganization of sets of narrative units; in short a retelling. Winterson's work brings this aspect of story to the fore, highlighting the indebtedness of new writing to old, and the interconnections between texts. In common with other writers in the postmodern mode, Winterson believes that there is no clear distinction between fantasy/fiction and the real, that the boundaries between them are fluid and shifting, and that narrative is the place where 'reality' is continually constructed and remade. Her work has consistently explored the themes of time as fluid and identity as multiple by exploiting the gap between fantasy and reality, and embarking on journeys through narrative space and time.[1] In Bakhtinian terms, the 'chronotope' featured in her work is that of physical and psychological alternate worlds, multiple realities which are characterized by 'gravity defying' tropes of weightlessness. Exploring both the operation of narrative and the motivation for storytelling, therefore, becomes a means of exploring aspects of human motivation and desire. Moreover, her use of intertextuality points to her love of stories and her valorization of their role in human life. For Winterson, stories represent more than a privileged site of play; as her work demonstrates, they represent a life-line or means of survival.

This chapter examines Winterson's use of intertextuality in *Light-housekeeping* as a means of exploring her key themes of the multiplicity of identity and reality and of the significance of narrative and storytelling. I will focus on the novel's two major intertexts, Virginia Woolf's *To the Lighthouse* and Robert Louis Stevenson's *The Strange Case of Dr Jekyll and Mr Hyde*, and make additional reference to a number of other works to which Winterson alludes, including Charles Darwin's *On the Origin of Species* (1859). Initially, I will set out a range of definitions of intertextuality and indicate how they will be used in the remainder of the chapter.

Defining intertextuality

Critics agree that intertextuality concerns the various kinds of relationship that exist between texts. As a general term, it may incorporate allusion, quotation, parody, pastiche and generic reworking. It is sometimes distinguished from the older term 'literary allusion', which is taken to mean a specific and direct verbal echo of one text by another, rather than the more general and diffuse mode of reworking implied by intertextuality. According to Hawthorn, the *intertext* is properly 'the text within which other texts reside or echo their presence' (126). However, in practice, the term has also been used of the *other* texts to which a particular text makes reference, so that Dante's *Inferno* becomes the intertext of Joseph Conrad's *Heart of Darkness*, which in turn becomes the intertext of *Apocalypse Now*. Montogomery *et al.* distinguish between a number of kinds of intertextuality including generic, parodic, and lastly poststructuralist accounts of intertextuality developed by Julia Kristeva and Roland Barthes. The term itself was coined by Kristeva, who views textuality as a 'permutation of texts, an intertextuality: in the space of a given text, several utterances, taken from other texts, intersect and neutralize one another' (cited in Hawthorn 126). Barthes goes even further: in his view all literary texts and indeed linguistic acts are intertextual recitations without origin or reference to external reality. In a famous formulation, he states:

> a text is ... a multi-dimensional space in which a variety of writings, none of them original, blend and clash. The text is a tissue of quotations drawn from innumerable centres of culture. (146)

This model of intertextuality is coterminous with the postmodern view of the text as ludic, parodic and multivocal. Of course, if all texts are intertexts, the original definition risks losing much of its meaning. Nevertheless it seems helpful to retain some conceptual framework and I will therefore adopt both Montgomery *et al.*'s distinction between literary allusion and radical intertextual reworking, and draw upon Rob Pope's further classification of modes of intertextuality. Pope distinguishes between explicit, implied and inferred intertextuality. *Explicit intertextuality* 'comprises all the other texts that are overtly referred to and all the specific sources the author has demonstrably drawn on' (236). *Implicit intertextuality* consists of passing allusions to other texts and is more subtle and indirect than explicit intertextuality. Finally, *inferred intertextuality* 'refers to all those texts which actual readers draw on to help their understanding of the text' (236). This last kind is obviously the most nebulous and difficult to prove, but is interesting to consider in relation to a writer such as Winterson whose work invites the reader actively to participate in its intertextual journeys through literary history.

Keeping the light: *Lighthousekeeping*

Lighthouse keeping is narrated by an orphan named Silver, who on the death of her parents is adopted by Pew, a blind lighthousekeeper in the imaginary Scottish town of Salts. Subsequently, Silver learns the history of the Cape Wrath lighthouse and the many stories that attach to it, including that of Babel Dark, a nineteenth-century Church minister in the town. Gradually, the reader learns Babel Dark's story; how he was born on the same day in 1828 that the lighthouse was completed; how he was named for the Biblical Tower of Babel; how as a young man he fell in love with and then abandoned a woman named Molly, who became pregnant. Babel subsequently becomes a minister and exiles himself to Salts. However, meeting Molly again by chance he realizes his mistake and begins a double life, spending ten months of the year in his Scottish parish unhappily married, and two months in Bristol with Molly and his child, a girl who like Silver is 'a child born of chance' (32), and like Pew is born blind and is to become the mother of a long line of Pews. Dark adopts the name 'Lux' while in Bristol and it is here that his happiest, light-filled days are spent. Dark's story ends after Molly realizes his betrayal and, heartbroken and disillusioned, he ends his life by walking into the sea. Pew and Silver are eventually forced to leave the lighthouse when mechanization is introduced; Silver travels first south to Bristol in search of Pew, and then to Capri and Athens in search of life and love. Following an interlude involving a breakdown and an encounter with an enigmatic female lover, the novel ends with Silver returning to the lighthouse and re-encountering Pew, who reaffirms both the importance of love and the power of stories.

Pew, the lighthousekeeper, is a timeless and mercurial figure who plays a major role in the novel's exploration of storytelling. 'There has always been a Pew in the lighthouse at Cape Wrath' (46), he tells Silver. He claims to have second sight and to have sailed in a ship that sank 200 years before. Like the lighthouse itself, Pew represents continuity, a constant in human affairs. Blind from birth, he lives in darkness but keeps the light alight, both by tending the lighthouse and by telling stories. Pew the lighthousekeeper is above all a storyteller, a purveyor of seamen's yarns and tall tales. Like Tiresias, another blind seer, he bears witness to events, unites opposites, and embodies contradictions. 'He was and he wasn't – that was Pew' (95), Winterson states, reminding the reader that stories are often about impossible things: 'the thing couldn't have happened, but it did' (127). What Silver learns from him is not merely how to operate the lighthouse, but how to tell stories: 'That's what you must learn. Both the ones I know and the ones I don't know' (40). Winterson develops the novel's refrain – 'keeping the light' – as a metaphor for storytelling:

> [E]very light had a story – no, every light *was* a story, and the flashes themselves were the stories going out over the waves, as markers and guides and comfort and warning. (41)

As in her other work, the novel insistently calls into the question the linearity and discreteness of narrative and the notion that stories can be said to begin or end. For example, in recounting the history of the Cape Wrath lighthouse, Winterson questions whether the story begins in 1828 when the lighthouse was built; in 1814 – when an Act of Parliament authorized the building of a lighthouse; in 1802 – the date of a terrible shipwreck off the coast; or further back to events in the life of the lighthouse's sponsor, Josiah Dark. This device of false starts, characteristic of metafiction, emphasizes the arbitrariness of narrative and the potentially limitless interconnections between stories.

As suggested, Winterson's use of intertextuality operates on many levels. Firstly, she makes playful use of character intertextuality. Pew the lighthousekeeper, Silver, the novel's female narrator, and DogJim, her pet, are of course named for the characters Blind Pew, Long John Silver and Jim Hawkins, from Stevenson's children's adventure novel, *Treasure Island* (1883). In an example of explicit allusion, Winterson invokes E. M. Forster's famous dictum 'Only connect', to describe the way lighthouses connect up across the world. As well as alluding to literary works, and drawing on the implications of contemporary scientific works such as Darwin's *On the Origin of Species* (implicitly alluding to intertextual allusions by writers such as John Fowles and A. S. Byatt), Winterson intertextualizes aspects of history and biography in imaginative and playful ways. For example, Robert Louis Stevenson's male relatives were indeed lighthouse engineers, and his grandfather Robert actually built the Cape Wrath lighthouse featured in Winterson's story:

> *Cape Wrath*. Position on the nautical chart, 58° 37.5°N, 5°W.
> Look at it – the headland is 368 feet high, wild, grand, impossible. Home to gulls and dreams. (12)

Built in 1828, the lighthouse was 66 feet tall and 523 feet above the sea at Cape Wrath, the northernmost point of mainland Britain. According to the Northern Lighthouse Board website, the name Cape Wrath, so suggestive of its stormy and forbidding location, and so suited to Winterson's purpose, actually derives from the Norse for 'turning point', apparently reflecting Norsemen navigational practice, turning their ships homeward when reaching it. Commenting on the history of the Stevenson family of engineers, Winterson writes:

> This was the day [1 February 1811] when a young engineer called Robert Stevenson completed work on a lighthouse at Bell Rock. This was more than the start of a lighthouse; it was the beginning of a dynasty. For 'lighthouse' read 'Stevenson'. They built scores of them until 1934 and the whole family was involved, brothers, sons, nephews, cousins. When one retired another was appointed. They were the Borgias of lighthousekeeping. (25)

In fact, Robert Louis also trained as an engineer, but ill-health prevented him following his father Thomas's career, and led him to take up first Law and then writing instead. In a series of bold and imaginative interconnections, Winterson has Babel Dark going to Salts in 1850, the same year that R. L. Stevenson was born, and Stevenson himself visiting Salts in 1886 when he discusses Darwin's theories with Babel Dark. Indeed, Darwin himself makes an earlier appearance in the town, dubbing it 'Fossil Town'. Of course, Winterson intends these fictional coincidences to be humorous ones, designed for the literary reader's amusement. There is no evidence of Darwin visiting the area, but Stevenson may well have done on family holidays in the Highlands and during visits to his father's and uncle's lighthouses. Stevenson spent weeks on the island of Erraid, off Mull, for example, when his father and uncle were building Dubh Artach lighthouse, completed in 1872. According to Winterson, 'Robert Louis came here [to Cape Wrath], as he came to all his family lighthouses' (26). And, in an interesting footnote to Stevenson's literary biography, he even wrote a history of the Stevenson family called *Records of a Family of Engineers*. In *Lighthousekeeping*, Winterson claims: 'The Stevensons and the Darks were almost related, in fact they were related, not through blood but through the restless longing that marks some individuals from others' (26). And, one could add, they are related intertextually, by the operation of Winterson's narrative. Finally, in an intertextual *coup de grâce*, Dark becomes in Winterson's text the very inspiration for *Jekyll and Hyde* as the rumour surrounding him causes Stevenson to explore in his fiction the theme of doubleness.

Arguably, the novel's most significant intertextual relations are with literary works by R. L. Stevenson and Virginia Woolf. *Lighthousekeeping* is premised on two sets of binary oppositions, which inform human culture in significant ways. The first of these is fixity and fluidity, symbolized by the lighthouse and the sea respectively, which Winterson establishes in the following terms:

> Look at this one. Made of granite, as hard and unchanging as the sea is fluid and volatile. The sea moves constantly, the lighthouse, never. There is no sway, no rocking, none of the motion of ships and ocean. (17)

This binary opposition refers intertextually to Virginia Woolf's *To the Lighthouse* (1927), a novel primarily concerned with the reconciliation of opposing principles, and which culminates in a momentous journey to a lighthouse and the completion of an artistic work. The second set of binaries, dark and light, symbolized by the two selves of the protagonist, Babel Dark and his alter ego, Lux, invokes Stevenson's *The Strange Case of Dr Jekyll and Mr Hyde* in its interest in split personality and the figure of the Doppelganger. Winterson's treatment of the two sets of binaries and their referents is moreover linked through the trope of light: the lighthouse's function is to light the passage of sailors, yet it does this by flashing a light at four-second intervals, therefore incorporating both light and dark.

Intertextualizing R. L. Stevenson's *The Strange Case of Dr Jekyll and Mr Hyde*

Stevenson's 1886 novel explores in exemplary fashion the theme of the doubleness of identity. Critics identify Stevenson's admiration for morally ambiguous heroes and anti-heroes, and point out the subtext of 'apprehension, sin and suffering' in his work, which has been attributed to a combination of the early influence of Calvinism and his ill-health (Drabble 938). But they also foreground Stevenson's delight in storytelling and romancing. Significantly, a radical Protestant upbringing and storytelling exuberance are also key features of Winterson's life and art. The main element that Winterson takes from Stevenson is his narrative of estrangement; both texts treat the theme of the strangeness or otherness of human identity. Winterson's character Babel Dark comes to see himself as 'a stranger in my own life' (*Lighthousekeeping* 64), while Jekyll learns to recognize:

> in my own person ... the thorough and primitive duality in man; I saw that, of the two natures that contended in my field of consciousness, even if I could rightly be said to be either, it was only because I was radically both. (*Jekyll and Hyde* 49)

And, like Winterson's Babel Dark, he desires and eventually finds a way to separate his two selves: 'If each ... could but be housed in separate identities, life would be relieved of all that was unbearable' (*ibid.*). Jekyll's life is in his own words, 'nine-tenths a life of effort, virtue and control' (51) just as Babel Dark spends ten months of the year as a dutiful minister in Salts. And, just as Dark's status as minister protects him, as a doctor, Jekyll can cover his tracks: 'I began to profit by the strange immunities of my position' (52).

However, Jekyll's two identities refuse to remain separate and discrete, and begin to cross over into each other's worlds. 'I was slowly losing hold of my original and better self, and becoming slowly incorporated with my second and worse' (55). Hyde is first caught knocking over a girl in the street and is traced back to Jekyll's house, and then Jekyll wakes up in his own bed as Edward Hyde. Similarly, Dark is seen by a traveller in Bristol. At this point in her narrative, Winterson directly quotes *Jekyll and Hyde* and draws the comparison between its tale of split personality and Babel Dark's double life:

'You understand me, Pew? I am Henry Jekyll.' He paused for a moment, looking at his hands, strong, long and studious. 'And I am Edward Hyde.' (187)

This episode intertextually invokes – and reverses – the moment in Stevenson's text when Jekyll looks down at his hand and realizes that he has woken as Hyde:

But the hand which I now saw, ... lying half shut on the bed clothes, was lean, corded, knuckly, of a dusky pallor, and thickly shaded with a smart growth of hair. It was the hand of Edward Hyde. (54)

Where Winterson's text differs significantly from Stevenson's is in providing details of her protagonist's other life. Jekyll has long indulged his 'low and shameful pleasures', but the reader is never told what these are. The implication, however, is that they are sexual in nature, one of any number of practices deemed unspeakable in Victorian society and left unsaid in Victorian literature. Similarly, Babel Dark's secret turns out to be sexual – his adulterous love for Molly; as Pew remarks: 'there's always a woman somewhere' (73). However, Winterson subverts the meanings of Dark's double life and his 'shameful pleasure' in a number of ways. 'The obvious equation was Dark = Jekyll, Lux = Hyde. The impossible truth was that in his life it was the reverse' (187). Winterson therefore transposes the meanings of dark and light in her postmodern reworking, inverting and blurring the binary. Dark is not so much like Jekyll, the better self, but Hyde, the debased and hateful incarnation, which is exemplified by his abuse of his wife, whom he 'treats like a dog', hitting and raping her and abandoning her at the Great Exhibition. Whereas, as Lux he becomes a somewhat better self, learning to love and trust another human being. The result, however, is as damaging as in Stevenson's tale: Molly 'had tried to earth him. Instead, she had split him' (101). And, keeping her in the dark about his family in Salts, he betrays her a second time.

At the end of Stevenson's text, finding himself 'still cursed with my duality of purpose' (57), Dr Jekyll takes the powders that will end his own life and transforms him into the diabolical Hyde permanently. Winterson's narrative differs slightly; Dark walks into the sea and ends the lives of both Dark and Lux. Her reading of the Stevenson text is interpolated into the novel:

'Do you know the story of *Jekyll and Hyde*?'
'Of course.'
'Well then – to avoid either extreme, it is necessary to find all the lives in between.' (161)

This may be interpreted as a plea to go beyond the binary and acknowledge the multiplicity of identity, much as Woolf urges in *To the Lighthouse*.

Intertextualizing science: Darwin and Freud

Underlying the theme of duality are two major discourses of nineteenth-
century and early twentieth-century thought: the Darwinian theory of
evolution and the Freudian theory of the unconscious. This develops
Winterson's well-established interests in scientific theory and science as
metaphor, tracing on a literary level what Darwin identified in terms of
human evolution: the interconnections and interrelationships between
things, whether these be species or texts. The novel may be seen as
mapping a kind of tree of life of stories; as she writes, a series of 'stories
layered by time' (39). Nineteenth-century science becomes the trigger for a
revolution in consciousness in both texts: chemistry in *Jekyll and Hyde*,
natural history in *Lighthousekeeping*. In one episode in Winterson's novel,
Babel Dark's dog falls down the Cliffside. Rescuing him, Dark discovers a
cave filled with fossils of ferns and seahorses, a find so significant in terms
of natural history that Darwin himself visits Salts to examine the fossils
(19). What it demonstrates to an astonished Dark is that the universe is
constantly evolving and transforming itself. Yet, Dark regrets the loss of a
stable, God-given world. 'That things might be endlessly moving was not
his wish' (119). Of Darwin, Winterson states, 'In nature, he found not past,
present and future, as we recognise them, but an evolutionary process of
change – energy trapped for too long – life always becoming' (150). What
she takes from Darwinism is not so much the 'fixity' of scientific laws but
the fluidity, variety and unpredictability of life that they point to. Pew
teaches Silver a similar lesson that 'everything can be recovered, not as it
was, but in its changing form': 'Nothing keeps the same form forever,
child, not even Pew' (150). Ironically, 'progress' comes to Salts and Pew is
retired from his job so that the lighthouse can be mechanized as indeed it
was in 1998. On his last day, Pew leaves Silver a first edition copy of
Darwin's *On the Origin of Species* and Stevenson's *Jekyll and Hyde* along with
Babel Dark's diaries.

    Moreover, in a fictionalized conversation, Dark and R. L. Stevenson
discuss split personality and atavism. Winterson imagines Stevenson's
enthusiasm for Darwinian theory as he speculates on its implications for
human identity:

> 'A man might be two men', said Stevenson, 'and not know it, or he might
> discover that he had to act on it. And those two men would be of very differ-
> ent kinds. One upright and loyal, the other, perhaps, not much better than
> an ape.' (164)

Here Winterson attributes to Stevenson a conception of the self that
combines Darwin's notion of evolution and Freud's theory of a self radically

split by the unconscious: 'Aren't we saying that there must be more to man than we choose to know, or indeed more than he chooses to know about himself?' (164). As a forerunner of Freud's theories of the ego, superego and id, or unconscious desire, Stevenson's text explores too the concept of repression and its inevitable failure: 'My devil had long been caged, he came out roaring' (56). Similarly, Dark clearly represents the 'dark' side of nineteenth-century scientific progress: the unexplained, shameful, irrational side, the side theorized most explicitly by Freud. And, partly prompted by his own guilt, in an example of Freudian disavowal, Dark's reaction is to repudiate Stevenson's words and insist on man's wholeness. However, Stevenson has heard the story of Dark's double life in Bristol and Dark finally confesses the truth, enabling Winterson's conceit that Babel Dark's life story becomes Stevenson's novel.

Winterson's text provides a coda to Darwin's theory of natural selection and the scientific principles on which it is based. She identifies 1859 as a key date in Western cultural history as the date of publication of Darwin's *On the Origin of Species*, and the completion of Richard Wagner's opera *Tristan and Isolde*. In classically structuralist fashion, she presents them as representing polar tendencies within the culture:

> Darwin — objective, scientific, empirical, quantifiable.
> Wagner — subjective, poetic, intuitive, mysterious. (169)

The novel is in part a meditation on these two poles and on how they may be reconciled. Although not endorsing Babel's dark and mystical world view, it nevertheless suggests that while evolution may explain the physical world, it cannot account for intangibles like human subjectivity and desire. As the narrator states:

> In the fossil record of our existence, there is no trace of love. You cannot find it held in the earth's crust, waiting to be discovered. The long bones of our ancestors show nothing of their hearts. Their last meal is sometimes preserved in peat or in ice, but their thoughts and feelings are gone. (170)

It is the task of the storyteller — and the poet and the composer — to 'trace love'. Yet, in doing so Winterson utilizes science as trope, and scientific discourse becomes the means of exploring such intangibles. Indeed her intertextual method of layering narratives may be seen in terms of the fossil motif, as she interleaves diverse stories of life on earth in the metaphorical cave of the text.

Intertextualizing Virginia Woolf's *To the Lighthouse*

Winterson's intertextual use of Woolf's *To the Lighthouse* is more muted and implicit than her use of *Jekyll and Hyde*, despite a direct allusion to Woolf's novel early on in the text: 'There was only forward, northwards into the sea. To the lighthouse' (19). The selfsame allusion to Woolf's contributes Winterson's title and the novel's major motif, the lighthouse; and through a combination of implication and inference, it contributes to some of its major themes: life as a journey, human striving, longing and loss. Woolf's representation of the lighthouse is a more externalized one than Winterson's: her characters never go inside it. For James, at the end of the novel, it is merely 'a stark tower on a bare rock' (193). However, throughout the text its appearance and meaning are determined by the perception and subjectivity of the viewer; as Lily states 'so much depends upon distance' (182). In a now often-cited passage of the novel, Woolf develops this radical interpretivist epistemology through the character of James:

> 'It will rain,' he remembered his father saying. 'You won't be able to go to the Lighthouse.'
>
> The Lighthouse was then a silvery, misty-looking tower with a yellow eye that opened suddenly and softly in the evening. Now —
>
> James looked at the Lighthouse. He could see the white-washed rocks; the tower, stark and straight; he could see that it was barred with black and white; he could see windows in it; he could even see washing spread on the rocks to dry. So that was the Lighthouse, was it?
>
> No, the other was also the Lighthouse. For nothing was simply one thing. The other was the Lighthouse too. (177)

This conception of the dual, indeed multiple, nature of things is echoed in Winterson's work. She shares the Woolfian and modernist denial of objective reality and the belief in the subjectivism and multifariousness of life. However, in this instance she pursues the implications of this further than Woolf, into the structure of the text itself. At the end of *To the Lighthouse*, the travellers achieve their goal and Lily the painter completes her artwork: 'It was done, it was finished ... I have had my vision' (198). There is a clear sense of an ending. In Winterson's postmodern textual universe there is no such closure. 'There's no such thing as an ending' (49), she writes; 'there is no continuous narrative, there are lit-up moments, and the rest is dark' (134); and 'the story of life' is simply 'one that begins again' (109). If, for Woolf, the lighthouse is a shifting signifier, in Winterson's text it is at once less forbidding and more comforting. As home to the blind visionary Pew and the orphan Silver, the lighthouse is not so much a symbol of phallic mastery as a beacon 'calling you home', a place of safety and small domestic rituals. Yet, paradoxically, in a playful, shifting postmodernist text, it also appears as an absolute value: a fixed point in a turning world. However, while the text acknowledges the importance of binary terms as organizing principles of culture, it works either to reveal their constant interplay or to blur the distinction between them, in order to emphasize the multiplicity of life and narrative.

Moreover, Woolf's exploration of 'masculine' and 'feminine' experience, representing the binary opposition between the objective and subjective modes, the rational and 'will to power' versus the emotional and relational, which are embodied in Mr and Mrs Ramsay, is echoed in Winterson's text in Babel Dark's split personality and his struggle between scientific and religious world views. Like Mr Ramsay, Babel Dark refuses to relinquish his rigid binary code and embrace difference. Using similar phallic imagery to Woolf, Winterson describes his final diary entry in which he aligns himself with the lighthouse: '*I stood firm. I stood firm. I stood firm*' (188). In one sense, Woolf's text could be said to 'mother' Winterson's, as Stevenson's and Darwin's 'father' it: through Woolf it is the female line of influence that emphasizes the unknowability and mystery of human experience, the male line through Darwin that asserts a world of empirical facts. Stevenson's *Jekyll and Hyde* is poised between these two opposites, acknowledging the irrational and unconscious aspects of human experience but unable to valorize them. In reworking Stevenson and Woolf, Winterson is gendering the relationship between the texts and, to some extent, regendering the narratives themselves. *Jekyll and Hyde* describes an archetypally male experience; similarly, *To the Lighthouse* represents a classic work of female modernism − a fluid, almost plotless text, foregrounding relationships, internal landscapes and the secret self. Winterson appropriates and transforms these gendered trajectories in order, as in her other work, to go beyond gender and multiply sexuality. In Woolf's text it is Lily Briscoe who, as a woman artist open to the feminine realm yet maintaining an aesthetic distance from it through her art, manages most successfully to resolve the binary opposition. In Winterson's text, it is Silver, another marginal and lonely figure, and a female lover of women, defined by her desire for both love and independence, who challenges convention and the fixity of identity. Silver, as a woman, faces the same dilemma as Babel Dark and, Winterson suggests, as all of us:

> What should I do about the wild and the tame? The wild heart that wants to be free, and the tame heart that wants to come home? (198)

It is the question of the need to belong versus the desire to break free, of constancy and familiarity versus difference and otherness, posed in different but connected ways by Stevenson's Dr Jekyll and by Woolf's Lily Briscoe, and by Winterson herself in the novel's intertextual meditation on identity, love and storytelling.

Notes

1. For example, in her novels of the late 1980s, *The Passion* and *Sexing the Cherry*, Winterson explores multiple conceptions of love, identity and selfhood in the contexts of carnival Venice during the Napoleonic Wars and mid-seventeenth-century London respectively.

Bibliography and further reading

Winterson, Jeanette. *Oranges Are Not the Only Fruit*. London: Pandora, 1988.
——. *The Passion*. London: Penguin, 1988.
——. *Sexing the Cherry*. London: Vintage, 1990.
——. *Lighthousekeeping*. London and New York: Fourth Estate, 2004.
Apocalypse Now. Film, dir. Francis Ford Coppola. Paramount Home Entertainment, 1979.
Bakhtin, Mikhail. *The Dialogic Imagination: Four Essays by M. M. Bakhtin*. Trans. Caryl Emerson and Michael Holquist. Austin, TX: University of Texas Press, 1994.
Barthes, Roland. 'The death of the author', in *Image-Music-Text*. Stephen Heath (ed.) and trans., London: Fontana, 1977: 155–64.
Conrad, Joseph. *Heart of Darkness*. London: Penguin Popular Classics, 1994 [1899].
Dante, Alghieri. *The Inferno*. New York: Signet, 2001.
Darwin, Charles. *On the Origin of Species*. London: Wordsworth, 1998 [1859].
Drabble, Margaret (ed.). *The Oxford Companion to English Literature*. Oxford: Oxford University Press, 1985.
Hawthorn, Jeremy. *A Glossary of Contemporary Literary Theory*. London: Edward Arnold, 1992.
Montgomery, Martin, Alan Durant, Nigel Fabb, Tom Furniss and Sara Mills (eds). *Ways of Reading: Advanced Reading Skills for Students of English Literature*. London and New York: Routledge, 1992.
Northern Lighthouse Board. 'Cape Wrath lighthouse.' 23 July 2005, www.nlb. org.uk/ourlights/history/capewrath.htm.
Pope, Rob. *The English Studies Book*. London and New York: Routledge, 1998.
Propp, Vladimir. *Morphology of the Folktale*. Louis A. Wagner (ed.), trans. Scott, Laurence. Austin, TX: University of Texas Press, 1968.
Stevenson, Robert Louis. *Treasure Island*. London: Penguin, 1994 [1883].
——. *The Strange Case of Dr Jekyll and Mr Hyde*. London: Penguin, 2004 [1886].
——. *Records of a Family of Engineers*. London: Heron Books, 1969 [1912].
Woolf, Virginia. *To the Lighthouse*. London: Vintage, 1992 [1927].

Section Four: Histories

Introduction

ROD MENGHAM AND PHILIP TEW

One of the most important growth areas in the literature of the last few decades has been historical fiction. This has ranged from popular equivalents of costume drama to a number of extraordinarily interesting and challenging explorations of literary genre. This section will be introduced with the brief examination of an exemplary work of post-millennial historical fiction, Barry Unsworth's *The Songs of the Kings* (2002). This analysis addresses certain themes relevant to the consideration of this sub-genre and its analysis in the chapters that follow, including its at least implicitly mythopoeic qualities and its rendition of accounting for the past.

Unsworth sets himself the task of rewriting the story of Iphigeneia, or rather of that episode at Tauris when the Greek fleet is waiting for a favourable wind to carry it over to Troy. The Trojan War is constructed as the imagined origin of modern political manipulation, of the abuse of language by those in power; as the mythical starting point for modern ideas of patriotic duty, national self-identity and the common good, all pursued as the merest pretext for economic and military expansion. The most powerful figures in this scenario are not warriors but advisors.

Ulysses, insignificant in terms of wealth, territory and military strength, is nevertheless the most influential character in the book, solely because of his rhetorical skills. It is Ulysses who generates the stories most people believe in, not Homer. The blind poet is seen here as a mere instrument; not the initiator of stories, but their adaptor, a skilled technician who adds to the stock of mythical tales a series of contemporary references and analogies under instruction from his political masters.

Literature comes into being precisely in order to circulate official versions of the truth. If it is not already clear how this set of relations might bear on contemporary issues concerning the role of fiction in an era when political and economic power depends on control of the flow of information, Unsworth makes clear the extent to which history as an unfinished process can be understood as a form of narrative for which there is no definitive version, only a succession of competing versions. *The Songs of the Kings* conforms to the model of historical fiction as a stratified text, not in respect of a particular geographical location (as in the writings of Adam

Thorpe and Iain Sinclair), but in respect of that moment when an Indo-European language and society passed from the conditions of an oral culture into the beginnings of literacy.

Paradoxically, the very process of writing down the stories of the *Iliad* and the *Odyssey* raised the spectre of a definitive version for the first time in the history of narrating their basic materials. For Unsworth, that would mean transfixing the dynamic relationship of official and unofficial versions, a relationship that he surveys sceptically, sardonically, but also elegiacally.

The elegiac imperative, together with its sardonic shadow, a shadow cast by modern knowingness, is also to be found in the works of Thorpe, Pat Barker, A. S. Byatt and Sarah Waters, where it is infused with the determination to reimagine the traditional or conventional patterns of commemoration and to reactivate the dynamic nature of a relationship between spokesmanship and testimony, between those stories that are remembered and those that are forgotten, between narratives of power and forms of resistance to that power.

Bibliography

Unsworth, Barry. *The Songs of the Kings*. London: Hamish Hamilton, 2002.

CHAPTER THIRTEEN

Pat Barker's *Regeneration* Trilogy

NICK HUBBLE

The ghosts of modernity

In Pat Barker's most recent novel, *Double Vision* (2003), a journalist surveys the site of a recent burglary and finds his stereotypical ideas of the reality of burglary undermined by unbidden images of rape and torture:

> One pool of blood in the kitchen, another in the living room, and everywhere, on every window, every door, every piece of furniture, clustering thickly around doorknobs and latches, grey fingerprints, handprints, thumbprints, everywhere, as if the house were suffering from an infestation of ghosts. (250)

Such moments in which characters become conscious of the repressed elemental forces straining against the constructed meanings of modern reality occur throughout Barker's fiction. In her first novel, *Union Street* (1982), 11-year-old Kelly Brown is scared by the appearance of a man in black on a fairground ghost train: simultaneously the lingering impression of a man she had met in the park earlier and the harbinger of her impending rape. Similar uncanny experiences occur in Barker's other early novels, including descriptions of séances in both *Liza's England* (originally published as *This Century's Daughter* in 1986, before being republished under Barker's original choice of title in 1996) and *The Man Who Wasn't There* (1989). This tendency has developed since the *Regeneration* trilogy – *Regeneration* (1991), *The Eye in the Door* (1993) and *The Ghost Road* (1995) – into a fully realized psychosocial landscape in which different planes of existence overlap and interact with different forms of class, gender and sexual consciousness. The wider transition in Barker's work, therefore, has been from the supernatural marking the imminent onset of unavoidable fate to its signifying a series of human possibilities, which haunt the present but do not always come to pass. The characters in her later fiction can see in more than one world and sometimes cross the borders between these domains.

For reasons of space, this chapter will not discuss her two most recent books, but concentrate on the trilogy and *Another World* (1998) in order to chart in detail how this transition came about. Barker playfully acknowledges this change in *The Ghost Road* during a scene remembered by the anthropologist-turned-military-psychologist, W. H. R. Rivers:

Hocart, though, was in a mood to tease. 'Why've I got death when you've got sex?' he wanted to know. 'Ghosts and sex don't go together. Now ghosts and *death* ...'

'All right, you can have ghosts.'

'*No* ...' Hocart began, and then laughed.

Not true anyway, Rivers thought. On Eddystone ghosts and sex *did* go together ... (133)

Rivers, of course, is a historical character, who we find at the beginning of the trilogy treating the equally historical war poets, Siegfried Sassoon and Wilfred Owen, and Barker's fictional creation, working-class officer Billy Prior, for shell shock at Craiglockhart hospital in 1917. From this point, the action broadens out to embrace the state suppression of pacifism and homosexuality as it follows its central characters through to the end of the war. The 'infestation of ghosts' across the trilogy ranges from the dead soldiers who appear regularly to Sassoon and others to the whistling of departing souls that Rivers recalls hearing years before during his anthropological fieldwork on Eddystone in the Soloman Islands. An indicative moment occurs during the first meeting between Owen and Sassoon at Craiglockhart, when Owen uses his sense for the supernatural to break through surface reality in a manner reminiscent of Barker's earlier novels:

Sometimes when you're alone, in the trenches, I mean, at night you get the sense of something *ancient*. As if the trenches had always been there. You know one trench we held, it had skulls in the side. You looked back along and ... Like mushrooms. And do you know, it was actually *easier* to believe they were men from Marlborough's army than to to to think they'd been alive two years ago. It's as if all other wars had somehow ... distilled themselves into this war. (*Regeneration* 83)

However, Sassoon's reply marks the appearance of a new kind of vision:

I had a similar experience. Well, I don't know whether it is similar. I was going up with the rations one night and I saw the limbers against the skyline, and the flares going up. What you see every night. Only I seemed to be seeing it from the future. A hundred years from now they'll still be ploughing up skulls. And I seemed to be in that time and looking back. I think I saw our ghosts. (*Regeneration* 84)

John Brannigan argues that by having Owen present the war as the distillation of all wars and the end of history, while Sassoon describes it from the perspective of the future as history in the making, Barker draws our attention to the 'displaced temporality' of the First World War and its consequences for the way we experience life today: 'The war is, at one and the same time, the repetition of the 'timeless' mythic story of Abraham and Isaac, and the decisive moment of epochal shift from the Victorian faith in progress and civilisation to the postmodern scepticism of the twentieth century' (Brannigan 52). A sense of this epochal shift is already present in the poems of Sassoon and Owen. In *Regeneration*, Barker nicely captures Sassoon's assistance with Owen's 'Anthem for Doomed Youth' (141–2, 156–8), the poem which did more than any other to show how the unprecedented ferocity and mass destruction of the war was too excessive to be contained within any conventional myth of generational sacrifice:

> What passing-bells for those who die as cattle?
> Only the monstrous anger of the guns.

Irony is used to fracture the combination of romantic literary language and traditional imagery in the symbolic order which had underpinned the cohesion of nineteenth-century society. This divorce from the possibility of ritual transcendence seems to render the soldiers as little more than the embodiment of passive suffering – an impression which is enforced by Owen's own suggestion that his dominant theme was pity (see Monteith 78; Garth 302) – and suggests that the field of human agency is strictly curtailed to domestic matters. The resultant crisis of representation has been felt ever since across all forms of Western culture, but most acutely when confronted by other events that pass beyond rational understanding such as the Holocaust.

However, many of the individuals caught up in these types of events – including both soldiers and poets of the First World War – have exhibited behaviour that flatly contradicts the retrospective imposition of passive victimhood. From the perspective of the future, as Barker has Sassoon imagine it, such human beings appear as ghosts who haunt modernity. The irony attendant on the reception of their own poetry condemning the poets themselves to become part of this myth of passivity has always been particularly apt with respect to Sassoon, who occasionally lets his anti-war mask slip:

> Sweet Sister, grant your soldier this:
> That in good fury he may feel
> The body where he sets his heel
> Quail from your downward darting kiss.

This poem, 'The Kiss', rarely appears in the anthologies of First World War poetry and in one place where it does, the school collection *Men Who March Away* edited by I. M. Parsons (37), a disclaimer by Sassoon is included (17). Yet, Barker has a sympathetic character in *The Eye in the Door* describe it as his best poem:

> I think that's the strongest poem he's ever written ... You know he's a tremendously successful and *bloodthirsty* platoon commander, and yet at the same time, back in billets, out comes the notebook. Another anti-war poem.

And the poem uses the experience of the platoon commander, but it never uses any of his attitudes. And yet for once, in that *one* poem, he gets both versions of himself in. (158)

One of Barker's aims in the trilogy is to include both such versions of the war poets. In *Regeneration,* Owen reconciles these apparently opposed viewpoints by finding a way to celebrate the 'pride in the sacrifice' of his doomed youth which does not collapse into War Office propaganda: 'There's a point beyond which you can't press the meaninglessness. Even if the courage is being abused, it's still ...' (157). This notion of a courage with the power to transcend the meaninglessness of war can also be found in the writing of another First World War veteran, J. R. R. Tolkien. John Garth's *Tolkien and the Great War* (2003) explains how Tolkien's experiences on the Somme were linked to his development of the concept of 'eucatastrophe' to describe the sudden turn, or escape from seemingly unavoidable defeat, which is not escapism or even success, but the movement of courage beyond meaning and, therefore, beyond fate (see 264–5, 293–4, 303–4). By rewriting the history of the First World War, Barker shifts the focus of our understanding from pity at passive suffering to wonder at this courage that goes beyond meaning – in Sassoon, Owen and Prior – so that success or failure and even life or death become irrelevant. By bringing these ghosts to the foreground, she holds up the dominant cultural representations of modernity to historical challenge.

Outside history

Barker's need to challenge the normative forms of cultural representation can be identified in her work before the trilogy. Her first two novels, *Union Street* and *Blow Your House Down* (1984), are uncompromising accounts of working-class women leavened only by sudden moments of eucatastrophe depicted with a Lawrentian intensity. For example, Kelly in *Union Street* (65) and Maggie in *Blow Your House Down* (170) both experience epiphanies figured by sunset bird choruses that allow them to transcend everyday horrors and gain control over their own lives. However, as critics such as Margaretta Jolly have noted, the depiction of the majority of the 'characters' own submission to and even complicity in their degradation' (Jolly 236) is so harrowing that there appears to be no solution for them in conventional political terms.

These books were not written to expose social problems and encourage reforms, but to critically examine gender roles and relations in the working class by focusing on the effect of historical strains on the generational cycles which reproduce and intensify patterns of behaviour. As Sharon Monteith points out in *Pat Barker*, the communities in these two books are communities in transition 'located between an industrial past and a post-industrial future' (5). On one level this means that the early books can be said to deal with the breakdown during the 1970s and 1980s of the relatively stable consensual society – with its class- and gender-based division of labour – that had been enshrined following the cultural upheaval of the First World War. However, on another level, they also raise the question as to whether that whole 60-year period was any more than a particularly prolonged process of transition. In *Union Street*, this idea is embodied in the 76-year-old Alice Bell, who relives the nodal moments of a working-class woman's life – girlhood (250–2), husbands (254), childbirth (259), mother's death (261) – in a series of flashbacks. In *Liza's England*, Barker returns to this device of embodying the transition from industrial past to post-industrial future in the life of one working-class woman. A striking illustration of this long transition is created by the realization of Stephen (64), Liza's gay social worker, that the big house in which he has a flat was the former home of the factory-owning family for whom Liza's mother did the 'rough cleaning' (28) before the First World War. This same idea, of a Victorian past underwriting a modern present, was treated rather differently by Barker 12 years later in *Another World*. In *Liza's England*, the possibility of an alternative fuller life outside history is present in Liza's and Stephen's shared dreams of the dancing figures on the outside of Liza's box of keepsakes, but there is no sense of escape from the bleak landscape of the present – in which Liza is killed as the result of a break-in by drunken youths – other than through individual transcendence. In *Another World*, the modern dysfunctional family of psychology lecturer Nick, his partner Fran, their young child and their other two children (one each) from former relationships, are decorating their huge Victorian house when they uncover an obscene mural of the house's original inhabitants:

> Victorian paterfamilias, wife and children: two sons, a daughter. Pinned out, exhibited. Even without the exposed penis, the meticulously delineated and hated breasts, you'd have sensed the tension in this family, with the golden-haired toddler at its dark centre. (40)

The obvious similarity to the modern family is rendered sinister by the discovery that the two elder siblings in the mural subsequently murdered their brother. A number of supernatural visitations seem, as in Barker's earlier fiction, to herald the unavoidability of the same fate for the modern-day toddler. Yet this possibility is counterbalanced and ultimately out-weighed by the story of Nick's grandfather, Geordie, a centenarian veteran of the Somme.

The character of Geordie allows Barker to embody the transition from industrial past to post-industrial future in a working-class man whose formative experiences occurred in the trenches of the First World War. The transition is charted by the different ways in which Geordie coped with his memories at different stages in his life: he refused to answer questions for decades and only began to talk in the 1960s, but then as his rarity value grew and demand increased, his willingness increased so that by the 1990s 'he was sought after, listened to, he had friends, interests, a purpose in life at an age when old people are too often sitting alone in chilly rooms waiting for their relatives to phone' (82). The reasons for these changes fascinate Helen, the oral historian introduced by Nick to his grandad, who concludes that he continually reworks his memories to fit in with changing public perceptions of the war. She urges him to address those areas which still remain hidden: questions of class, masculinity and sexuality. Yet, as Geordie insists, and Nick comes to realize, his memories do not change: 'For Helen, memories are infinitely malleable, but not for Geordie. Geordie's past isn't over. It isn't even the past' (241). The fact that Geordie's tendency to continually relive the moment when he killed his fatally injured brother in no man's land is diagnosed as a symptom of post-traumatic stress disorder only provokes Nick to anger:

> It's too easy to dismiss somebody else's lived experience as a symptom of this, that, or the other pathology: to label it, disinfect it, store it away neatly in slim buff files and prevent it making dangerous contact with the experience of normal people. But suppose, Nick wants to shout at rows of faceless white-coats, suppose you're wrong and he was right. Suppose time can slow down ... Suppose Geordie experienced time differently, because, for him, time was different? (271)

Barker exposes the dominant myths and cultural discourses of modernity with a re-enactment of the past that becomes an act of the present – an act of radical human agency because, in the Nietzschean sense, beyond good or evil.

Early in the novel we learn how Nick and Geordie's recent trip to the battlefields and cemeteries of northern France had been part of an attempt by Geordie 'to graft his memories on to Nick' (74). By the end of the book, this process has been completed and an inter-generational transition has occurred similar to that between Liza and Stephen in *Liza's England*. The difference from the earlier book is that here the landscape of the present *does* seem to have altered decisively – as signified by the decision of Nick's stepson Gareth not to rub Nick's toothbrush round the inside of the toilet bowl as usual (274) – so that there is a clear prospect of things changing for the better. This is because by coming to understand that the past is really another part of the present, the characters learn that it 'never threatens anything as simple or avoidable as repetition' (278) and thus escape from the mechanisms of historical fate.

However, the characters' increased capacity to act freely outside history also lies in their greater ease with their own sexuality. Nick and Fran might sometimes be repelled by each other's bodies and sexual desires but they are fully aware of them as part of their everyday lives, which is to say that they are conscious of what formerly would have been con-sidered unconscious drives. Therefore, they are not shocked by the openly displayed sexuality of the Victorian family in the mural they uncover, and so ultimately remain immune to its potential uncanny power. Freud argues in 'Beyond the Pleasure Principle' that time and space are abstract ideas produced by the way that consciousness is constructed and so have no value in the workings of the unconscious (see 295–7, 299–300). Therefore, it is not coincidental that as the wider sexual awareness of post-industrial British society has radically weakened the once-firm dividing line between consciousness and the unconscious, so the hold of clock and calendar time has also diminished. Geordie experiences the past as 'like falling through a trapdoor into another room, and it's still going on' (264–5). Nick comes to learn that sexuality provides a different means of crossing the border as not only Geordie's memories are grafted to him but also Geordie's sexual desire for Helen. This is only consummated after Geordie's death, when Nick and Helen listen to the tape in which he describes how he killed his brother, and so find themselves transported beyond the modern boundaries of time and space. Ultimately, it is this sexual experience that allows Nick to understand that Geordie's condition is not pathological because it shows him how one can move outside history.

Regenerative pastoral

Regeneration was originally intended as a single novel. Only after Barker failed to achieve any 'sense of completion' despite repeatedly rewriting the final chapter did she decide to extend the project into a trilogy (Stevenson 175–6). Monteith suggests that this extension responds to the challenge of 'saying the unspeakable': 'in *The Ghost Road* she has Prior assay that, if the war were to last a hundred years, there might be found a language to say it in' (Monteith 67). However, if we read the war through Barker's eyes as not some sort of irruption into modernity but actually an intensification of the ongoing twentieth-century transition from an industrial past to a post-industrial future, we can observe an underlying process that has lasted for more than a hundred years. From this perspective, Barker's use of contemporary idiom, such as Prior describing walking towards a line of machine guns as 'sexy' (*Regeneration* 78), is not so much 'to ensure that the reader never loses sight of the fact that the meaning of the First World War persists and changes for each generation' (Monteith 69) as to indicate that we *do* now possess a language capable of 'saying the unspeakable': a language of sexual- and self-awareness that can penetrate the borders of the unconscious. This is demonstrated throughout the trilogy by the way that Prior is continually able to articulate exactly those questions of class, masculinity and sexuality that Geordie is unable to address in *Another World*. In this respect, the latter novel is closer to social realism, while the trilogy deploys the more self-consciously fictional device of inserting a character with late-twentieth-century sensibilities into an otherwise naturalistic depiction of the First World War.

Like other Barker characters, Prior's function at one level is to relive certain archetypal working-class experiences but, because he is free from the contextual boundaries of the period where he has been located and is — in the words of his father — 'neither fish nor fowl' (*Regeneration* 57) in terms of class, sexuality and gender, he is able to represent not so much working-class consciousness as the working-class unconscious. Various stages of which are recapitulated by his sexual encounters across the trilogy: breaking all taboos with Mrs Riley who had breast-fed him as an infant (*The Eye in the Door* 118); farcically coupling with his girlfriend Sarah while her mother is at the cinema (*The Ghost Road* 79–83); achieving communion with the German enemy through sex with a teenage French boy in a newly liberated village (247–8). However, his most telling liaison is with a fellow officer in *The Eye in the Door*. Realizing that Charles Manning cannot 'let go sexually with a social equal', Prior removes his uniform jacket, lights a cigarette, roughens his accent and transforms himself 'into the sort of working-class boy Manning would think it was all right to fuck' (*The Eye in the Door* 11). The potential antagonism of the situation is then exacerbated by Manning taking Prior into a servant's bedroom.

The hierarchical ordering seems obvious but events confound the reader's expectations as it is Prior who proceeds to take the active role and Manning who subsequently admits that 'I needed that ... I needed a good fucking' (14). The revolution proceeds full circle when the pair eventually agree to 'turn and turn about' (17). Prior reflects on the complexity of this interaction as he strokes Manning: 'how impossible it is to sum up sex in terms of who stuffs what into where. This movement of this hand had in it lust; resentment, of Manning's use of the room among other things; sympathy for the wound; envy, because Manning was *honourably* out of it' (13). This self-awareness allows the sexual encounter, which would otherwise be confined to a moment outside time and space, to become the basis of lasting mutual recognition: transcending the false equality of equivalent social rank because it highlights inequality and difference to the point that they become desired by, and thus fully interchangeable between, both participants.

It is precisely the absence of such mutuality in the psychoanalytical encounter with Rivers which arouses Prior's ire: 'All the questions from *you*, all the answers from *me*. Why can't it be both ways?' (*Regeneration* 50). This is a valid criticism of psychoanalysis: the fact that a hierarchical relationship is always maintained between analyst and patient shows how its purpose is always the restoration of the traditional symbolic order and not the recognition of its insights which interrogate that order. It is this hierarchical bias which accounts for the otherwise paradoxical process of curing shell-shocked soldiers in order to send them back to the war, which was responsible for their condition in the first place. However, this does not mean that Barker endorses the widely held view that Sassoon's return to France represents a defeat: 'defeat by therapy and by the framing of his anti-war protest as neurosis' (Monteith 56).

For, as she shows, while Rivers employed psychoanalytical techniques, his essential understanding was quite different to that of conventional psychoanalysis, taking its cue from the experiments on nerve regeneration he had conducted with the neurologist Henry Head before the war. They had cut Head's radial nerve and spent five years charting its regeneration. The sensation returned in two stages: the protopathic, an extreme all-or-nothing response, was gradually overlaid by the epicritic, in which proportionate response was restored. The ambiguity of this duality is revealed by Rivers' reflections on the pilomotor reflex, by which the hairs on the back of the hand raise:

> For Head it was awakened by poetry, for Rivers, more than once, it had been the beauty of a scientific hypothesis ... What had intrigued Rivers most was that human beings should respond to the highest mental and spiritual achievements of their culture with the same reflex that raises the hairs on a dog's back. The epicritic grounded in the protopathic, the ultimate expression of the unity we persist in regarding as the condition of perfect health.
>
> Though why we think of it like that, God knows, since most of us survive by cultivating internal divisions. (*The Eye in the Door* 232–3)

As Rivers is aware, the disassociation demanded by society places an intolerable burden on the individual. This burden is exacerbated in an individual like Sassoon, who has internally divided into pacifist anti-war poet and bloodthirsty company commander. Rivers realizes that the more extreme the first side of Sassoon's character is allowed to become – as it has with his public protest – the more unbearable the second side will become to him. Therefore, Rivers identifies Sassoon's protest as a neurosis which has to be treated because otherwise it will lead to an irreconcilable breakdown. What Rivers does gently but persistently is to reconcile Sassoon to the military side of his personality for the good of his own psychic health, as in the scene where he gently persuades him to change out of his pyjamas and into his uniform (261). Barker does not so much privilege therapy over war protest, as privilege a regenerative under-standing of psychic healing over Freudian therapy, which remains subordinate to a hierarchical order.

Monteith and Nahem Yousaf relate this regenerative component in Barker's fiction to her use of the pastoral form. Referring to the 'soldier-poet' as a figure consciously combining protopathic with epicritic sensi-bilities, who is alive to the 'chaos of feelings' and so capable of witnessing hope in the misery of war, they argue that a similar dialectic 'is carried over in the war photographer's facility for standing both inside and outside a moment to extrapolate meaning from it' (Monteith and Yousaf 297). Ronald Paul has also discussed Barker's work in terms of pastoral, and cites William Empson's description of the 'essential trick of the old pastoral, which was felt to imply a beautiful relation between rich and poor', in order to argue that 'classic First World War fiction' depends on the 'pastoral conventions of such fictionalised encounters between high (officers) and low (soldiers)' (Paul 149). However, a different way of thinking this through would consider how Empson's *Some Versions of Pastoral* classifies these 'low' and 'high' characters as operating in a pastoral text at the first and second levels of 'comic primness' – 'double irony in the acceptance of a convention' – but also allows for a third level where the enjoyer gets the joke at both levels:

> For this pleasure of effective momentary simplification the arguments of the two sides must be pulling their weight on the ironist, and though he might be sincerely indignant if told so it is fair to call him conscious of them. A character who accepts this way of thinking tends to be forced into isolation by sheer strength of mind, and so into a philosophy of Independence. (Empson 171)

It can easily be seen how this position describes Prior's situation in the trilogy but it is also readily apparent how the pastoral form provides a means for a regenerative reconciliation between protopathic (low) and epicritic (high) sensibilities, so that the two can pull equally on what, therefore, becomes a holistic individual. Tolkien's concept of eucatastrophe turns on a similar double irony by which the modern individual, whose only defence against the horrors of war lies in the ironic detachment of considering everything meaningless, is transfigured by an ironic downturn of fate which threatens to make everything really meaningless. The disassociation caused by modern life can only be regenerated by going beyond fate, meaning and irony. However, this is not to say that it is necessary to go to war to be healed.

The strain of disassociation is as great on Rivers as it is on any of his charges, but he seeks reconciliation by returning not to the trenches but to memories of his anthropological expedition to the Soloman Islands. He first seems to find the necessary epiphanic moment of self-affirmation in the final chapter of *Regeneration*, by recalling an incident in which a group of natives recently converted to Christianity began to direct his own questions back towards himself:

> And I suddenly saw that their reactions to my society were neither more nor less valid than mine to theirs. And do you know that was a moment of the most *amazing* freedom . . .
>
> . . .
>
> And suddenly I saw not only that we weren't the measure of all things, but that *there was no measure.* (242)

Yet in retrospect, this is shown as a false position which Rivers rejects in *The Ghost Road*:

> And with that realisation, the whole frame of social and moral rules that keep individuals imprisoned – and sane – collapsed, and for a moment he was in the same position as those drifting, dispossessed people. A condition of absolute free-fall. (120)

The change in emphasis is unmistakeable and recognizes that the position described in the first version is in fact really just an affirmation of a modern, detached, ironic, consciousness. Indeed, it looks very much dependent on the pastoral convention of a fictionalized encounter between high (ethnographer) and low (native) and perhaps is one reason why Barker remained less than happy with the ending of *Regeneration*. The alternative model of self-reconciliation through mutual affirmation that she advances in *The Ghost Road* eliminates hierarchical values by going beyond the boundaries of modern cultural representation. The core moment occurs when Rivers and the healer, Njiru, hold hands crouched together in a dark cave as thousands of screeching bats flock past them:

> There had been two experiences in the cave, and he was quite certain Njiru shared in both. One was the reaching out to grasp each other's hands. But the other was a shrinking, no, no, not shrinking, a *compression* of identity into a single hard unassailable point: the point at which no further compromise is possible, where nothing remains except pure naked self-assertion. The right to be and to be *as one is*. (170)

Here, both participants feel equally the pull of sensibilities. This ontological moment allows Rivers to look back to Njiru for the inspiration to cope with the almost impossible dilemma of serving as a military psychologist. Njiru finds the means to reconcile the dilemmas imposed upon his own patriarchal society by the British colonial power's suppression of head-hunting, and the presence of two British anthropologists among them taking notes on all their activities. Specifically, he breaks the impasse, where traditionally a dead chief's widow must remain incarcerated in a confined space until the tribe brings back a head, by instead abducting a small boy, who is allowed to live. Subsequently, at the meeting where Rivers hears the whistling of ghosts, the dead chief's soul is able to depart. Looking back on that meeting, Rivers realizes 'that the questions the ghosts had asked had all been questions the living people wanted answered' about the purpose of the white men and whether they were harmless or would offend the spirits (211). Likewise, he reflects on how the ghosts who had appeared to Sassoon at Craiglockhart had asked him: 'Why was he not in the line? Why had he deserted his men?' (212). Ghosts ask the questions that people cannot ask for themselves – the fundamental questions that lie at the heart of individual and social dilemmas. Once the questions are answered and the dilemmas solved or reconciled, then the ghosts depart. Through the processes of mutual recognition which Rivers undergoes with Sassoon, Prior and Njiru, Barker is able to gradually disentangle class, race, sexuality and gender from their dominant hierarchical contexts and move towards answering the questions thrown up by the disruptive and disassociative pressures of the long transition from pre-industrial to post-industrial society. Therefore, while her earlier work turns on the eucatastrophic experiences of individual men and women, the trilogy is able to close with a collective act of regeneration, as Njiru appears to Rivers and performs the exorcism by which the ghosts of modernity are allowed to depart in peace.

Bibliography and further reading

Barker, Pat. *Union Street*. London: Virago, 1982.

——. *Blow Your House Down*. London: Virago, 1984.

——. *The Century's Daughter*. London: Virago, 1986. Republished as *Liza's England*. 1996.

——. *The Man Who Wasn't There*. London: Virago, 1989.

——. *Regeneration*. London: Viking, 1991.

——. *The Eye in the Door*. London: Viking, 1993.

——. *The Ghost Road*. London: Viking, 1995.

——. *Another World*. London: Viking, 1998.

——. *Border Crossing*. London: Viking, 2001.

——. *Double Vision*. London: Hamish Hamilton, 2003.

Brannigan, John. *Orwell to the Present: Literature in England, 1945–2000*. Basingstoke: Palgrave Macmillan, 2003.

Empson, William. *Some Versions of Pastoral*. Harmondsworth: Penguin, 1995.

Freud, Sigmund. 'Beyond the Pleasure Principle'. in *On Metapsychology*. Penguin Freud Library 11. Angela Richards (ed.). Harmondsworth: Penguin, 1984: 275–338.

Garth, John. *Tolkien and the Great War*. London: HarperCollins, 2003.

Jolly, Margaretta. 'Towards a Masculine Maternal: Pat Barker's Bodily Fictions', in *Critical Perspectives on Pat Barker*. Sharon Monteith, Margaretta Jolly, Nahem Yousaf and Ronald Paul (eds). Columbia, SC: University of South Carolina Press, 2005: 235–53.

Monteith, Sharon. *Pat Barker*. Tavistock: Northcote House, 2002.

Monteith, Sharon, Margaretta Jolly, Nahem Yousaf and Ronald Paul (eds). *Critical Perspectives on Pat Barker*. Columbia, SC: University of South Carolina Press, 2005.

Monteith, Sharon, and Nahem Yousaf. '*Double Vision*: Regenerative or Traumatised Pastoral?', in *Critical Perspectives on Pat Barker*. Sharon Monteith, Margaretta Jolly, Nahem Yousaf and Ronald Paul (eds). Columbia, SC: University of South Carolina Press, 2005: 283–99.

Parsons, I. M. (ed.). *Men Who March Away*. London: Heinemann, 1965.

Paul, Ronald. 'In Pastoral Fields: The *Regeneration* Trilogy and Classic First World War Fiction', in *Critical Perspectives on Pat Barker*. Sharon Monteith, Margaretta Jolly, Nahem Yousaf and Ronald Paul (eds). Columbia, SC: University of South Carolina Press, 2005: 147–61.

Stevenson, Sheryl. 'Interview with Pat Barker', in *Critical Perspectives on Pat Barker*. Sharon Monteith, Margaretta Jolly, Nahem Yousaf and Ronald Paul (eds). Columbia, SC: University of South Carolina Press, 2005: 175–84.

CHAPTER FOURTEEN

'The Loom of the Inordinate': A. S. Byatt's Woven Realism

WENDY WHEELER

Human experience has two sides. The 'right' side is learned articulate language and abstract thought (mind). The other side is inordinate (i.e. 'excessive' and 'illegitimate'), embodied experience – involving learned knowledge, impossible to convey fully in articulate language – called 'tacit' by Michael Polanyi. The former derives from the latter via the branching tree of analogy and metaphor, as George Lakoff and others have argued (Lakoff and Johnson 1980; Lakoff 1999) but does not ultimately map on to it. As Friedrich Nietzsche pointed out, people forget that truth is 'A mobile army of metaphors, metonyms and anthropomorphisms, ... which after long use seem firm, canonical and obligatory' (46–7), thus easily mistaking words and ideas for concrete, hypostatized, reified things. Of course, embodied experience lives in the brain too – largely in the right hemisphere – where intuitive, gestalt thought develops, and from where aesthetic and spiritual apprehensions doubtless also arise. Experience, like the book and the text – from the Latin root *textus* leading to 'tissue', 'textile' and 'weave' – is woven. But literature is, perhaps, especially interested in exploring the inordinate side of things.

Self-consciousness is clearly part of the problem. The body visibly decays and dies, but consciousness that the self-aware mind must die with it is deeply uncongenial to most people. Thus, to natural enchantment is gradually added other forms: story, myth and the paradox (*credo quia absurdum est*) of the leap of faith which is both intellectual and intellect-denying, and also close to madness (*A Whistling Woman* 120). The body, reifications of language, fear of death and fantasy are all *humanly real*. One of the oddest things about the modern idea of reality and realism is that it should exclude, and make illegitimate and unspeakable, so much of very ordinary (that is, very ordinarily strange) human experience.

A. S. Byatt's interest in reality and its accurate depiction means that the strange aspects of ordinary life must be woven into such an account. Meditating in *Still Life* on 'the difficulties of writing about strangeness' (72), Byatt suggests that the difficulty lies in the tendency of language to run 'in old clichés' (*ibid.*). Wordsworth, she adds, 'much mocked, thought himself back to an innocent vision, told us that grass is green and water wet because he had reached beyond familiarity to some primal wonder that these things were so and not otherwise, to some mythic sense that he was giving or finding the words for the things, not merely repeating' (*ibid.*). Realism, for Byatt, perceives the human experience of reality as more than the everyday world of objects, vaguely complicated by 'psychology', and embraces the mythic or magical. The novel – always 'a world in the head' (Byatt and Sodré 37) – is where the human difficulty of discovering what Ignês Sodré calls 'a meaningful internal world' is reworked and reimagined via psychical objects – people, places and things – rendered in the discourses and metaphors of the fictional world (38).

T. S. Eliot places the rending of the loom's fabric in the seventeenth-century 'dissociation of sensibility' (*Passions of the Mind* 9). In *Still Life*, in 1965, Frederica, in love with the poet-don Raphael Faber, considers a hypothetical PhD thesis on the dissociation of sensibility 'that occurred between Shakespeare and Donne, who felt their thought as immediately as the odour of a rose, and Milton, who did not' (345). Perhaps it would be truer to say that Milton's *Paradise Lost* has not so much lost touch with the embodied and immediate feeling of words-as-experience as it offers, instead, a *rendering* of this falling apart as both terrible *and* heroic.

The seventeenth-century scientific revolution sundered the web which mythic thought had tried to weave between grammar and the flesh. Renaissance thought and art attempted a new human-centred realism, out of which modern science grew. Increasingly what was real was the measurable world. Simultaneously, the instruments of perception, however much they extended biological perception and neurological conception, always returned to biological restrictions of the senses. The Frederica Potter quartet, *The Virgin in the Garden* (1978), *Still Life* (1985), *Babel Tower* (1996) and *A Whistling Woman* (2002), opens in 1953 with the new Elizabethan Age, the dualistic and mechanistic world ushered in by a new technological scientific revolution. Both the logical positivists' idea of language as describing a world solidly revealed by the senses, and the idea that human perception is itself essentially passive, are repeatedly questioned in all four novels – as indeed they were during the period (1953–80) covered by the quartet. The final novel in the series touches on the philosophy of Wittgenstein, whose early work, the *Tractatus Logico-Philosophicus*, influenced the logical positivists. The novel includes the appearance on Frederica's television show of the psychologist and philosopher Richard Gregory, whose *The Intelligent Eye* (1970) – first appearing as a BBC TV series of lectures in 1968–9 – discussed the way in which perception is actively built by evolution and in experience, rather than simply given or reflected (*The Whistling Woman* 136).

Thus reality and the realism which sought to describe it entered into informed public debate in the 1960s – as represented by Frederica's television show *Through the Looking Glass*. The anarchic wish of 1960s youth to blow up both reality and the rules of grammar, represented by the irresponsible intellectual utopianism of the Anti-University, and the flesh-denying Manicheism of the religious cult in *A Whistling Woman*, cannot be an adequate response to the complexities of human experience. Humanity is both mind and body – as the title of the North Yorkshire University conference held in the novel reminds us. The theme of interrelating mind, body and reality, especially concerning the history of gender differences, runs throughout the quartet.

The destabilizing of earlier Newtonian and Enlightenment beliefs about reality produce aesthetic and theoretical explorations of forms of derealization; this happened previously in modernist responses both to Freud and to Einstein. The Freudian Unconscious undid the confidence of the Cartesian *cogito*, as quantum mechanics undermined the idea of the objective determinacy of matter. That reality and its perception is more complex than positivism's account is not an argument against reality, but one for attending more closely. Thomas Kuhn's influential *The Structure of Scientific Revolutions* (1962) argues that scientific accounts of truth and reality are determined by discursively supported paradigms of knowledge, and emphasizes the relationship between language and reality in accurately rendering truth. Competing theologies of materialism and spiritualism inform the multi-disciplinary Mind and Body Conference of *A Whistling Woman*, and the mixture of New Age spirituality and revolutionary Marxism at the Anti-University.

By 1978, when *The Virgin in the Garden* was published, postmodernism was relatively well established as an intellectual movement, and fighting its way onto university curricula. Grounded in anti-positivism, and thus suspicious of all truth claims, whether moral or scientific, as 'constructed in language', postmodernism drew on the Enlightenment revolutionary, and then Nietzschean legacy of suspicion of any axiological claims. On this account, only the supposedly determining materiality of articulate language finally mattered. Suggestions that some kinds of experiences might be important to human beings *qua* humans were derided as naïve humanism; the evidence of the body and evolution was dismissed as 'biological determinism' or ignorance of psychical complexity. And, of course, there was sufficient truth in all this (the idea of truth never *really* went away) to make it plausible. *Babel Tower*, written during the early to mid-1990s when neuroscience was addressing the reason/madness distinction explored in the emergence of Romanticism from within Enlightenment, is inter-cut with extracts from *Babbletower*, a novel-within-the-novel which uses mythic allegory to explore the terror and madness resulting from absolute rational choice and the overthrow of all human valuations and orderings in pursuit of existential freedom.

As the title of her study of Iris Murdoch indicates, Byatt understands that human life involves only 'degrees of freedom'. Recounting, in *Degrees of Freedom*, the influence of Murdoch's essay, 'Against Dryness', in which Murdoch dismisses both the positivist (i.e. liberal) and the existentialist idea 'that human beings are "solitary and totally free" and that the fundamental virtue is "sincerity" ... or "truth to oneself"', Byatt reports Murdoch's insistence, instead, on 'the hard idea of truth' (*Degrees of Freedom* 5; *Passions of the Mind* 24). This 'electrified' her because '[h]owever initially attractive, even apparently "true" the idea might be that all our narratives are partial fictions, the wholesale enthusiastic acceptance of that way of thought removes both interest and power, in the end, from both art and the moral life' (*Passions of the Mind* 24). Does one read in order to discover that art is just about itself — although it is always about itself too, because every writer and artist thinks about form and information — or does one read (or watch) also to know about the world? Byatt concludes:

> During my time as a writer such solipsistic ideas of our experience of the world have increased largely in power. So that, whilst it was once attractive (*séduisant?*) to think that whatever we say or see is our own construction, it now becomes necessary to reconsider the idea of truth, hard truth, and its possibility. We may be, as Browning said, born liars. But that idea itself is only wholly meaningful if we glimpse a possibility of truth and truthfulness for which we must strive, however, inevitably, partial, our success must be. I do believe language has denotative as well as connotative powers. (*Ibid.*)

Realism is, of course, a materialism, and historically its importance accompanies a growing interest in the depiction of (increasingly ordinary) human experience, and a related decline in the explanatory power of myth. But Byatt's metaphor of the loom of the inordinate (*A Whistling Woman* 102, 110), which I have analogized as the underside, as it were, of the human weave, alerts us to the actual indivisibility of human experience. In *A Whistling Woman*, Frederica, struggling as intellectual woman in a pre-feminist era, writes 'laminations' in which her thoughts and experiences are layered together, with a cleverly ludic commentary of the William Burroughs cut-up method, thus exposing the ludicrousness of her divided self in a male dominated world. Not until the novel's end, in an epiphanic reworking of the death of Bergotte from Proust's *Remembrance of Things Past*, does Frederica embrace rather than resist what David Abram has called 'the spell of the sensuous' (*passim*).

In *A Whistling Woman*, the possibly schizophrenic, charismatic cult leader Josh Lamb (also known as Joshua Ramsden) experiences the loom of the inordinate. Following his deeply religious father's murder of his wife and daughter, inspired by God's call to Abraham to sacrifice Isaac (Genesis 22: 6, 7, 8 — the text marked for him by his father from prison — source also of Kierkegaard's meditation on faith in *Fear and Trembling*), and the father's subsequent judicial hanging, Josh begins to experience dissociated states and hallucinations. It is during these, springing out of 'the grey fog of normality and unknowing that his aunt had tried to weave to preserve him, or herself, from the memory and the knowledge of the horror' (101–2), that Josh first experiences the tapestry's other side, woven, as it were, on 'the loom of the inordinate':

> Now and then ... he saw the dark open again, great crevasses where the busy warp and weft flailed and hurtled. Or looking into a shop window in the street

he would see his own reflection, and behind it, not the odd car, no ordinary passers-by, no policeman, but the roaring and rushing of the loom of the inordinate. There was no mirror in his bedroom, indeed, there were no mirrors in his aunt's house. She was against Vanity. So he saw himself little. (102)

Josh envisions the loom's doubleness, which is echoed elsewhere in the novel in the theme of difference and identity played out in the mono-zygotic twins John and Paul Ottokar – one of whom is Frederica's lover. Tellingly, Josh's 'double loom' vision first arises in Mr Shepherd's Latin class where the teacher expounds on the ways in which Latin roots expose the analogies and metaphors by which a word's etymological journey into its present meaning may be traced. Mr Shepherd warns the boys that this understanding of the metaphorical nature of linguistic evolution 'should cause you never again to take English for granted as the language of common sense' (108). Josh quickly succumbs to the intimation, explored in literature and psychoanalysis but literalized in psychosis, that language has a fearful fecundity only contained by the conventions of common sense. Madman rather than poet, Josh sees that language is capable of many meanings:

> For something that wove language on two looms, the visible commonplace and commonsense, and the inordinate, the extra-vagant (outward-wandering) invisible underside of the tapestry, was letting him glimpse messages. (110)

Josh, 'seeing himself little', is caught in infantile trauma and incapable of seeing himself as one among similar others. This leads to 'magical' intuition (and the vision of the loom's inordinate unruliness), rather than to normal human empathy. It is echoed in Marcus Potter's similar ignorance (also paternally derived) of the ordinariness of psychical confusion and conflict. It is as if, Byatt indicates, the modern paternal myth of a disenchanted world is always secretly matched by its mythical and magical other. Josh and Marcus's fathers are poles apart, but also secretly linked in their 'theo-logical' commitments: frank religion in the case of Josh's father; socialism born of the Dissenting tradition in the case of Bill Potter. Both produce visionary sons who are mystified by their confused experiences of reality.

Byatt does not suggest or imply that the meanings which Josh or Marcus derive from their visions of the inordinate are unreal. Rather, she implies that reality itself may be stranger than common sense allows. In *Still Life*, the representation of strangeness as art continues in the focus on Van Gogh, but, increasingly, the strangeness of science enters too, introduced in Gerard Wijnnobel's reflections on science, art and interdisciplinarity in the new University of North Yorkshire (Wijnnobel becomes its first Vice-Chancellor) (333), and also in Marcus's dreamlike and healing meditations on phyllotaxis. Unlike the refrigerator which killed his sister Stephanie, and which he failed to switch off with sufficient alacrity, Marcus begins to find his demented visionary mathematical mind 'earthed', and possibly warmed, by consideration of a living tree. This passage from chapter 21, 'A Tree, of Many, One', is a significant point at which Byatt brings the supposed unreality of the inordinate loom into conjunction with contemporary discourses of scientific reality. Like some nascent Buddha beneath the tree, Marcus meditates:

> He touched its thick hide, neither flesh warm nor stone cold. Most of the form of a tree is dead cells, standing, contained in a thin sheaf of living, dividing, watery cells below the bark, with the pushing exploratory cells shape-shifting at the questing ends of twigs and roots. The leaves were alive: he plucked one of the suckers, clear gold-green, strongly-veined, saw-edged, rough-surfaced yet shining, asymmetrical at the base. ... He knew there was an inner geometry ... but he began to see an outer geometry.
>
> Carefully contemplated, the growth of leaves from twigs, twigs from limbs, limbs from bole, showed to a geometric eye a persisting regularity in all this gnarled idiosyncrasy ... Marcus stared and mapped, stared and mapped, learning the tree ... Always before Marcus had thought of geometry as something spun from his mind across the threatening, shapeless mass of the world, reducing it to his order.
>
> ...
>
> When he had become ill, he had had a time of terror in a field of pouring light, had felt himself to be some kind of funnel through which the light must flow, his eye a burning glass. He had devised a kind of geometric scheme to make the thing safe to think about, two intersecting cones, at the centre of which his eye, his mind almost accidentally were. He held his hand against the tree-skin, working out that he was back in the same place, seen differently. ... Only he was not afraid, moreover, for two clear reasons. One was that the tree, the tree itself, was the intersection, the meeting cones between light and earth.
>
> ...
>
> The tree seen was solid geometry, meeting light. The tree, thought about, was contained and moving force and energy, stable yet changing, consuming and not consumed. (291–2)

Marcus's disorderliness, his mathematical, scientific ungroundedness, is earthed by the vision of nature's patterns – phyllotaxis – not held together by his own troubled body-mind, but solidly there outside him and still. He is no longer the rushing and roaring shuttle of the loom himself, but sees its production of order out of seeming chaos in nature itself. In *A Whistling Woman*, in the company of the Wittgenstein philosopher Vincent Hodgkiss who will become his warming lover, Marcus begins to articulate the mystery of the Fibonacci numbers which describe mathematically how complexity evolves from simplicity – and pattern, self-similarity and difference emerge in the world in nature and in culture and language:

> I want – to look at how numbers – *do* – inhere in things. I want to understand why certain things grow in the Fibonacci spiral. Twigs around branches,

branches round the stem of trees. Daisy flowers and sunflowers. Some snails and pine-cones. You'd need a combination of maths, and physics, and cell biology, and ... I want to solve phyllotaxis. (220)

One might say that this is also the nature of desire, of life's striving for itself. The move from bodily desire towards abstraction and impartiality, is, of course, the move of language and the intellect. But the body, and physical and moral connectedness, cannot be forgotten. Frederica, spiky, difficult, and suspicious of the gradual poetic pleasures of suggestiveness and implication (*Still Life* 4, 12), only at the end of *A Whistling Woman* begins to exercise desire. But Marcus's novel expression of what he *wants* – 'to solve phyllotaxis' – opens the possibility of desire articulated in both the mind and the body.

Byatt initially intended to write *Still Life* without metaphors. Of course, she found she couldn't. Like Marcus, she found that language, like natural life, is full of pattern and productivity. Language springs from our embodied being and doing, but in everyday life we tend to suppress its metaphorical productivity. Literature enables such illicit aspects of language, producing from similarity difference. Thus language proliferates meaning both over time (in its developing etymological life), and at any particular time – in a spoken sentence, a poem, a novel where bursts of generative activity can occur, constantly weaving newly articulated patterns.

Byatt's own interest in metaphor and 'the mimesis of things' led her to Paul Ricoeur's *The Rule of Metaphor*: 'Metaphor, a figure of speech, presents in an *open* fashion, by means of a conflict *between* identity and difference, the process that, in a *covert* manner, generates semantic grids by fusion of differences *within* identity' (*Passions of the Mind* 15; Ricoeur 252). This, plus the timely reading of Proust's *Remembrance of Things Past*, gave her some sense of how a novelist could effectively handle the idea of the self – evanescent but continuous – through its constitution in objects: both people but also, less obviously, things. Not only things simply named by small bright words, but by adjectives, personifications, and the opening up of the *double* space between the realistic description of experience and metaphor, which is 'both an experience and an act, both the reception of mental image *and* a deliberate act of understanding. It is to perceive identity and difference simultaneously and dependent on each other' (*A Whistling Woman* 15).

Writing in *Passions of the Mind* on George Eliot, Byatt has noted that Eliot's realism is 'partly a moral realism rejecting "compensation" [predominantly the compensations of religion] and other consoling doctrines, and partly a related technical realism, a desire for accuracy' (84–5). However, fidelity to human experience demands the inclusion of subjective experience. Modern narrative approaches this through the generative capacity of metaphor and the mimesis of objects which constitute a consciousness and a life. Realism (like scientific discourse) has problems with the (illicit) *strangeness* of human experience. Life is in very many ways not ordinary at all, but extraordinary. As Richard Todd notes, 'Byatt has long been attracted to Murdoch's view that "reality ... 'is more, and other, than our descriptions of it'"' (Todd 65 citing *Degrees of Freedom* 11).

In the past, the extraordinary was to some extent contained, represented and legitimized in myth, magic and religion. Following the Enlightenment, it has increasingly fallen to art (and in part to psychoanalysis) to provide spaces for weaving on the loom of the inordinate. Byatt has interwoven such episodes of strangeness into her own fiction, a manner of writing explicitly opposed to what Murdoch describes as the modern problem of having 'been left with far too shallow and flimsy an idea of human personality ... which produces a picture of man as a "lonely, self-contained individual"' (*Degrees of Freedom* 4). Against this 'dryness', Byatt's fiction follows Murdoch's prescription that 'the novel, to return to its imaginative power, must pit against "the consolations of form, the clear crystalline work, the simplified fantasy-myth", "the now so unfashionable naturalistic idea of character"' (*Degrees of Freedom* 5). In other words, in modernism, Eliot's 'consolations' of religion can become T. S. Eliot's 'consolations' of form and fantasy-myth. But the naturalistic idea of character, for Byatt, must also include what the Victorians called the more than – or super – natural, which she prefers to render less problematically as the inordinate.

In the Frederica Potter quartet, as elsewhere in Byatt's fiction, this takes the form of depictions of strange fits of passion: various kinds of knowing or unknowing possessions – of art by life, of madness, and of myth. In *The Virgin in the Garden*, the mythic element is supplied by both the similarity and the difference between the first and second Elizabethan ages, with the Virgin Queen's deployment of mythic iconography (both Catholic and classical: she is Mary, Flora, Diana and Astraea) contrasted with Frederica's clumsy attempts at seduction and defloration. Frederica herself is a maddening character who continues to exasperate various people throughout all four novels. Her brother, Marcus, is both maddening and maddened: a budding mathematician whose numbers churn in poetic forms. Still characterized as an *idiot-savant* at the opening of *Still Life*, which takes one of its major themes from the life and works and madness of Vincent Van Gogh, Marcus's problems with reality implicate him in responsibility for the accidental death of his sister Stephanie – something the reader finds it hard to forgive. Thus the reader is also maddened. Stephanie's death, occasioned by the attempt to rescue a sparrow lodged behind the fatally unearthed refrigerator, is thus framed by Bede's allegory of life as the sparrow flying from darkness, through the warmth of the king's hall, out to darkness again. This, significantly, is also the novel's epigraph.

In *Babel Tower*, the mythic element takes the form of a political quest narrative – Jude Mason's allegorical novel *Babbletower* – in which Enlightenment rationalism is pushed to its Sadean extremes in the story of the founding of a utopian community which culminates in terror, torture and madness. Its author's name – a point made in the book's trial for obscenity – recalls Hardy's rather different handling of the same theme of the conflict between aspiration, desire and reality in *Jude the Obscure*. In *A Whistling Woman*, the realist story is intercut with Agnes Mond's Tolkien-like allegory of Artegall's quest, finally achieved through his ability to translate the language of the Whistler's, Carteresque bird-women who have chosen to fly free and whose terrible language kills ordinary men.

In the closing pages of *A Whistling Woman*, which is so informed by the image of the endlessly wakeful Whistlers, Frederica visits the Mauritshuis at The Hague to make a TV programme on Vermeer's *View of Delft*. Frederica's life seems to be falling into disarray. She is pregnant and, just before entering the Mauritshuis, discovers that her and her son Leo's 'family' with Agatha Mond and her daughter Saskia is shortly to be ended by Agatha's newly revealed relationship with Gerard Wijnnobel. The latter, gnomically, but perhaps with reference to the coming of Enlightenment following the counter-Reformation, describes Vermeer's painting (in which the viewer, under cloud, sees sunshine arriving, and quite evidently coming closer and closer, in little patches of yellow light on the city across the water) as 'A mystery of survival and renewal' (418); but all Frederica feels is a pregnant 'drowse of defeat', as she falls very deeply and very briefly asleep in front of the painting. This seems like the symbolic death of the wakeful whistling woman.

Frederica awakes, however, to an epiphany in which, momentarily, she seems to be in the gold promising light of the painting: 'She was in a calm place where golden buildings stood above dark water, where the sky was blue and still, the stone was pink, time was very quietly arrested' (418). Both the arresting of time, and the preceding brief discussion of the novelist Bergotte's death before the *View of Delft* in *Remembrance of Things Past*, take us back to Proust and to Bergotte's epiphany in that novel when considering the extraordinary detail of the famous little patch of sunnily illuminated yellow wall in Vermeer's painting. This produces in Bergotte an arresting moment, shortly before his heart arrest and death, in which he realizes that his own work has been 'too dry':

> At last he came to the Vermeer which he remembered as more striking, more different from anything else he knew, but in which, thanks to the critic's article, he remarked for the first time some small figures in blue, that the ground was pink, and finally the precious substance of the tiny patch of yellow wall .... 'That is how I ought to have written,' he said. 'My last books are too dry, I ought to have gone over them with several coats of paint, made my language exquisite in itself, like this little patch of yellow wall.' (n. pag.)

Bergotte, Proust tells us, 'was not unconscious of the gravity of his condition' in which there appeared to him a celestial scales where his own life hung in one pan, and the perfect little patch of yellow wall in the other: 'He felt that he had rashly sacrificed the former for the latter'. This, in turn, takes us back to Byatt's revelation, in *Degrees of Freedom*, of Murdoch's polemic against dryness. The latter is an argument against the modernist reduction of language in art to a 'smallness, clearness, self-containedness' which

> admires the work of art in so far as it is whole and complete, containing its own terms of reference, not depending upon any resonance outside itself for its statement. The practitioners of 'dry' art admire myth and symbol, precision and coherence; they would, theoretically, be more excited by an interpretation of one of Shakespeare's plays which offered them a beautifully plotted, 'containing' framework of themes and recurrent symbols, than by one which placed its main emphasis on Shakespeare's skill in reproducing the accidental, the idiosyncratic happenings of life, or his power to arouse in the audience an immediate emotional attachment to Falstaff. (3)

The point, in other words, is not simply to be an observer and creator of formal perfection (Vermeer's painting of Delft is certainly that), but to know, too, that the artist has placed the viewer in the cold waiting for the sun which has already bathed the further reaches of the city. The importance of the little patch of yellow wall is not simply to do with the balance of forms, shapes, light and shade, but also that it signifies the closeness of the sun and the nearness of its warmth to the viewer placed under the great dark cloud which dominates the top of the painting. The point is that the viewer should be Frederica, sensuously *in* the world of the painting, not Bergotte who forgot yellow warmth until the moment it was leaving him.

Byatt's work is beautifully plotted, mythically resourceful and resonant, and provisioned with a framework of themes and recurrent symbols. Although it does not disavow the modernist past, it seeks to maintain a 'resonance outside itself' by reference to both contemporary cultural themes and to everything unruly about life, which the loom of the inordinate expresses. Marcus's mathematical and precise dryness may be wetted by the rising sap of the Fibonacci tree (and Vincent's matching bodily attentiveness, despite his own modernist, Wittgensteinian, intellectual interests), but Frederica's epiphany is tied very precisely to the competition within her between the whistling woman's fearless 'masculine' courage and this same courage expressed in a decidedly contemporary female awareness of 'reality'. Later, back on the Yorkshire moors, and having decided in favour of human warmth and an infant's prejudice, Frederica considers the connections:

> She looked at the earth under her feet, and the cobwebs and the honey-scented gorse, and the peat, and the pebbles, and thought of Luk's world of curiosity. She thought that somewhere — in the science which has made Vermeer's painted spherical waterdrops, in the humming loom of neurones which connected to make metaphors, all this was one. And in front of her, another creature, another person, contained in a balloon of fluid, turned on the end of its cord, and adjusted to the movement. (421)

This emotional adjustment in Frederica, set against the movements of the moor, sky and sea, returns to the sensuous body to find both its own motivation and also the whole galaxy of felt connections to the world. The wholesomeness of the body, in other words, is the necessary counter-balance to ungrounded intellectual abstraction.

This, then, would seem to be a good description of Byatt's realism, which wants to account for both sides of the loom: precision and disorder, pattern and passion, the figure in the fabric, and the threads which hang beneath. Readers have objected to the quartet's hanging ending, at the close of *A Whistling Woman*, with Frederica returning to Luk, and neither having 'the slightest idea what to do'. Yet the affirmed messiness ('Everyone laughed. The world was all before them, it seemed. They could go anywhere' [421]) seems precisely the point. Doing the right thing, Byatt seems to suggest, does not depend on having a realistic plan, but on the possession of confidence about how reality is constituted and viewed. Such confidence is expressed in Luk's assurance – which ends the narrative – that 'We shall think of something'.

Is this ending, apparently affirming a reconstituted if not entirely normal family, a betrayal of Frederica's intellectual life and independence? The Prologue of *Still Life*, set at the Post-Impressionism exhibition at the Royal Academy of Arts in 1980, suggests otherwise, as ten years after the close of *A Whistling Woman*, Frederica is still a public intellectual. But spirit-ually speaking has Frederica bowed before the coarse realities of life as it is 'really' lived, and thus lost the integrity of paying attention to the correc-tions of literature – as an attempt to give expression to the inordinate – alongside the grosser corrections of life?

Surely such a conclusion cannot be justified. The phrase 'the world was all before them' also recalls Milton's closing lines of *Paradise Lost*, as Adam and Eve descend from Eden. Eve too has thought of death, of denying the seeds of life, and has similarly fallen into an exhausted sleep before opting in favour, not of the romance of the gardens of paradise, but of life, human struggle and the generations to come (*Paradise Lost*, Book XII). Frederica is leaving the garden in which she began, and the fall into knowledge is not only human but literary. Because literature – unless you think it is just a dry piece of perfected form – is the pre-eminent place where what Roland Barthes calls the crudeness of knowledge (of organized knowledge as science, for example) can be corrected by a due attention to subtlety, and to the excess of world over word in which the nuances must nonetheless be caught. Barthes writes, '*La science est grossière, la vie est subtile, et c'est pour corriger cette distance que la littérature nous importe*' (Barthes 18; also Sontag 465). In *Literature and the Taste of Knowledge*, Michael Wood translates this as 'Knowledge is coarse, life is subtle, and literature matters to us because it corrects this distance' (35). In a similar vein, Wood also notes J. L. Austin's observation of 'the innumerable and unforeseeable demands of the world upon language' (35). Finding meaning in a fallen world, in a fallen language, is hard labour: the task that God lays upon both Adam and Eve. It is both a coarse real task and a subtle interpretative one: knowledge in life and in literature, and, in both – where, indeed, Frederica really is for the reader – on each side of the loom's ceaseless seductive and textual weave.

Bibliography and further reading

Byatt, A. S. *Degrees of Freedom: the Early Novels of Iris Murdoch*. London: Vintage, 1994 [Chattos & Windus, 1965].

——. *The Virgin in the Garden*. London: Vintage, 1994 [Chatto & Windus, 1978].

——. *Still Life*. London: Vintage, 1995 [Chatto & Windus, 1985].

——. *Passions of the Mind*. London: Vintage, 1993 [Chatto & Windus, 1991].

——. *A Whistling Woman*. London: Vintage, 2003 [Chatto & Windus, 2002].

——, and Ignês Sodré. *Imagining Characters*. New York: Vintage, 1997 [London: Chatto & Windus, 1995].

Abram, David. *The Spell of the Sensuous*. New York: Vintage, 1997 [Pantheon, 1996].

Barthes, Roland. *Leçon*. Paris: Seuil, 1978.

Hardy, Thomas. *Jude the Obscure*. Harmondsworth: Penguin, 1998.

Kierkegaard, Søren. *Fear and Trembling/Repetition*. Princeton, NJ: Princeton University Press, 1984 [*Fear and Trembling* 1843]. Trans. Howard V. Hong and Edna H. Hong.

Kuhn, Thomas. *The Structure of Scientific Revolutions*. Chicago, IL: University of Chicago Press, 1962.

Lakoff, George, and Mark Johnson. *Metaphors We Live By*. London: University of Chicago Press, 1980.

——. *Philosophy in the Flesh: the Embodied Mind and Its Challenge to Western Thought*. New York: Basic Books, 1999.

Nietzsche, Friedrich. 'On Truth and Lies in an Extra-Moral Sense', in *The Portable Nietzsche*. Ed. and trans. Walter Kaufmann. Harmondsworth and New York: Penguin, 1976: 42–7.

Polanyi, Michael. *The Tacit Dimension*. London: Routledge & Kegan Paul, 1967.

Proust, Marcel. *The Captive*. Vol. 5 of *Remembrance of Things Past*. Trans. C. K. Scott Montcrieff. London: Chatto & Windus, 1941. Online version accessed 1 November 2005, http://etext.library.adelaide.edu.ac/p/proust/marcel/p96c/index.html, 2003, n. pag.

Ricoeur, Paul. *The Rule of Metaphor*. London: Routledge, 2003.

Sontag, Susan (ed.). *A Barthes Reader*. London: Jonathan Cape, 1982.

Todd, Richard. *A. S. Byatt*. Plymouth: Northcote House, 1997.

Wood, Michael. *Literature and the Taste of Knowledge*. Cambridge: Cambridge University Press, 2005.

CHAPTER FIFTEEN

Fiction's History: Adam Thorpe

ROD MENGHAM

One of the most important defining characteristics of modernism was its transformation of time-scale. The basic template for nineteenth-century fiction was human longevity, or enough of it for the development (or stasis) of character to become evident. Variations were already in place in novels chronicling the succession of generations in a single family, or in the habits of a writer like Hardy who would place the usual measures in the context of several different durations, ranging from fractions to the immensely extended periods of geological change. In the early 1920s, the temporal setting for Adam Thorpe's novel *Nineteen Twenty-One* (2001), pivotal texts were being written that would shrink the scale of significance down to that of a single day. The contraction of scale was illusory, of course. The protagonist of *Mrs Dalloway* would recall her early adulthood on the first page, opening up a perspective that converts the text into an ellipsis of the *bildungsroman*.

In *Ulysses*, the crowding of thought and incident into a 24-hour period seems to give priority to the momentary and the contingent, but patterns emerge in the form of shadows cast by related material that is up to 3,000 years old. In the 1980s and 1990s, one major consolidation in literary fiction that reflected a vogue in more commercially viable forms of writing entailed an effect of historical layering, the juxtaposition of successive episodes in the history of a particular place. History came to mean most when embedded in geography. From the complexities of Iain Sinclair to the simplicities of Edward Rutherfurd, the text was organized in terms of the superimposition of different historical epochs. This was a modernist idea, of course, despite its appearance in texts more readily asso-ciated with postmodernism.

The chief legacy of an Eliotic notion of tradition is to be found in the construction of narrative in British writing of the last two decades. At times, it becomes the motivating force of the project, as in Peter Ackroyd's *English Music* (1992). But attention to place in fiction is impossible to realize without immersing the reader in circumstantial detail, whose texture and volume resist appropriation by theories of cultural inheritance. This is, in a sense, the agenda of Woolf's *Between the Acts*, where the village pageant – that popular version of modernism's meshing of history and geography – is constantly emerging from and being overwhelmed by atoms of meaning that always seem about to settle into a definite pattern, but then fail to do so.

The best contemporary novels in this vein weigh continuity against discontinuity, typology against uniqueness. Thorpe's *Ulverton* (1992) is a case in point: as reader, you remain uncertain whether the village is to be seen primarily as a fragment of England, or as the centre of its own universe. The organizing point of view is difficult to assimilate; it is not that of narrator or of character, but of any occupant of an imaginary set of coordinates. As in an archaeological excavation, the stratigraphy of a given site is obtained only by an act of simultaneous destruction and creation.

The pattern of settlement in one phase is rendered visible by obliterating any overlying patterns. The fictional reconstruction of an earlier period of history is the more convincing the less it appears to depend on contemporary modes of perception. It is a modern interest in the past that vivifies it, and yet the modernity of that interest is ultimately what obscures the nature of the object under review. In the mid-nineteenth-century section of *Ulverton* (whose episodes range from the Civil War to the late twentieth century) a lady photographer describes the opening of an Egyptian tomb, whose wall paintings are exposed to light for the first time in 3,000 years: 'as if breath was stirring within them, and their parts were being touched into swelling fact' (186). Unfortunately, it is the modern intrusion which ensures the deterioration of these images: 'it is the sudden shock of the air, and the evil properties of our own breath, that is causing the damage to the pigment' (186). Any historical truth which survives this contact does so randomly and unpredictably. Seeds from the tomb are transported to Ulverton, where they are kept in a drawer for 100 years and then planted successfully in the mid-twentieth century. This penultimate phase of the novel revolves around the assembling of artefacts for inclusion in a time capsule.

The idea is that the capsule will be buried and then retrieved by future archaeologists who will use it to recover the history of the society that produced it. The chief exhibit is a text written by the originator of the project, but neither the text nor any of the other objects takes into account the relations of power and desire that infuse the whole process of collecting and burying the artefacts. The unofficial, disregarded narrative of the secretary responsible for administering the project is the only source of this information.

The village of Ulverton returns in Thorpe's fiction as the main setting for most of the events recounted in *Pieces of Light* (1998). However, the spatial relations of this novel are not radial, but polarized between the Wiltshire Downs and a colonial backwater in West Africa, close to Mount Cameroon. The temporal relations involve a registration of physical and cultural change in the environs of Ulverton, between the 1920s and the 1990s, while the evocations of Bamakum are all recollections of the 1930s, projecting an Africa of the mind that remains forever the same. The most obvious pretext for this polarization is the protagonist's departure from the Africa of his early childhood to an England of prep schools and holidays spent in the houses of relatives. Although the attachment to Ulverton increases through successive decades, it is never as magnetic as the desire for a locale that is never revisited. The failure to return to Africa only serves to intensify the longing for an original home, located partly in landscape, buildings and objects, and partly in one particular phase of a relationship.

But if the biography of Hugh Arkwright supplies the most obvious links between Britain and Africa, it is not the only source of the novel's divided attention. In some ways more powerful, although more obscure, the perception of Africa as the original starting point for homo sapiens is part of the novel's fascination with the distant origins of society, religion and language. The mysterious sequence of events explored from different angles in the five sections of the book can be accounted for in different ways: as the outcome of individual pathology, as the imprint of supernatural influences, as the distorted reflection of local mythologies, and as the echo of ritual practices with universal resonance.

One possible explanation for the long-drawn-out succession of disappearances and murders that make Bamakum and Ulverton alternative settings for the same story seems on the face of it the most likely. The possibility that Arkwright himself is the source of the trouble is prepared for meticulously in the details of his isolation as a child, his early separation from his parents, the disappearance of his mother, his resentment of the uncle with whom he is made to live, and the torment he suffers when his beloved Rachael abandons him for this same uncle. The memoir of childhood with which the book opens reflects carefully and painfully on the grounds for Arkwright's acute sense of rejection, although the adult perspective brought to bear on these early events tempers the child's bewilderment by projecting a sense of resignation in the formal control of a carefully organized narrative. However, the impression of emotional security derived from this carefully paced storytelling is disturbed by the subsequent diary section with its volatility and touches of arrogance, defensiveness, paranoia. Clearly, the adult Arkwright has equipped himself with an armature of professional expertise and celebrity-status, enclosing a deeply vulnerable core of childish need.

Paradoxically, his reputation as theatrical guru rests on his reviving antique systems of gesture marketed as contemporary with Shakespeare. On his own admission, this theatrical archaeology does not guarantee a return to authenticity, but relies on a tradition of conjectures and back-formations. As a solitary child, Arkwright had used similar gestures while reciting Shakespeare to himself in the secluded 'theatre' of an Ulverton beech wood; the constant rehearsing of emotional crises, of traumatic separations and healing reunions of the kind that Shakespeare's plays are so well stocked with, cultivated an ambition for scripting relationships, ensuring their adherence to a pattern, their final unfolding into restitution and fulfilment. But the chief benefit the adult derives from instituting these rigid systems of meaning is to contain ambiguity, defuse the unpredictable, render human behaviour completely legible. A childhood of misreadings precipitates the need for an infallible method of reading. One way of guaranteeing that infallibility is to alter the original text of human behaviour, to intervene in other people's lives in order to render unavoidable their conformity to a chosen pattern.

The diary section, infused with the director's self-confidence in manipulating human words and actions, is succeeded by a series of letters from Arkwright to his dead mother; these documents form an elliptical confession of sorts, although they do not admit responsibility for any of the crimes they seem all the time to be moving in the direction of. Written from within some form of psychiatric institution, their entire premise is the need for a complete candidness in the elaboration of a 'talking cure', and yet, as the final section of the novel makes clear, the letters remain silent on decisive points, obscuring our knowledge of the 'unspeakable' that is disclosed almost casually in the last few pages.

The final section of the novel consists of letters from Arkwright's mother to his uncle. Although they predate his birth, they contain information that represents his life in an entirely new light. Until this point, the central mysteries of the novel have concerned his mother's disappearance, his need to know whether disappearance necessarily means death, and his growing suspicion that the ghost of his mother has returned to the vicinity of Ulverton. All of these conundra diminish in significance when it is discovered that his mother is not in fact his true parent, when he is made to realize that her abandonment of him was preceded by an original abandonment by his biological parents, the District Officer, Hargreaves, and the missionary's daughter, Grace. His only knowledge of his natural father and mother is through hearsay. The genetic link seems confirmed by his replication of Hargreaves' blindness in one eye (they are both probably sufferers from hereditary glaucoma). But the lack of direct insight into the characters of both Grace and Hargreaves makes Arkwright seem like the child of colonialism itself. The constant movement backwards and forwards from centre to periphery in the history of British colonial expansion has ensured a magnification of selected aspects of English culture at a remove from England itself, a distorted version of Englishness that is then transplanted back to the original source. English culture of the last 200 years has evolved under the influence of fictions of Englishness cultivated abroad.

Arkwright's entire life has been based thoroughly and fatally on a fiction of the family romance, as much as the milieu in which he has been educated and acculturated depends on a patriotism derived from estrangement.

The novel's powerful intimations of the supernatural are gradually dispelled by the sporadic detective work of Arkwright, on the trail for clues concerning the apparition of the 'Red Lady' that he associates with the woman he believes to be his mother. But what is striking about this process of demystification, this provision of rational explanations for what had seemed not to make sense, is the insight it gives into the means by which superstitions are generated and mythologies sustained. The dismantling of beliefs reveals nothing more strongly than the desire to believe and the quickness of the imagination to frame stories in which enigmatic phenomena are the guarantee of shelf-life. Ghost stories are about revenants, about those who return, their textuality equally a record of what has happened in the past, and a prospect of what may happen in the future. Ray Duckett's activity as an assiduous collector of folklore is only the most tangible example of a communal impulse to keep alive narrative templates that can accommodate the desires of successive generations to give more than fleeting and subjective meanings to the places they inhabit.

The main focus for all such attempts to establish a geography of fiction, to trace particular stories and beliefs back to a physical place of origin, to demonstrate the relation between intelligibility and locality, is the contradictory uncle-figure of Edward Arnold. Revered by superannuated dowsers, by furtive members of the Ancient Order of Druids, and by amateur drama producers obsessed with the traditions of mumming, Arnold is both ridiculous and menacing, a fraud with influence, a facile antiquarian taken seriously by archaeologists like Alexander Keiller (the excavator of Avebury) and by the proselytes of Nazism. Arnold's insistence on the survival of primitive values, both in the ritual practices of third-world countries, and in the legends and superstitions attached to specific English places, is neither detached nor irrelevant to the growing interest in territorial identities pursued with sinister energy during the 1930s. Although he draws the line at the anti-Semitism of German visitors to his annual gatherings celebrating the winter solstice, his belief in the efficacy of sacrifice is expressed in terms that are dangerously close to the political registers of Nordic or Aryan identity politics:

> 'Sacrifice isn't sacrifice unless you miss what you're sacrificing. A sheep is pathetic – unless it's your last sheep and you're starving. God gave His only begotten Son. He didn't really, because God is an invention, but Jesus knew the ropes. He outwitted the gods at their own game and they've never recovered.'
> I didn't really understand this thing about Jesus and the gods, but I pretended I did.
> 'Who would *you* sacrifice, then?'
> 'All depends on what I wanted from the gods.'
> I thought for a moment.
> 'To make the wildwood spread faster.'
> He gave a little start. I knew he thought of the wildwood as a sort of seed, the seed of the great forest that was going to cover Britain from end to end, as it did long ago before farmers cut it all down – except for the bit in our garden. That's why I wasn't allowed in.
> 'That's a good example, Hugh. I would have to please the gods an awful lot, wouldn't I? Yes, in that particular case, I would do as your Africans do. Nearest and dearest. Give my favourite child, or my wife, or whatever.'
> 'You haven't got children, and Aunt Joy's dead.'
> He looked at me steadily, puffing on his pipe. I felt my stomach go queer.

'That leaves me,' I added, trying to turn it into a joke.

'What?'

'I'm your nephew. I'm next.'

He nodded almost without moving his head, still staring into my eyes, as if I had sparked off a train of thought or given him the start of an idea. (122–3)

This exchange between nephew and uncle acquires significance within more than just this scenario. To begin with, it implants dread in the impressionable boy, less through fear that he will be victimized himself, than by entertaining the possibility that his mother's disappearance is somehow traceable to his uncle's fixation. But what it also allows for is the relay of fantasies, the transmission of half-baked theories of cultural inheritance, propagated in a series of publications and through the emulation of Arnold's followers. The popularity of his theories is owing partly to their easily assimilated and easily adapted conversion of local into general significance. Geared always to reconciliation with the land, to the consecration of specific terrain, Arnold's sacrificial ethos is what redeems the home turf from banality, invests the provincial with universal meanings. Its power derives from its translatability (often literally: from English into German, for example); its capacity to migrate, despite its being earthed, in every sense, in the lore of the land, in the cultivation of spirit of place. This mobility is what makes it so dangerous, in the scope it offers to those dispossessed of value in a modern setting to substitute an archaic scheme of significance that will reward their loyalty.

The exchange also touches on the core of Arnold's desires and ambitions: his dream of restoring the 'wildwood' to its primeval state and extent. This reversal of the movement of history would require an apocalyptic erasure of modernity. Crossing the threshold of catastrophe is part of the teleology of fascist discourse during the 1930s. The post-historical resurgence of the forest is envisaged in terms that replicate the enhancing of local detail into universal significance, in the expansion of the patch of woodland 'in our garden' into an enormous tract covering Britain 'from end to end'. The primacy of wilderness means the displacement and devaluing of the human. This flight of the imagination is what connects together English woodland and African jungle. Arnold's glib allusion to 'your Africans' and their customs makes the connection by a quite different route. What gives the ethos of sacrifice its totalizing scope is not so much a perception of universal forms of human behaviour, as a recognition of the reach of colonialism. Colonialism is what makes Ulverton and Bamakum part of the same cultural landscape, a global system of values that combines the familiar with the exotic, the domesticated with the feral.

If the African outpost is assumed to be the ultimate source of the violence invading the lives of the novel's characters, its inclusion within the dynamics of colonialism allows for the possibility that the reverse may be true: the long scars on the back of the servant Joseph are only the most obvious signs that the relationship between savagery and civilization is confused. The literary historical associations of dark and light inherited from Joseph Conrad's writing about Africa in *Heart of Darkness* (1899) are refracted into the 'pieces of light' that enter an eyeball gradually losing its sight. Darkness is in the eye of the beholder. Thorpe's novel explores the dark histories of self, of community, of customs, revealing the patches of light within them as illusory, as nothing but fictions, even though the power of fiction is what drives the characters to lead the lives they do. As one theory after another is abandoned, the protagonist gets no closer to distinguishing truth from fiction, but is drawn ever more forcefully towards recognizing the extent to which his life is ruled by a conflict of fictions.

In the end, the most deadly fictions are those whose repercussions reach beyond the text of the novel. Arnold's theories may be fabricated, marked as inauthentic, but they are not fictitious in the sense of being historically inaccurate. The topographical writing of the 1930s is often diverted into similar currents of rhetorical excess. The identification of chalk downland as the site of continuity with the traditions of the 'authentic hill-people' is matched exactly by the claims of H. J. Massingham's *English Downland* (1936):

> The burial tump was the house of the dead reborn and with the stone circle, also sepulchral in origin, a kind of emblem of eternity, or at least of life that travelled through death and on and on like the ridges of the chalk into the western sky. Archaic rites of fertility and resurrection were hardly science-proof. But they were concerned with the elementals of life and death and their monuments are appropriate to the curves and sweeps of the bare down that shake off the confinement of the vale. Barrow and height on which it stands symbolise alike the marriage of heaven and earth. (13–14)

This appeal to the permanent, even metaphysical, status of a culture rooted in landscape, is as rhapsodical in its celebration of indigenous forms as more openly political versions of a discourse of origins. These are the fictions of racial identity that authorize the historical realities of sacrifice, the 'archaic rites' brought back into use.

If the exceptional value of literature is its ability to preserve and transmit the structures of thought and feeling that material evidence can only hint at and may mislead us about, it is hardly surprising that in *Nineteen Twenty-One*, Thorpe's projection of an 80-year-old reality should rely heavily on the implications of literature. The text is almost an anthology of glimpses at the works of E. M. Forster, Virginia Woolf, D. H. Lawrence, T. S. Eliot, James Joyce and others. There is a perverse logic in Thorpe's moving from the construction of a modernist version of history in *Ulverton* to the assembling of a fictional history of modernism; or rather, of the moment of modernism, since the text filters many of the concerns of modernist writers but shows these emerging from strata of disregarded material. The basic premise of *Ulverton* is sustained concentration on the history of a single place, a premise overturned in *Nineteen Twenty-One*, which concentrates on a single, extended historical moment that is given various settings in England and France. The history of modernism cannot be grasped without an understanding of the role of displacement, in its fictional scenarios and in its scenes of writing. The constant exchange of settings that marks the experience of reading a novel like *Women in Love* (as opposed to the rootedness of most of the characters and relations in *The Rainbow*), is matched by the itinerant condition of its author, whose cultural mobility is typical of a period in which the most authoritative writing is identified with the radical dislocations of the exile and émigré.

Thorpe's selection of themes and characters is informed by scholarship that converts his text into the fictional equivalent of New Historicism. This might make it look more of an academic exercise than it is, were it not that the protagonist's mentality is thoroughly literary, and his own lack of originality increases the plausibility of his dependence on the preoccupations of other, contemporaneous writers. The laboriousness of his imagination lags behind that of his creator. A Jewish intellectual from Derbyshire, Joseph Monrow wears both his Jewishness and his regional identity lightly, until a chance encounter with a physical double leads him to define more sharply the edges of his own personality. The doppelganger, Hubert Rail, also has artistic ambitions – he is a painter – but fewer advantages: he is less solvent than Joseph, more authentically embittered, a slightly more unsettling version of Forster's Leonard Bast. Joseph has many other doubles: literary shadows such as Septimus Smith, Stephen Dedalus, Prufrock. His incompleteness as a character is accounted for in cultural terms, with his marginal status as a Jew being paralleled by Hubert's uncertain class position. But the most insurmountable barrier to completeness is the one constructed by the psychosexual challenge of the First World War. A pacifist who dreams of being a hero, Joseph is called up in the final weeks of the conflict, only to be gassed in a training exercise before he ever reaches the front. His own hysteria in the dug-out threatens the lives of his companions, and induces in him a sense of shame and inadequacy that permeates his subsequent existence. His masculinity is shorn as effectively as the truncated member of another of the complementary characters, the villager Samuel. Joseph's great writing project is to be the definitive novel about his generation's experience of the war. But his focus on the lives and deaths of combatants, with its disregard for the strata of civilian life, neglects much of the kind of evidence that Thorpe himself carefully sifts.

Thorpe's approach to the reconstruction of a historical moment recognizes the extent to which such moments are always focused elsewhere, themselves already caught up in a narrative trying to make sense of a different epoch. His own brilliance as a writer shows in the scrupulous patience he exercises as a literary archaeologist, recognizing the incompleteness of any interpretation, realizing the need sometimes to wait years, understanding only in the unfolding of a later project the scope of an earlier set of finds. The two novels about Ulverton offer the most obvious case in point. In poetry, Thorpe's most impressive achievement so far has been the sequence 'From the Neanderthal', published in 1999 but reacting to the author's own excavation, 23 years earlier, of a greenstone hand axe dated to 135,000 BC. Few writers have a literary imagination as meticulous as Thorpe's, refusing finally to let go of their work, holding onto its possibilities almost indefinitely.

Bibliography and further reading

Thorpe, Adam. *Ulverton*. London: Jonathan Cape, 1992.
——. *Pieces of Light*. London: Jonathan Cape, 1998.
——. *From the Neanderthal*. London: Jonathan Cape, 1999.
——. *Nineteen Twenty-One*. London: Jonathan Cape, 2001.
Ackroyd, Peter. *English Music*. London: Hamish Hamilton, 1992.
Conrad, Joseph. *Heart of Darkness*. London: Penguin, 1995 [1899–1900/1902].
Joyce, James. *Ulysses*. London: Secker & Warburg, 1994 [1922].
Lawrence, D. H. *The Rainbow*. Harmondsworth: Penguin, 1976 [1915].
——. *Women in Love*. Harmondsworth: Penguin, 1976 [1921].
Massingham, H. J. *English Downland*. London: B. T. Batsford, 1936.
Woolf, Virginia. *Mrs Dalloway*. London: Hogarth Press, 1990 [1925].
——. *Between the Acts*. London: Hogarth Press, 1990 [1941].

CHAPTER SIXTEEN

Prior Knowledge:
Sarah Waters and the Victorians

MARK WORMALD

Interviewed in 1994, Jeanette Winterson identified the nineteenth century as a low point in the history of attitudes to sexual identity. A period of intense and inhibiting 'anxiety about sexual difference and about sexual propriety', it produced, in Winterson's view, a damagingly narrow range of artistic expression. Interrupting a vigorous tradition of bold cross-dressing in the opera as in Shakespeare,

> What you can have in the nineteenth century is music hall, even music hall camp, and you can have pantomime, but ... [w]e're not supposed to believe in it, we're not supposed to be troubled by it, it's supposed to be a joke. (Wachtel 145)

Winterson was not amused. Imaginative champion of what, since 1994, has become confirmed as 'queer culture', she argues for the necessity of sexual dissidence, of perversities defying normative conventions, whether heterosexual or indeed homosexual. A passage in Casanova's diary about the attraction he and other lusty heterosexual men felt for a castrato prompts this comment:

> Of course that is creating emotion around the forbidden, which is also what art does, to go into those forbidden places and say, well, what do you really feel? ... Our queer culture is working now in the same direction: lesbians are no longer afraid of saying, well, I think that man's really sexy. And this is a good thing. It's breaking down rigid notions of sexual identity, whether homosexual or heterosexual. But of course we haven't got there first, we're just returning to something which the nineteenth century very kindly stamped on for us. I'm not fond of the nineteenth century. (Wachtel 146)

And it was evident that what she regarded as the rigid proprieties of the period's fiction were at the heart of that antipathy:

> I think it's very odd when critics talk about the nineteenth-century novel as something which is alive and trendy and important when it was a construct for

the nineteenth century. It was thoroughly kicked over, and quite right too. If you want to read nineteenth-century novels, there are plenty for you to read, and you may as well read the real thing and not go out and buy a reproduction. (141)

As the last of these comments implies, Winterson knew she was in a vocal minority. Readers have ignored her advice. At least since 1969, and John Fowles' *The French Lieutenant's Woman*, responses to, commentaries upon or pastiches of Victorian novels have been remarkably successful, and have often proceeded from an unusually close if sometimes ironically realized dialogue between the academy and the novelist. From Fowles via A. S. Byatt and David Lodge, to Charles Palliser and Michel Faber, these novels have also responded with a variety of wit and detail, identification and scepticism to what we know, since Steven Marcus, of *The Other Victorians*, and, since Elaine Showalter, of the *Sexual Anarchy*, in matters of culture and gender in the later nineteenth century. Few other forms of contemporary fiction have presented a coincidence of desire *for* the novel with desire *in* the novel so compellingly as these learned romances or looser, baggier monsters – among them both postmodern reflections on what it is to possess, and misappropriate, Victorian literature and the hidden sex-lives of its heroes (Flint *passim*), and what John Sutherland has called the 'neo-Victorian low-life high-filth novel' (*ibid.*; Sutherland 28).

The popular historical novels of the lesbian scholar and novelist Sarah Waters constitute a uniquely powerful challenge to Winterson's assumptions. For they insist on inhabiting and exploiting the conventions that Winterson despises. All three of Waters' books resemble the 'reproductions' Winterson has no time for: scrupulously researched and differentiated period romances, set in successively earlier decades of the nineteenth century, they exploit in turn, and with the benefit of late-twentieth-century critical perspectives, the literary and cultural paradigms of a period Waters knows well enough to ventriloquize and thus to test. Her writing presents a series of eminently readable first-person narratives, committed to the page by women whose texts embody and bring to vivid life episodes in the history of sexuality. These may or may not be 'real', but in Waters' hands they manage to escape the limitations of the genres which inspired them. These range from the homosexual subcultures of Victorian decadence at the *fin-de-siècle* that Waters had researched for her PhD, through the discourses and culture of spiritualism and the Foucauldian panopticism of the women's prison at Millbank in the 1870s, to a mischievous rearrangement of the elements that Wilkie Collins had deployed in *The Woman in White*. Waters subjects each of these overlapping sets of material to what her own scholarly work calls 'resistant rereading' (Waters 1995: 214; Waters 1996: 186), and seduces the many readers of her novels into questioning their own attitudes to desire in and for narrative.

In the course of this chapter, I shall be illustrating the range of contexts and conventions that Waters enlists and exploits in her writing, and arguing that it is her subtle and playful approach to these conventions and to the larger question of genre, in both of the periods she writes between, that makes her fiction so accessible, as well as so challenging.

The presence of these contexts, as well as the challenge that Waters has begun to pose to Winterson, is clear enough to any prospective reader of the Virago paperback edition of *Tipping the Velvet* (1999). Sandwiched between two puffs from reviewers – the *Daily Telegraph*'s opinion that 'This could be the most important debut of its kind since that of Jeanette Winterson', and another invitation to 'Imagine Jeanette Winterson on a good day collaborating with Judith Butler to pen a Sapphic *Moll Flanders*' – is a single sentence from the text itself. Even before we discover its context in the novel, it is clear, from the way it treats its setting, how misleading those comparisons with Winterson really are:

> Piercing the shadows of the naked stage was a single shaft of rosy limelight, and in the centre of this was a girl: the most marvellous girl – I knew it at once! – that I had ever seen. (*Tipping the Velvet* 12)

This sentence has of course been highlighted to produce in the novel's prospective readers exactly what that rosy limelight achieved for its narrator: a swift seduction, and a taste of the 'saucy, sensuous and multi-layered historical romance' that the blurb beneath it promises.

Yet even before we discover its context, in the novel's opening chapter and the 'old-fashioned music hall', the Palace at Canterbury, and before we discover the crucial fact of the narrator's own sex and origins – Nancy Astley is an oyster-girl from Whitstable – it is clear that that sentence has another purpose: to alert readers to the games and tricks, redressings as well as cross-dressings, that they can expect from the narrative. This is, palpably, writing that flirts, rehearsing the conventions of its obvious occasion through a rather subtler and textured literariness, which lies rather ironically, even implausibly, over the voice of an oyster-girl from Whitstable. Here, it borrows and inverts the clichés of heterosexual desire, on that 'naked stage', in order to flaunt them with knowing perverseness to serve this moment of homosexual rapture. It may also be seizing something else. Readers may begin to question Nan's choice of epithet for 'this most marvellous girl'.

Who is responsible, novelist or narrator, for the inversion of Wordsworth's 'Marvellous boy', or the poet Chatterton, variously regarded as an earlier, brilliant bringer to life of a remote past, or a forger? And what, if anything, are we to make of it? It is too early to know; but there is no disguising the sheer excitement, the sense of the 'marvellous', that attends this ambiguity. Here in Waters' music hall is none of the merely camp jokiness that Winterson saw in Victorian conventionality; instead, Waters is seducing her readers into believing in the possibility of the kindling in that limelight of genuine erotic desire, a desire that inhabits the codes of Victorian theatricality only to move beyond them, into territory at once darker and more compelling, because unresolved. And a curiosity about the forms that the expression of this desire will assume in the shadows beyond that 'shaft' of light is one of the components that unite narrator and reader in their progress through the novel.

Tipping the Velvet sates this curiosity. Nancy's picaresque story allows the startling, because often explicit – 'naked', indeed – staging of scene after scene of sexual activity, most of it dissident, illicit; much, but not all, lesbian. Nancy finds herself in all sorts of positions, physically and socially, in the extravagant permutations of her notably theatrical sexual career: from a carefully controlled and disguised first love with this 'most marvellous girl' Kitty, for whom she acts first as theatrical dresser and as undressing lover, then as music hall partner, only to be jilted by her manager; via the dissolute and despairing period in which, masquerading as 'gay' rent-boy ('gay' here properly carrying its Victorian meaning as prostitute), she performs acts of oral sex for clients who think her male; onto a position of bondage to a mistress, Diana, whose classical name and effortless opulence introduces Nancy to a bizarre subculture of lesbian sadomasochism that mimics the male homosexual cultures, orchestrated around models of 'Greek love', of the *fin-de-siècle*; and finally towards her true sweetheart Florence, for whom Nancy plays a variety of roles from housekeeper to passionate lover. Yet throughout the narrative is driven by an authority, and an urgency, that makes this a much more seriously motivated per-formance than the indulgent fantasy that this summary, or the subsequent television adaptation, may suggest.

The sources of that authority and urgency lie in the research that Waters undertook for her PhD, and in the articles they became; these articles also reveal the transformation this material undergoes in her passage from criticism to novel, as well as the motivation for the construction of this fictional world. In her criticism, she has made clear the fascination of the period for her, describing 'the late nineteenth century' as 'that decisive moment in modern homosexual definition and organization', and arguing in her study of Victorian and Edwardian representations of Antinous, handsome attendant to the Roman emperor Hadrian, that 'each offers us a glimpse of the narratives and fantasies around which the literary homosexual community structured and powered itself' (Waters 1995: 194, 195). This was, she writes, 'a fin de siècle culture saturated with discourses of sexual transgression to which, spectacularly, homosexuals both con-tributed and fell victim' (225). And these are the discourses with which *Tipping the Velvet* is saturated.

Writing recently against the genre of lesbian historical romance, which often resorts to an ahistorical and apparently unquestionable desiring body as irresistible imperative for the discovery, in secret, of a sexual identity thought impossible, incompatible with the dominant patriarchal culture, Waters and Laura Doan have insisted upon the importance of recognizing the power to locate, define and mark off 'the cultural discourses by which bodies and desires are constructed' at any point in history (Doan and

Waters 18). One important part of Waters' critical project has been to extend and refine the work begun by such lesbian literary historians as Terry Castle, whose influential reading of Sylvia Townsend Warner's *Summer Will Show* (1936) as 'exemplary' in its 'subverted triangulation, or erotic "counterplotting"' of the construction of canonical narrative around male homosociality, or even male homoeroticism, tended to play down Warner's engagement with the historical setting of her story, in the Paris of 1848 (Castle 74). Waters is concerned to identify 'a distinctly *lesbian* tradition of historical fantasy and speculation' in which Warner figures as an important but not exceptional player; from the short stories of Renée Vivien, via other writers of the 1930s such as Maude Meagher, and on to the early novels of Jeanette Winterson, Waters sees a continuing role for the construction of 'lesbian romance in the interstices of historical narrative' (Waters 1996: 117).

However, the seriousness of Waters' historical scholarship, and the scrupulousness of her engagement with critics, and novelists, whose historicism might be regarded as superficial, does not mean that Waters simply imports the dominant cultural discourses of the *fin-de-siècle* into *Tipping the Velvet*. As her survey of representations of the Antinous trope and narrative reveals, in the 1880s and 1890s the bulk of these representations were authored by men; it was only in occasional, suggestive but indirect responses to the trope by writers such as the American poet Annie Adams Field, in reading whom scholars need to rely on the biographical evidence of long same sex cohabitation rather than her writings to infer lesbianism, that women began to explore this, out of what has proved an enduring sense of the paucity of archetypes from history and literature for their own sexuality: 'With relatively few recognized or prestigious historical models and traditions of their own, lesbians have been frequent visitors to classical scenes of erotic male bonding' (Waters 1995: 211–12). It was not until 1912 that the novelist Kate Everest staged her own bold reversal at book length of an earlier, male version of the Antinous narrative, 'displaying in the process a remarkable familiarity with the topography of male homosexual fantasy' (225).

Yet this familiarity is just what Waters' heroine displays 20 years earlier. On the night they meet, when Diana lives up to her name and hunts Nan down, extracting the silk padding from the crotch of her trousers, she asks: 'Did you think you could play at Ganymede forever?' (*Tipping the Velvet* 249). By the climactic last night of their relationship, this schooling in models of Greek love and pederasty, through the staging of tableaux and a little deft reading, has evidently paid off: to mark Diana's birthday, Nancy selects for her what she thinks will be the perfect present:

> a marble bust of the Roman page Antinous. I had taken his story out of a paper at the Cavendish [Club], and had smiled to read it, because – apart of course from the detail of Antinous being so miserable, and finally throwing himself in the Nile – it seemed to resemble my own. (308)

Nancy's caveat has two functions. First, it alerts the reader to a local dramatic irony available to Nancy's hindsight, remembering this from the vantage point of a different and more socially equal happiness that she achieves with Florence. The resemblance is more complete than she knows. Later the same night, Nancy too will be miserable, ejected from Diana's house after being caught *in flagrante delicto* with the maid Zena, rescued but still vulnerable victim of the reformatory and member of Diana's household, whom her mistress has just savagely insulted, and to whose defence Nancy has risen and now fallen.

But there is a larger purpose in Waters' act of literary appropriation, selective response and *homage*. Her own prior knowledge of the period, its savage social inequalities, as well as the necessary consequence of those inequalities for the imagined lives of women forming precarious, unstable and at times necessarily undocumented lesbian relationships, alerts her to the fact that such relationships are constructed by forces most powerfully expressed through oblique, displaced, narratives. Nancy has learned this too. The experience of its different forms, that Nancy's own career has given her, thus allows her to reflect variously with ironic self-consciousness and with bitter plangency on the roles she finds herself playing. Thus, trying to make herself the ideal housekeeper for Florence and Cyril, she clasps at the baby of the house: the sight of Florence's expression, 'strange and sad, but also desperately tender', makes her think: 'Blimey, I was wasted in male impersonation, I should have been in melodrama' (372). But in later discovering the depth of Florence's own unrequited love for Lilian, Nancy reflects:

> I had thrust myself upon her and her brother, and thought myself so sly and charming; I had thought that I was putting my mark upon their house, and making it mine. I had believed myself playing in one kind of story, when all the time, the plot had been a different one. (398)

This sense is also caught through beautifully polished, and literally reversible, authentic images, such as the little picture of Eleanor Marx that Nancy has cleaned for Florence, and which she now turns and 'read the back of it: *F.B., my comrade*, it said, in large looped letters, *my comrade for ever. L.V.*' (398).

These closing pages of *Tipping the Velvet* suggest the techniques that she would refine in her next two novels: producing genuinely involving and surprising dialogues and domestic interiors in the shadow of a social, political and literary culture that the clarifying perspective of history allows us to know better than its immediate consumers, but which still has the capacity to reverse our expectations as well as to comfort them. Here, a lesbian friend recounts a joke she had made, in the first months of 1895, to the woman she admires in her workplace, a printing office:

> 'When she raised her eyes to me I held out my hand to her. I said, 'Are you Sue Bridehead? My name's Jude ... '

Florence laughed: they all had just been reading the latest chapter of that novel, in a magazine; I daresay Annie would not have made the joke, had she known how the story would turn out. Now Florence said: 'And what did she say to that? That she wasn't sure, but thought Sue Bridehead might work at the other office?'

'Not at all. What she said was: *Allelujah!* Then she took my hand and – oh, then I knew I was in love, for sure!' (408)

This knowing, informed, ironic but still emotionally valid misreading and inversion of a canonical text, as it were from within, and by women who are as printers themselves responsible for the distribution of types and texts, aptly condenses the effects Waters would go on to produce in *Affinity* and *Fingersmith*. Both of these novels retreat from her first book's explicitness – a gesture, certainly, to their settings, in the 1870s and the 1860s respectively, but also to the effects to be wrung from the discourses of the times. In *Affinity*, educated Victorian literary culture meets the intriguing possibilities of fraud and revelation to be found in the surviving accounts of the working-class spiritualists of the 1870s, young women empowered by the revelations they claimed to offer in making the dead speak again and materialize before their wealthy clients (Owen *passim*). *Tipping the Velvet* inhabits the terrain, and the plot, of Collins and Dickens, veering between Briar, a corrupted form of Collins's Limmeridge House, Lant Street in the Borough, where Messrs Sawyer and Allen, alias Nockermoff had done their worst in *Pickwick*, and Holywell Street, where the great Victorian bibliographer of pornography Edward Ashbee had his own work printed (Marcus 34–76; 65). Both novels dramatize confinement, in their representations of the women's prison at Millbank and a female asylum respectively. Both split their narratives between two women narrators, whose lives are brought into a relation that relies on mutual suspicion and desire. Both, through these alliances, succeed in snaring the reader into a complicity, sympathy and then a sensation of having succumbed to an always suspected reversal of expectations. And both turn on the power of women to exist, and to write, within and against the structures of power and history that seem to subjugate them entirely.

If both deploy prior knowledge, it is *Affinity* that does so more unsettlingly, and it is thus with this novel that the remainder of this essay will be occupied. As with *Tipping the Velvet*, *Affinity* combines, sometimes uneasily, a determination to incorporate the fruits of research into a culture and a period, for a serious purpose and with genuinely shocking results, with a mischievous and notably self-conscious series of allusions to canonical literature. Presenting much of the narrative through the secret diary of the Lady Visitor of the women's gaol at Millbank, Margaret Prior, allows Waters to use Foucault's studies of nineteenth-century surveillance and prisons, and of the history of sexuality, as a framework for another potential lesbian romance, as Margaret becomes fascinated with one prisoner, the spiritualist medium Selina Dawes, convicted for fraud and assault after the mysterious death of her wealthy patron. The structures of surveillance within the prison's pentagonal wards, and through the gazes and glances of matrons and visitors upon their charges, combine to form an effectively panoptic culture. Though we do read occasional brief diary entries of Selina's own, glimpses of life with Mrs Brink and her maid Ruth, all of these are dated from before her imprisonment, 'are significantly printed in smaller font size, and ... give no indication as to her present self' (Kohlke 160). The prisoner's individual identity seems to have been diminished, relegated to its irretrievable past.

Waters suggests that this culture of control reaches further still. Margaret's narrative reveals analogies and overlaps between the intrusive surveillance of the Millbank prisoners, and the oppressive subjection to patriarchal expectations and matriarchal scrutiny in her own comfortable domestic sphere. Middle-class women like Margaret, who was forced to suppress her feelings for her friend, Helen, when she became her sister-in-law, and whose violent emotional and physical reaction to that loss and to her father's death are presented to the world as a mistake in medication rather than the suicide attempt that would have led to the conviction of a woman from a lower class, are also revealed as victims of this seemingly ubiquitous but skewed gaze. Yet that gaze, we may realize, is our own: we are as readers of her secret diary – often composed late at night, and at great haste, under the influence of chloral and then laudanum – ourselves complicit in the culture that prompted it, which constrains its author, and which it continues to exhibit.

Still, our involvement in this wider literary complicity remains as enjoyable as it is compromising. This is due to Margaret's literariness. It is, then, a pleasure confirmed when she compares the unreliability of her own evidently hazy perceptions with those of another recent and better known victim of drug-induced amnesia: in searching in vain for the locket in which she keeps a lock of Helen's blonde hair, Margaret speculates: 'Perhaps I rose and seized the locket and placed it somewhere like Franklin Blake in *The Moonstone*' (*Affinity* 90–1). Margaret herself conspires in the patronizing elaboration of this network of literary allusions and references, and extends it, in her growing relationship with Selina, whose apparently uncanny knowledge of the detail of Margaret's life from within her cell proves the basis of the affinity that the two come to claim for each other. Margaret proposes Aurora Leigh and Marian Earle as romantic alter egos for herself and Selina, and though she forgives her companion's failure to recognize a quotation from Keats's *The Eve of St Agnes* (1884; *Affinity* 300–1), it seems clear, for most of the novel, that its narrative is constructed to resonate pleasingly within the prior knowledge available to readers for whom the literary is as familiar as it is to her.

Yet Margaret, as spinster, is also trapped by her failure, as writer, as character, to become either the character or the author to whom, as her mother knows, she has aspired: 'You are not Mrs Browning, Margaret ... You are not, in fact, Mrs Anybody. You are only Miss Prior' (252–3). And it is actually this sense of marginalized privilege, within a familiar circle but occluded by it, that makes Miss Prior a suitable (and aptly named) guide to the overlapping discourses of the early 1870s. One diary entry, for 23 October 1874, demonstrates how artfully Waters exploits this particular form of prior knowledge. Margaret leaves the British Museum after a morning reading prison histories in the middle of a fog so thick that the reading-room had to be closed. In the context of her brooding – she has also been remembering childhood stories and ghosts – what happens next opens and expands, as well as condensing, these questions of familiar unrealities; it proves that the fog Margaret steps through can accommodate perspectives and creatures beyond the prehistoric megalosaurus of the start of Dickens's *Bleak House*. Indeed, it can be the medium by which a remote image is restored and renewed, by dint of its proximity to its literary archetypes.

> I thought it even rather marvellous, to emerge from the museum and find the day become so grey and thick, and so unreal. I never saw a street so robbed of depth and colour as Great Russell Street was then. I almost hesitated to step into it, in fear that I would grow as pale and insubstantial as the pavements and the roofs.
>
> Of course, it is the nature of fog to appear denser from a distance. I did not grow vaguer, but stayed sharp as ever. There might have been a dome about me then, that moved when I did – a dome of gauze, I saw it very clearly, it was the kind that servants set on plates of summer cakes to keep the wasps from them.
>
> I wondered if every other person who walked along that street saw the dome of gauze that moved when they did, as clearly as I saw mine. (126)

Through such precise observations, Prior's narrative enables readers to recognize that the environment of her own prescribed predicament is also a space of overlapping, indeed potentially endlessly proliferating subjectivities. The medium that teases us to recognize the world she inhabits also reminds us of the constructs that constrain our imagination of that world.

The rest of the diary entry substantiates this, by confronting the novel's other very particularly dated sense of its own medium. As Alex Owen has shown, the early 1870s were vigorous years for spiritualist mediums. Out of the fog looms another reading room, that of the British National Association of Spiritualists. There, in the pages of *The Spiritualist*, Margaret finds accounts of Selina's early career and then of her trial and conviction. Waters provides verbatim extracts alongside Margaret's own summaries of the material she finds in the reading room, much of it serving to undermine Selina's own accounts of the glamour and excitement of her gift in giving voice to the spirits of the departed through séances and 'dark circles': these phenomena strike Margaret now as resembling 'garish tricks for petty payments, like a music-hall turn.'

Much more impressive, in every sense, are the wax casts of limbs left by the materialized spirits, among them the bloated hand of Selina's own 'spirit-control', Peter Quick (130). The novel never resolves the enigmatic status of Peter Quick, though his name is surely chosen to evoke distracting memories and anticipations of Henry James's bestial butler-ghost in *The Turn of the Screw*, Peter Quint. Quick's testimony, as Mr Hither the librarian confirms, could never be heard in court, but his physicality, reproduced in 'the bulging wax' of the cast, compels Margaret's fascinated attention, in the hideous contrast it provides with Selina's

> own slender fingers, the delicate bones that move in her wrists as they arch and dip above the putty-coloured wool of prison stockings. The comparison was horrible. I became aware of myself suddenly, stooped low before the cabinet, misting the dull glass with my quick breaths. (131)

Mr Hither observes of these casts, 'They *are* a little queer, aren't they? But rather marvellous, for all that?' And the chapter closes with a knowing reprise of this contrast: first, in an oral account, from an old lady who happens to be in the reading room, and has attended Selina's séances, of the appearance of Peter Quick, for all his roughness of manner 'the queerest, quaintest sight you ever saw' (151); then of a portrait of him, by 'a spiritual artist ... as he appeared for the dark circles at Mrs Brink's house.' This, Margaret reflects, 'might be comical, if it were not so queer' (154).

Many elements in this diary entry, itself a cabinet of curiosities, recur in the pages of Waters' narrative, from fog to mist to wax to dreams. All share the malleability, the impressibility and ductility of wax, which like Waters' writing itself manages to take vivid and apparently authentic period form only to melt and assume a new and unexpected fluency. Shortly after her visit to the reading room, Margaret is intrigued and then horrified to discover a smear of wax inexplicably on the floor of Selina's cell (187). In a moment of deranged despair, she interprets this as the remnant of a stream of wax seeping through London and the locks of the gaol the night before, only to solidify in the form of Peter Quick, for an embrace with Selina that proves the indissoluble affinity between medium and control (188). Waters keeps the more modest, but brilliantly appropriate explanation for the novel's ingenious denouement. That drop of wax was actually another mark of textual authenticity, secrecy and complicity – the sign of one of many letters of an ongoing correspondence between Selina and her conspirator, written at night, by the light of a candle whose wax then seals it, smuggled out by one of the Millbank matrons, who is convinced that Selina has brought back her dead child to her, even to the point of providing an oddly familiar curl of yellow hair in a locket.

And the identity of the conspirator? The novel provides two answers. The straight one, as it were, fits the logic of Waters' own criticism as well as her fiction, which continually gives voice, and control of a text, to those women whom history has left mute. In this case, it is the voice, and agency, of a servant. That Margaret treats servants as a class, and takes their protection entirely for granted, is one quiet implication of her description of her passage through the fog, with its translucent but self-centred 'dome of gauze, that moved when I did', and which ' – I saw it very clearly [–] was the kind that servants set on plates of summer cakes to keep the wasps from them.' The conspirator turns out to be someone whom Margaret has had daily opportunities to see very clearly, but has chosen to look right through. This is her own maid, whom readers have known only as Vigers: efficient, muscular as her name suggests, but also, it is assumed, barely literate. But Vigers is also Selina's Ruth: Selina, we realize, has depended for her own cultivation of Margaret's sympathies on a correspondence beautifully contained, suggested but invisible within the novel itself. Ruth Vigers is the author of those letters; they were written after herself doing what we have, and reading the secrets of Margaret's diary, as they unfolded in their instalments. It was Vigers who spirited away that locket; Vigers who, on the night of the Eve of St Agnes, may or may not have bedded Selina in the servant's quarters directly above Margaret's own agonizingly frustrated wait for the woman she thought would materialize before her.

However, there is another candidate, deliberately at odds with any one reading of the novel as marvellous or queer, comic or quaint, who makes a single appearance in the text, but who in her very absence, as invasive commentator or identifiable presence in its apparently conventional pages, nevertheless makes a strong case to be the controlling medium of this richly complex and enjoyable fiction. Selina dreams she awakes in her coffin, already buried. As she lies very still,

> there came a whispering voice beside me, it came against my ear & made me shiver. The voice said 'Did you think you were alone? Didn't you know I was here?' I looked for the person that spoke, but it was too dark for me to see them, there was only the feeling of the mouth close to my ear. I couldn't tell if it was Ruth's mouth, or Mrs Brink's, or Aunty's, or someone else entirely. I only knew, from the sound of the words, that the mouth was smiling. (281)

'Someone else entirely': however tempting it might be to rise to this teasing invitation, and identify the smiling mouth of Sarah Waters herself, the breathy, characteristically sensual signature is deliberately not, or not just, that of the postmodern author engaging in metanarrative communion with her subjects. Instead, it is the mark of the familiar compound ghost, both intimate and unidentifiable, that Sarah Waters conjures in her historical fictions, from nineteenth-century material and its much more recent critical and novelistic interpretations. The pleasure she takes in these notably contemporary dialogues with the dead, like the pleasure she communicates to such a range of readers, is as palpable as that smile in the dark.

Bibliography and further reading

Waters, Sarah. 'The Most Famous Fairy in History': Antinous and Homosexual Fantasy.' *Journal of the History of Sexuality*, 6:2, October 1995: 194–230.

———. 'Wolfskins and Togas: Maude Meagher's *The Green Scamander* and the Lesbian Historical Novel.' *Women: A Cultural Review*, 7:2, Autumn 1996: 176–88.

———. *Tipping the Velvet*. London: Virago, 1998; paperback, London: Virago, 1999.

———. *Affinity*. London: Virago, 1999.

———. *Fingersmith*. London: Virago, 2002.

Alderson, David, and Linda Anderson (eds and introd.). *Territories of Desire in Queer Culture: Refiguring Contemporary Boundaries*. Manchester: Manchester University Press, 2000: 'Introduction' 1–12.

Byatt, A. S. *Possession: A Romance*. London: Chatto & Windus, 1990.

Castle, Terry. *The Apparitional Lesbian: Female Homosexuality and Modern Culture*. New York and Chicester: Columbia University Press, 1993.

Doan, Laura, and Sarah Waters. 'Making Up Lost Time: Contemporary Lesbian Writing and the Invention of History', in *Territories of Desire in Queer Culture: Refiguring Contemporary Boundaries*. David Alderson and Linda Anderson (eds and introd.). Manchester: Manchester University Press, 2000: 12–28.

Faber, Michel. *The Crimson Petal and the White*. Edinburgh: Canongate, 2002.

Flint, Kate. 'Plotting the Victorians: Narrative, Post-Modernism, and Contemporary Fiction', in *Writing and Victorianism*. J. B. Bullen (ed.). London: Longman, 1997: 286–305.

Fowles, John. *The French Lieutenant's Woman*. London: Cape, 1969.

Kohlke, M.-L. 'Into History through the Back Door: the "Past Historic", in *Nights at the Circus* and *Affinity*.' *Women: a Cultural Review*, 15:2, Autumn 2004: 153–66.

Llewellyn, Mark: ' "Queer? I Should Say It Is Criminal": Sarah Waters' *Affinity* (1999).' *Journal of Gender Studies*, 13:3, November 2004: 203–14.

Marcus, Steven. *The Other Victorians: a Study of Pornography and Sexuality in Mid-Nineteenth-Century England*. London: Wiedenfeld and Nicolson, 1966.

Owen, Alex. 'The Other Voice: Women, Children and Nineteenth-Century Spiritualism', in *Language, Gender and Childhood*. Carolyn Steedman, Cathy Urwin and Valerie Walkerdine (eds). London: Routledge, 1985: 34–73.

Palliser, Charles. *The Quincunx*. Edinburgh: Canongate, 1989.

Showalter, Elaine. *Sexual Anarchy: Gender and Culture at the Fin de Siècle*. London: Bloomsbury, 1991.

Sutherland, John. 'Hoist that Dollymop's Sail.' *London Review of Books*, 24:21, 31 October 2002: 28–9.

Wachtel, Eleanor. 'Jeanette Winterson', in *More Writers and Company*. Elaine Wachtel (ed.). Toronto: Alfred A. Knopf, 1996: 136–49.

Index